全国高等院校研究生英语核心教材系列

研究生英语核心教材

——综合教程(下)

主编　陈锵明

对外经济贸易大学出版社

图书在版编目(CIP)数据

研究生英语核心教材.综合教程.下/陈锵明主编.
北京:对外经济贸易大学出版社,2009
ISBN 978-7-81134-313-7

Ⅰ.研⋯ Ⅱ.陈⋯ Ⅲ.英语－研究生－教材 Ⅳ.H31

中国版本图书馆 CIP 数据核字(2009)第 003626 号

研究生英语核心教材——综合教程(下)

陈锵明 主编
责任编辑:刘小燕

对 外 经 济 贸 易 大 学 出 版 社
北京市朝阳区惠新东街 10 号 邮政编码:100029
邮购电话:010－64492338 发行部电话:010－64492342
网址:http://www.uibep.com E-mail:uibep@126.com

唐山市润丰印务有限公司印装 新华书店北京发行所发行
成品尺寸:185mm×260mm 17.25 印张 398 千字
2009 年 3 月北京第 1 版 2009 年 3 月第 1 次印刷

ISBN 978-7-81134-313-7
印数:0 001－5 000 册 定价:34.00 元(含光盘)

出版说明

"全国高等院校研究生核心教材系列"是对外经济贸易大学出版社联合华东师范大学、中国人民大学、香港中文大学、山东大学、山东师范大学、福州大学等高校的骨干教师共同编写,适用于我国各地区全日制研究生使用的一套全新立体化教材。

我国研究生教育迅猛发展,非英语专业研究生英语教学面临新的挑战。为培养新时期合格的外语人才,根据全国高等院校研究生外语教学研究会 2007 年出台的修订大纲《非英语专业硕士/博士学位研究生英语教学基本要求(试行)》,我们联合上述院校的骨干教师编写了这套适用于我国各地区全日制研究生使用的"全国高等院校研究生核心教材系列"。

本套教材由《研究生英语核心教材—综合教程(上)》、《研究生英语核心教材—综合教程(下)》、《研究生英语核心教材—听说教程》、《研究生英语核心教材—写作教程》、《研究生英语核心教材—翻译教程》组成。

本套教材编写的基本原则是注重培养学生的语言交际能力。《非英语专业硕士/博士学位研究生英语教学基本要求(试行)》辩证地阐述了语言学习和能力培养的关系,提出研究生英语教学应"确保语言基本功训练,但以培养学生语言交际能力为主要目标"。本套研究生英语教材在选材、编写及练习的设计方面都体现了"扎实的基础训练,突出的能力培养"的目标。

对外经济贸易大学出版社
外语图书事业部
2008 年 7 月

前　言

　　《研究生英语核心教材－综合教程(下)》是为研究生公共英语课程编写的教材。

　　在研究生阶段,学生已初步掌握了英语"听,说,读,写,译"的基本技能。相对而言,学生英语阅读能力较强而口头与笔头表达较弱。本教程着重点之一是通过针对课文设计的一系列问题的提问,让学生对课文表达的观点,思想,以及涉及的事件在教师的引导下,与同学和教师进行由浅入深的的探讨,在课堂对答交流中,提高学生口头上用英语陈述自己观点和论点或反驳对方的观点和论点的能力,培养学生在学术领域或在较高的层次上与国外同行用英语进行交流的能力。

　　本质上,语言是文化的载体,英语语言学习,即是认识英语文化的过程。在研究生阶段,学生思想业已成熟,善于思考,喜欢探究。因此,以思想内容为主导(content－driven)的课堂教学方式,可以在语言学习同时,既欣赏西方文化,又获得思想交流与碰撞的愉悦。

　　从这点出发,本书共分十个单元,各个单元之间题材与体材尽量不一,但每个单元都由三篇同一个主题的文章组成。每单元的第一篇,设计了一系列基于课文以及由课文进一步延伸的问题。随后的两篇同一主题的泛读文章为第一篇的问题提供不同的观点与视角,以利于论题做更深入和广泛的讨论,因此也可视为第一篇的有机组成部分。

　　所选课文尽量语言质朴流畅,具有一定的思想性。让学生认识到,好的英语往往是质朴的英语,质朴的语言往往更能表达复杂丰富的思想。

　　本教程配有词汇,语篇,以及翻译练习,所选练习基本与课文主题相关,让课文所讨论的问题在口头问答的基础上得到笔头上的强化。

　　本教程编写分工如下:

　　主编负责制定本教程具体编写方案、各单元的选材、修改、润饰以及最后审订。

　　各单元参编人员如下:

第 1 单元	陈锵明	第 6 单元	王　冰
第 2 单元	周叔瑾	第 7 单元	陈艳鹃
第 3 单元	徐朝晖	第 8 单元	黄莉青
第 4 单元	张凤群	第 9 单元	俞婷婷
第 5 单元	张　莹	第 10 单元	叶艾莘

　　恳请读者对本教材的疏漏和不足之处给予指正。

　　本教程配有辅导用书和课件等立体化教学资源,供教师教学参考(见书末赠送课件说明)。

陈锵明

2008 年 11 月於榕城

Contents

Unit 1

The Unabomber

本单元课文综述

Text 精读 The Unabomber《邮包爆炸案》节选自 1996 年 4 月美国联邦调查局破获的一起延续多年的系列爆炸案的报道。凶手竟是曾毕业于哈佛大学的数学教授卡可辛斯基（Kaczynski）。卡可辛斯基辞去教职后自建木屋独居于山野，随后多次邮寄炸弹，炸死三人，致残二十多人。卡可辛斯基的行为究竟出于什么目的？卡可辛斯基是个恐怖分子，极端环保主义者，或仅仅是个疯子？

Passage One 泛读 The Disease of the Modern Era《现代社会病》是《大西洋月刊》在线编辑 Sage Stossel 与哲学家 Alston Chase 就《邮包爆炸案》进行的访谈。

Passage Two 泛读 Solitude《独处》选自美国作家亨利·梭罗的作品。梭罗同样曾就读于哈佛，也曾自建木屋独自野外生活，但他对大自然的独特体验为美国人民留下了丰厚的精神遗产。

ext

The Unabomber

Ted Ottley

1. Kaczynski

He lives in a ten by twelve cell. He escaped the death penalty. He's **given cooking tips** to a secret agent and written a screed on how Oklahoma bomber Timothy McVeigh **got it wrong.** In short, he's full of **gratuitous** advice on how to run the world.

He's Unabomber Ted Kaczynski — one of society's most **obnoxious.**

His biggest worry? People will call him crazy.

He was born Theodore John Kaczynski in Chicago, on the 22nd of May 1942.

He has one younger brother, David. His mother Wanda was widowed in 1990 when her husband Richard learned he had terminal cancer and **took his own life.**

Wanda and David **were left to wonder** how this son and brother evolved from brilliant academic to America's **most wanted terrorist**. His mother had to face the cruel reality that her firstborn bombed, killed and maimed innocent people for nearly eighteen years — in a **mindless crusade against** progress.

2. Student of Destruction

It was May 25th 1978.

A carefully wrapped parcel lay on the ground of the engineering department parking lot at the University of Chicago. It bore red, white and blue stamps **commemorating** playwright Eugene O'Neill. It was addressed to engineering Professor E. J. Smith, Rensselaer Polytechnic Institute in Troy, New York.

It appeared to be an undelivered parcel returned to its sender — Professor Buckley Crist of Northwestern University in nearby Evanston Illinois.

Without questioning how it had arrived at a different institution, the finder contacted Professor Crist.

Professor Crist claimed to **have no knowledge of** the parcel, but had it **couriered** to him anyway. But when he saw it the following day, he noticed it hadn't been addressed in his own handwriting. This made him suspicious enough to call in campus cop Terry Marker.

Ironically, there was some joking — "Maybe it's a bomb!" But the joke soon soured when Marker opened the parcel. It exploded in his hand and he became the first person to be scarred by the Unabomber's handiwork.

Fortunately, the injury was slight, mainly because the bomb was an amateurish piece of construction. Had it detonated with the full force its maker obviously intended, Terry Marker and those around him could well have sustained serious — if not fatal — injuries.

The university called in the ATF (Bureau of Alcohol, Tobacco and Firearms) and they immediately **proclaimed** the bomb the work of an amateur for several reasons.

It was based on a piece of metal pipe — about an inch in diameter by nine inches long. But the pipe was packed with something definitely not kept by the average home handyman — smokeless explosive powders. Its primitive trigger device was a nail tensioned by rubber bands. There were two other distinctions. The box was hand made of *wood*, as were the plugs that sealed the pipe ends. This was an unusual touch — pipe bombs usually use threaded metal ends that can be bought in any large hardware store — they make sure the pressure inside the pipe builds up enough to "bubble" the pipe until it swells enough to explode. Wooden ends simply don't have the tensile strength to cope with the pressure. The other components could well have been **scavenged** from any junkyard.

For now, the Unabomber was simply thought of as "the Junkyard Bomber".

Just why Professor Crist had been targeted was unclear. Theories ranged from a prank **gone wrong** to a disgruntled student **paying the professor back for** a poor grade.

The whole **scenario** was a strange "double-play" designed to confuse. The bomber had made it appear that Crist sent the package to Smith, and, undelivered, it had been returned to an institution neither one belonged to.

The ATF filed their photos and findings and embarked on a series of **wild goose chases.** As yet, there was no reason to suspect a serial bomber had made his first appearance.

3. Come Fly with Me

American Airlines flight 444 originated in Chicago. Its passengers, **en route to** Washington, D. C. suddenly heard a loud "thud" from the baggage area of the Boeing 727.

There, in a parcel, a household barometer had been **rigged to function** as an altimeter. When the plane reached 35,500 feet, the device completed an electrical circuit that **ignited** a mass of gunpowder. The makeshift bomb began to smolder in the hold. Passengers gasped for breath as smoke poured into the main cabin. Oxygen masks dropped as the crew prepared for an emergency landing at Dulles International Airport, Virginia.

Passengers and crew evacuated via the escape slide, and twelve were rushed to hospital where they were treated for smoke inhalation. When the source of the explosion was examined, it was a homemade bomb — again in a wooden box — that had been air mailed from Chicago. Clearly, the bomber could not know which flight would carry his parcel, so authorities concluded it was not a specific attack on American Airlines.

But the Chicago area bombings stopped, and the bomber lay silent for 16 months. Law enforcement agencies had started to relax, and speculated their man may have died, been jailed for another crime or **suicided**. Others only hoped he'd blown *himself* up!

No such luck ... In 1993 he was back with a whole new arsenal — and **a newfound vengeance.** On December 10th 1994, advertising executive Thomas Mosser flipped through mail that had arrived during a business trip. There was a parcel addressed to him, naming his previous employer, Burson-Marsteller.

In spite of the incorrect spelling of his previous employer's name, Mosser opened the **meticulously** wrapped parcel. Immediately a violent explosion rocked the house and Mosser's life was over. His head was **all but severed** from his body, his hand barely connected with his fingers, and his abdominal wounds were **mammoth.**

The bomb itself had been more vicious than any before — packed with razor blades, metal and nails it was designed to **lacerate** and **pierce** Thomas Mosser beyond recognition.

His wife, Susan described the blast saying, "... a thunderous noise resounded throughout the house ... a white mist was pouring from the kitchen doorway ... when the mist settled to the floor, a horrifying image emerged. My husband's body, face up on the floor, his stomach slashed open, his face was partially blackened and **distorted**. Blood. Horror ... I dialed 911 and screamed 'I need an ambulance! '" "It was supposed to be the day my family picked out a Christmas tree. The day we celebrated Tom's latest promotion.

Instead, it was the day my husband was murdered — the day I had to tell the children 'Daddy is dead.'"

The same day several people received letters from the Unabomber. The last letter received that day was to Warren Hoge at *The New York Times*. It threatened:

"... since we no longer have to confine the explosive in a pipe, we are now free of limitations on the size and shape of our bombs ... we know how to increase the power of our explosives and reduce the number of batteries needed ... we should be able to blow out the walls of substantial buildings.

Clearly we are in a position to do a great deal of damage. And it doesn't appear that the FBI is going to catch us any time soon." The letter then made its core demand. They would stop the bombings if a respected paper would print its 35,000-word "*Manifesto*". It ended with:

"If the answer is satisfactory, we will finish typing the manuscript and send it to you. If the answer is unsatisfactory, we will start building our next bomb."

4. Madman's *Manifesto*

After consulting **Attorney General** Reno and **FBI Chief** Freeh, *The New York Times* and *The Washington Post* decided to publish the Unabomber's **rambling and repetitive rant**. The papers agreed with Freeh and Reno — surely someone would recognize the writer by his choice of words or philosophy.

One of its more **deranged** sentences runs in the *Manifesto*, "In order to get our message before the public with some chance of making a lasting impression, we had to kill people."

He pronounced the Industrial Revolution as "a disaster for the human race" as was the use of technology.

All over America, scholars and students studied the *Manifesto*, hoping to find some clue that would pinpoint the Unabomber — *and* **reap** the one million dollar reward for identifying him.

One man — *David Kaczynski* — came to the sickening realization that the *Manifesto's* writing style and philosophy closely matched that of his older brother Theodore (Ted) Kaczynski.

David and his wife Linda were **devastated** by the thought that Ted could have spent 18 years terrorizing and killing so many innocent people. But the more they read, the more similarities they discovered.

Most telling was the Unabomber's reversal of the saying "You can't have your cake and eat it too." Writing about the negative consequences of eliminating industrial society, the Unabomber wrote: "... you can't eat your cake and have it too. To gain one thing you have to sacrifice another." Ted's quirky use of the aphorism was precisely the way he — and his mother — had always phrased it.

There were many other similarities — far too many for David to ignore. So, after much soul searching, David and his wife Linda felt they had a moral **imperative** to make contact with the FBI before more harm could be done.

Still, they had to be sure. So they contacted an old friend — private investigator Susan Swanson — to **enlist** her help. They told Susan they thought a "friend" could be the Unabomber, and asked her to have some of Ted's writings analyzed and compared with those in the *Manifesto*.

Swanson **came back with an answer** David hoped he'd never have to hear. After linguistic experts and profilers evaluated and compared the writings, they concluded the same person probably wrote them. So, David and Linda made the painful decision to **take their concerns to** the FBI.

Six weeks later, on April 13th 1996 the task force arrested Ted Kaczynski at his **ramshackle cabin** outside Lincoln, Montana. The tiny dwelling was crowded with proof **that** they'd found the Unabomber.

5. Back to Court

Final sentencing took place on May 4th 1998. The defendant and victims were allowed pre-sentencing statements — Kaczynski went first.

He complained that the prosecutors had distorted his motives and beliefs:

"... purely political. By **discrediting** me personally, they hope to discredit the ideas expressed by the Unabomber ... I only ask that people reserve their judgment about me ... until all the facts have been made public."

Understandably, his victims' responses were unsympathetic. Susan Mosser, whose husband Tom was killed in December 1994, made a strong statement as she described the killing:

"Nails. Razor blades. Wire. Pipe. Batteries. Everyday household items. Pack them together, explode them with the force of a bullet from a rifle, and you have a bomb. Hold it in your hand while it is exploding, as my husband Tom did, and you have unbearable pain ... Please, your honor, lock him so far down that when he does die, he'll be closer to hell. That's where the devil belongs!"

The last victim to speak was Nicklaus Suino, injured in 1985. He spoke of the ongoing traumatic conditions the bombing left him with and reflected on the death penalty:

"If there ever was a model candidate for the death penalty, Mr. Kaczynski is that candidate ... however, the most important goal for me in seeing him prosecuted was to ensure that he is unable to send his dangerous packages to anyone else." Observing the bomber's strange evolution, he observed: "He has actually become the very thing he once seemed to fear. Not a victim of progress, but an empty machine, devoid of conscience . . . ."

Kaczynski received four consecutive life sentences in a maximum-security jail. He was transferred to the Colorado "Supermax" facility, where he will spend the rest of his life — and simply **fade into oblivion.**

Retrieved from *http://www. crimelibrary. com/* 8 – 30 – 2005

New Words and Phrases

Unabomber		源于"University and Aviation Bomber",因其针对的主要目标为大学和航班而得名
cooking tips		烹饪技巧
screed	*n.*	lengthy writing 冗长的文章
get (sth. or sb.) wrong		misunderstand 误解
gratuitous		free 免费的
obnoxious	*a.*	extremely unpleasant 可憎的
take one's own life		kill oneself; commit suicide
were left to wonder		一直迷惑不解
most wanted terrorist		被通缉的恐怖分子
mindless crusade against progress		fight against 不顾一切地反对
commemorate	*v.*	in memory of; in honor of; to remember; to mark
have no knowledge of		have no idea of
proclaim	*v.*	declare; announce 宣布
scavenge	*v.*	在废弃物中寻觅
a prank gone wrong		hoax 恶作剧出了轨
pay back		报复
wild goose chase		chase the wild goose futile chase 徒劳的追求,无益的举动
en route to		on the way to
rigged to function		fixed, to serve as 装配
ignite	*v.*	detonated; set off
with a newfound vengeance / with a vengeance		with great violence or force; to an extreme degree 猛烈的;极度地
meticulously	*adv.*	extremely careful and precise
all but severed		nearly severed; nearly cut off

lacerate and pierce	*v.*	cut and penetrate
distorted	*a.*	misshaped；deformed；disfigured
manifesto	*n.*	declarration 宣言
Attorney General		（美国）司法部长
FBI Chief		联邦调查局局长
rambling and repetitive rant		不着边际的激昂的演说
deranged	*a.*	insane
reap	*v.*	obtain
devastated	*a.*	feel very shocked and upset 震惊心烦意乱（精神或感情上）
most telling	*a.*	明显的
imperative	*n.*	an obligation；a duty 责任；义务
enlist	*v.*	to persuade sb to help you
ramshackle cabin		shaky 摇摇欲坠的小屋
plead guilty		认罪
discrediting		败坏……的名声；怀疑
fade into oblivion		forgotten；sink into obscurity, to pass out of sight or existence 渐为（世人）忘却
fade	*v.*	逐渐淡出，逐渐消失；disappear gradually
vanish	*v.*	尤指迅速地消失；突然不见，disappear quickly

 **About the author**：After graduating in Communications Arts, Ted Ottley began his career as an English teacher in London. He went on to become a copywriter（广告词撰稿人）, then creative director with a London advertising agency. He returned to his birthplace Canada and continued his writing career. He contributed（投稿）to all media advertising, theatre, and broadcasting. He currently devotes most of his time to journalism and fiction, and has two books in progress.

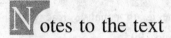otes to the text

1. 邮包炸弹杀手卡可辛斯基

A one-time math professor at the University of California, Berkeley, waged a deadly campaign against technology. He believed the system reduces people to gears in a machine, and takes away their autonomy and freedom. He moved in a cabin that he built himself near Lincoln, Montana in 1971.

卡可辛斯基在他的 Unabomber Manifesto 中表达了反对科技并希望回归原始社会的主张。他写道："工业革命及其后果对于人类来说是场灾难。尽管工业革命延长了我们这些生活在所谓"发达"国家的人的生命,但是它却导致了社会的不稳定,使人生没有实现感,使人类屈从于种种耻辱的行为之中,最终导致大范围的心理失衡而且对自然界造成了严重的破坏。技术的持续发展将使这种情况更加恶化。它将进一步使人类屈从于更为无耻的行为并对自然界造成更为严重的破坏。而且,假如这种社会能够存活的话,某些后果将是不可避免的:我们将永远无法对这一社会进行改革以阻止它对人类的奴役,对人类尊严的剥夺。因此我们需要发起一场对工业社会的革命,这不是一场政治革命,它的目标不是去推翻一个政府而是去颠覆现今这个社会的经济和技术基础。"他写道:"为了使我们的理念能够传达给公众,并获得持久的影响力,我们不得不杀人。"

2. 卡可辛斯基语录:"The reason I dropped out of the technological system is because I had read about other ways of life. Jane Austen wrote that happiness is always something that you are anticipating in the future, not something that you have right now. This isn't always true. Perhaps it is true in civilization, but when you get out of the system and become re-adapted to a different way of life, happiness is often something that you have right now."

3. **Kaczynski's trial**:案犯审判颇为曲折。他的辩护律师决定以卡可辛斯基精神失常为由,来挽救他免判死刑。但卡可辛斯基不同意,他认为那是对他的思想的扭曲和侮辱。他要求解雇他的辩护律师,在法庭亲自为自己辩护。那么法庭将面临尴尬的局面:法庭只能将他的观点视为疯人呓语;既然是疯子,审判疯子又有失合法性。最后他同法官达成一项十分特殊的辩诉协议。Kaczynski wanted to stand trial in order to draw attention to the ideas expressed in his manifesto but his attorneys decided that a mental status defense was their only real chance at saving their client's life. But Kaczynski would not agree to it; he broke off meetings with defense psychiatrists. Undeterred, his lawyers found experts who based their diagnoses on Kaczynski's philosophy and his reclusive, hermetic lifestyle. Frustrated, Kaczynski eventually allied himself with prosecutors and sought to fire his lawyers, asking to represent himself. Although the court-appointed psychiatrist found Kaczynski sane, the presiding judge denied his request for self-representation. Thus, faced with an unacceptable alternative (i. e. , a trial in which his ideas were dismissed as the ravings of a madman), Kaczynski agreed to a plea bargain. In exchange for the government's agreement not to seek the death penalty, Kaczynski acknowledged responsibility for 16 bombings between 1978 and 1995.

4. **The plea bargain** (辩诉达成交易):
The terms of the agreement stipulated (规定) that Kaczynski plead guilty (认罪) to the deaths of all three men killed by letter bombs he mailed in return for a guarantee that he will not be executed, Kaczynski agreed to accept life in prison or a federal psychiatric facility without the possibility of parole (假释). As part of the plea agreement, the government is requiring that Kaczynski's future earnings go to pay restitution (赔偿) to the families of his victims. The agreement spares Kaczynski not only the death penalty —

the evidence that he was the Unabomber was overwhelming from the beginning — but it also enables him to avoid being portrayed in court as a madman, something he vehemently opposed. It also allows the prosecution to avoid giving the impression that it was trying to execute a man who is mentally ill.

5. **David Kaczysnki**：举报人，Ted Kaczysnki's brother who reported Ted to the FBI, said in an interview in an effort to save his brother's life: Our interest from the beginning was to protect life and if this government were to process this like a cold and calculative machine, I would have to conclude that my faith in that system was misplaced. David Kaczynski told the Post, "What would a future family member in a similar situation think if I were repaid with my brother's death. It would be the ultimate disincentive for anyone else to cooperate with our justice system. "

6. **David Kaczynski's $1 million**

When David received the one million dollar reward for uncovering the bomber, his selfless nature again surfaced — half the money went immediately to bomb victims and their families. The balance was needed for the mammoth legal bills the family had covered.

7. **Oklahoma bomber Timothy McVeigh**：俄克拉荷马州俄克拉荷马城爆炸案案犯提摩西·麦可维。1995 年 4 月 19 日，俄克拉荷马州俄克拉荷马城爆炸造成了联邦大楼等 324 座建筑被摧毁或损坏，86 辆汽车被毁坏，168 人死亡，853 人受伤。这是 9·11 事件前，美国本土发生的最严重的恐怖主义事件。1997 年 6 月 2 日，主犯 Timothy McVeigh 被陪审团裁定 11 项罪名成立。6 月 13 日，同一陪审团推荐死刑。2001 年 6 月 11 日早晨 7 点 14 分，提摩西·麦可维（Timothy McVeigh）在印地安纳州被注射处死。

8. **Bureau of Alcohol, Tobacco and Firearms**：美国联邦酒精、烟草和枪支管理局

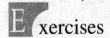

Exercises

I. **Answer the following questions based on Text and the words and expressions listed below are for your reference.**

1. **Which group or groups of words would you use to describe Ted Kaczysnki? Why?**

  a hermit / recluse；

  brilliant professor / academic / mathematician；

  mad / crazy / mentally ill / unsound / disordered / insane；

  a person of great social conscience; environmental extremist / naturalist，

  a social misfit; a person of anti-society / progress / science / technology / civilization / industry

2. **How much do you know about his family**?

A single-parent family / broken family / loving

caring / uncaring / close family; widowed mother; father committed suicide; family

with violent history; attached to his brother

3. **Why is it that he was worried about being called crazy**?

thought to be insane / his ideas discredited / dismissed lightly

his ideas to be taken seriously / an insult to his intelligence.

4. **What is the "double-play" designed by Ted Kaczysnki to confuse the police**?

University of Chicago; Professor Smith of Rensselaer Polytechnic Institute in Troy,

NY; Professor Crist of Northwestern University / in Evanston Illinois

sender / sendee / finder / addresser / addressee

5. **Describe the construction of the first bomb.**

Amateurish piece of construction; Pipe; trigger device; metal ends;

The pressure inside builds up / swell enough to explode

6. **What theories did the police come up with to try to account for Professor Crist being targeted**?

a prank gone wrong / a joke turns sour / pay the professor back for / get even with

7. **Why was Ted Kaczysnki's manifesto allowed to be published**?

recognize / identify / find the clue

8. **How was David Kaczysnki able to relate the manifesto to his brother Ted Kaczysnki**?

Similalities / resemblance

9. **Did Ted Kaczysnki plead guilty in the court because he finally found his conscience, and Why**?

Make his ideas known

10. **Comment on the court speeches by the victims and their family.**

II. Further questions for discussion.

1. Why do you think Ted Kaczysnki, a Harvard educated professor ends up as an anti-technology extremist?

2. What would you do if you were in the position of David Kaczysnki?

3. Comment on David Kaczysnki's taking his concerns to the police.

4. What's your comments on the court sentencing of Ted Kaczysnki to life in prison instead of death?

5. How do you interpret Ted Kaczysnki's real motive?

III. Vocabulary study.

1. **Word in Use.**

1) **get sth. / sb. wrong**: to make a mistake in the way you answer or understand

something   算错,误解

No real harm will be done should you get it wrong first time, but you will have to start from the beginning again.

Don't get me wrong on this, this is not in any way meant to be a criticism. What we're trying to do here is to sit down and get it better organized.

I'm not sure that honesty's a word which I would use. Don't get me wrong. I'm not suggesting that a salesman is dishonest.

2) **commemorate**: *vt.* to remember officially and give respect to a great person or event, especially by a public ceremony or by making a statue or special building. (Remember, honor, mark, celebrate) 纪念

The idea of making a special flower picture to commemorate a particular wedding anniversary works very well.

Such arches were erected to commemorate important military or domestic happenings, or in memory and respect of generals and emperors.

The four men who allegedly planned demonstrations to commemorate the 1988 flag-raising, were sentenced to terms between 6 and 12 years.

3) **call in**: to ask someone to come to help in a difficult situation 求助

British detectives were called in to conduct a fresh inquiry.

Environmental health officers have been called in and are now treating the problem.

Professional hunters called in by police were today searching for a great white shark that killed a scuba diver on his honeymoon.

4) **embark on / upon sth**: to start something, especially something large, important, or new 开始

But by the summer of 1984 the marriage began to break down and Mrs Martin embarked on an affair without her husband's knowledge.

She was often forced to spend months apart from her husband as he embarked on long tours.

Labor has now embarked on a leadership election.

5) **wild goose chase**: an attempt to accomplish something impossible or unlikely of attainment 无法达到目的的;徒劳的

Instead of that, he had become involved in what was most likely a wild goose chase.

They deliberately sent me on a wild goose chase.

Police said, "He lied and took us on a wild goose chase."

6) **speculate**: to guess possible answers to a question when you do not have enough information to be certain 推测

A spokesperson declined to speculate on the cause of the train crash.

Your students may have seen you play a sequence without sound then rewind for a second viewing, or pause to speculate about what might happen next.

It would be futile to speculate what might have been achieved had these two separate teams felt able to cooperate.

7) **pick out**：to recognize, find or make a choice among different people or items in a group 挑出

The critics picked him out as the outstanding male dancer of the decade.

I can't remember now who it was from but I'd been picked out and given a valuable prize.

8) **devoid of**：lack or be without something that is necessary or usual 缺乏

Their apartment is devoid of all comforts.

"Did you do your homework last night, Hank?" she asked in a voice devoid of real inquiry.

His mind would become totally clear and his reactions devoid of any hesitation.

2. **Word Distinctions.**

1) **escape, escape from**

课文中 He escaped the death penalty. 他逃过死刑,其涵义是他没有被判处死刑;

但 He escaped from the death penalty. 他判了死刑,但逃掉了。

选择以上适当的词填空:

He cut a hole in the wall and _____ the prison.

The police lay in wait around his house, but he did not return that night and _____ capture.

A lion has _____ its cage.

She was lucky to _____ serious injury.

He narrowly (= only just) _____ a fine.

His name _____ me (= I have forgotten his name).

Nothing important escapes _____ notice / attention.

2) **search, search for**

选择以上适当的词填空:

The police spent the whole week _____ the missing boy.

They _____ the suspect before he had time to destroy the document.

I've _____ every of my pocket, but I can't find my key.

The detectives _____ the house all over, there is no sign of the stolen goods.

She _____ her mind / memory for the man's name, but she couldn't remember it.

People who are _____ inner peace sometimes turn to religion.

3) **approve**, **approve of**

选择以上适当的词填空：

Obviously he did not _____ smoking but he had to accept it in the situation.

We had to wait months for the city council to _____ our plans to extend the house.

I thoroughly _____ what the government is doing.

The court _____ the sale of the property.

3. **Decide the meanings of the following words by matching each word in Column A with the word or expression in Column B that is similar in meaning.**

A	B
1) obnoxious	a. extremely large
2) mammoth	b. deliver
3) courier	c. very unpleasant or rude
4) enlist	d. ignite
5) reap	e. suicide
6) manifesto	f. solicitate
7) devastated	g. deformed
8) distorted	h. harvest
9) take one's own life	i. destroy
10) detonated	j. declaration

4. **Try to write a brief story with the following crime-related words and phrases.**

lawbreaker, criminal, wanted, caught, arrested, charged with, tried, sentenced, put into prison, serve time in prison, death penalty

IV. Translation

1. **Put the following Chinese expressions into English.**

   1) 暴力犯罪   2) 判终生监禁   3) 辩护律师   4) 不服罪

   5) 被起诉   6) 守法公民   7) 通缉要犯   8) 法网恢恢,疏而不漏

2. **Put the following Chinese sentences into English with the words or phrases in the brackets.**

   1) 我花了一个小时计算那道题但还是算错了。(get it wrong)

   2) 人们塑了一个雕像以纪念这位诗人的百年诞辰。(commemorate)

   3) 警察直升飞机被叫来搜索在三周内洗劫五个加油站的武装劫匪。(call in)

   4) 他是否给那些即将开始表演生涯的人们一些忠告?(embark)

   5) 正当他们对下一步行动感到迷茫时,总部来电说他们现在的搜寻是徒劳无益的。(wild goose chase)

   6) 政府把坠机事件归咎于技术故障,而国外媒体揣测直升机是被火箭击落的。(speculate)

7）回顾两人一起生活这许多年，他们很容易发现那些导致他们婚姻破裂的倒霉时刻。（pick out）

8）地板是硬石头铺的，墙是石灰刷的，房间里没有一件家具。（devoid of）

3. Put the following Chinese paragraphs into English.

1995 年 4 月 19 日上午 9 时，美国俄克拉荷马城中心，"轰"的一声巨响，只见火光冲天，浓烟滚滚，响声和震动波及数十英里之外。瞬间，一座 9 层高大楼的 1/3 墙倒顶塌，500 名政府官员和职员在这里上班，许多人惨死废墟之中。

官方说，这是美国 75 年来最严重的一次恐怖主义制造的爆炸事件。联邦调查局当天发布紧急通缉令，并悬赏 200 万美元将嫌疑犯捉拿归案。

1995 年 8 月 10 日，提摩西·麦可维（McVeigh）被联邦政府指控 11 项罪名，包括 8 项一级谋杀。10 月 25 日，政府表示将寻求死刑。1996 年 2 月 20 日和 1997 年 6 月 2 日，陪审团裁定 11 项罪名成立。6 月 13 日，同一陪审团推荐死刑。2001 年 6 月 11 日早晨 7 点 14 分，提摩西·麦可维在印地安纳州被注射处死.

4. Put the following quotes into Chinese.

1）All violence is not power but the absence of power. —— Emerson

2）Nothing enduring can be built on violence. —— Gandhi

3）Violence is an admission that one's ideas and goals cannot prevail on their own merits. —— Eward Kennedy

4）Political power grows out of the barrel of a gun. —— Mao Tse Tung

5）Nothing has ever been established except by the sword. —— Napoleon

5. Translate the following passage into Chinese.

The Oklahoma City bombing trials raise questions more interesting than the answers they provide. How, in four years, can an army sergeant and Green Beret aspirant turn so violently against the government he served? If there had been no Waco（城市名）, would there have been no Oklahoma City? Did McVeigh want to be captured? Why did the government only bring charges against three men in connection with the bombing, when compelling evidence suggests that others played significant roles in the crime? We do not have clear answers to any of these questions — but some possible answers to these and other intriguing questions have come into better focus in the years since the McVeigh and Nichols trials.

V. Comment on the structure of the text.

Understanding the macro structure of a text is essential in building reading competence.

The text is a feature report（专题报道）which tells the longest and the most expensive hunt for a serial killer in the US. It appears in the online courtroom TV news.

A feature report is usually composed of three parts：a headline（标题）, lead（导语）and body（正文.）

Headlines play a vital part in kindling a spark of interest in the reader. They are usually short, dramatic or sensational, aiming to produce "eye-catching" effects by making use of different linguistic devices. In the headline of the above report, "**Ted Kaczynski: The Unabomber**", the writer coins a new word "UNABOMBER" to draw the readers' attention. The word "unabomber" is a blend of three words: *university*, *aviation* and *bomber*, referring to the bomber who directed his target of attack at university teachers and aviation staff.

The news lead (usually the opening paragraph of a news report) is like a mini-story, it gives the gist of the whole news event, consisting of just one sentence in most cases. All other paragraphs that follow the lead are supporting paragraphs, providing specific details. The basic elements of a new item contain information about the six w's — who, what, where, when, why and how. The news lead usually contains the first few w's and leaves the rest to the supporting paragraphs. The lead of this text features the who and what of the event.

The body is the detailed presentation of a news event. The facts are usually arranged in three different ways: (1) in chronological order (in the order of time sequence); (2) according to the relative importance of the specific details: the most important thing comes first, then follow the less important ones; (3) in a way that combines (1) and (2): it begins with a summary of the general event and then provides the details in chronological order. The body part of this text is arranged in the order of time sequence. The paragraphs of a news report are usually very short, many of them consist of only one sentence that gives one specific detail. Subheadings (副标题) are used to help readers focus on particular aspects of the new item.

Extended Exercises

1. **In the following article, some paragraphs have been removed. Choose the most suitable paragraph from the list A-E to fit into each of the numbered gaps. There is ONE paragraph which does not fit in any of the gaps.**

An Insider's Guide to Teen-Speak

I speak ordinary adult English, and my daughter was brought up to do the same. By 12, she was quite good at it. She could conduct conversations, answer complex questions, tell jokes and give directions. But within a year, she began to practise Teen-speak. Although it has an English vocabulary, Teen-speak is a difficult language. At first, it seems to make sense. You nod and smile, believing that you know what has been said. Only later do you discover that you understood nothing you were told.

1) _____

Depending on the tone used, a harmless response such as "Great" can mean (a) *Great*; (b) *Not that again*; or (c) *You've ruined my life*. The answer "Sure" never indicates simple agreement, as in regular English. Depending on duration, "Sure" means: (a) *That's just what I'd expect from an old person*; (b) *You don't know what you're talking about*; or (c) *You've ruined my life*. "Yeah" has the same range of meanings, but in this case the briefest version has the most devastating intent.

2)＿＿＿＿＿＿＿＿＿

Simple Teen-speak remarks rarely mean what they seem. "I've cleaned my room" means *The mess that was in the middle of the floor has now been moved to the edges of the room*. "Janet's mother said it was OK with her" means *If you agree, Janet thinks she can get her mother to agree*. Statements about clothing are particularly dangerous. "I have nothing to wear" means *The laundry I have been hiding for two weeks is now so well hidden even I can't find it*. "Everybody's wearing them" means *I saw them on a music video*. "It's not too cold" means *I've lost my coat*.

3)＿＿＿＿＿＿＿＿＿

Don't venture any further into the subject of school, because the next step is foolhardy: "When did you do your homework? You've been watching television ever since you got home." The answer will be "I did it in my free periods." This means *Since I have already spent an hour at school pretending to do it, why should I spend another hour pretending to do it again?*

4)＿＿＿＿＿＿＿＿＿

Even if the subject turns serious, Teen-speak has a word — or several words — for it. When you raise a problem, the common teen response is "I'll take care of it," which means *I am willing to act as if I take this seriously if you are willing to act as if you believe me*. "I don't want to talk about it" means you've touched a nerve, and *If you insist on talking about it, I'm going to do a ten-minute soap opera and give you a headache*.

5)＿＿＿＿＿＿＿＿＿

Even after you think you've mastered Teen-speak, you will never understand it completely. All teenagers occasionally slip back into ordinary speech. They do this to trap you. If they catch you translating when you should just be listening, it's an incredible victory for their side. As a reward, they get to say "You never listen to me!"

A: I am assured by friends whose children are now ambassadors and bank executives that, at some point, it ends. But whether that day comes before or after the Nobel Prize is not clear. Either way, a rudimentary understanding of Teen-speak can make a parent's life more comfortable.

B: If you insist on bringing a serious discussion to some kind of conclusion, you can make your point and then ask "Do you understand?" But then you leave yourself open for one of Teen-speak's ultimate remarks: "Whatever. " It means *Why are you still talking when it is obvious that I have stopped listening?*

C: Of all the Teen-speak responses, however, the most important is "OH". When it is pronounced with a rising pitch and quick stop, "Oh" signals an impending expenditure, as in "Oh, I lost my runners" ($90) or "Oh, I need a new computer book ($23.50). "

D: Asking questions about school gets you another wave of Teen-speak. The usual answer to "How was school today?" is "OK. " In this context, "OK. " means *Don't ask.* It you then ask "What did you do at school today?" the answer is always "Nothing. " This is one of the few times when teenagers are saying exactly what they mean.

E: The words teenagers use with one another (cool, bad, awesome, etc.) have a variety of meanings. The keys to understanding them are tone, duration and pitch — a little like Chinese.

F: Since teenagers, like humming-birds, must eat twice their weight in food each day, much of what they say is acoustically distorted by the inside of the refrigerator. Even if you master the refrigerator echo, what you hear is also coded Teen-speak. "There's nothing to eat" means *We're out of junk food.* "I haven't had anything to eat" means *Hamburgers, chips and milkshakes don't count.* "Is this all that we're having?" means *Green things don't count.* "I just made myself a sandwich" means *The leftover roast you were saving for tonight's dinner fitted nicely between two pieces of bread.*

After Michael Anania, *Reader's Digest*, July, 1992

2. **Identify the five ways of beating career blues by grouping the following numbered paragraphs into effective sections and choose the most suitable subheading from the list A-E for each way.**

Beat Those Career Blues

1) Overcoming career blues is largely up to you to do what you can to initiate a change in attitude. Here are five ways to get started.

2) Richard Germann, a career management consultant often tells unhappy clients to fantasize about their dream job — everything from what they would really like to be doing to what sort of office environment they prefer. This encourages people to formulate their own definition of job satisfaction. Without that definition or goal, it's easy to feel down at work.

3) To do this exercise, break your ideal job into the smallest possible parts. If you see yourself as a junior executive working under a great boss in marketing, when in fact

you're a clerk working under a tyrant in purchasing, look for "stepping stone" goals that will advance you to the next position.

4) For example, you might first see whether you can get a transfer to a different section of purchasing to escape the tyrant. Or why not go for a low-level position in marketing? Then get some additional training or schooling so that you look like a good executive candidate. At the very least, find out what qualifications you will need to move up the ladder. Developing and following your own plan of action is one of the biggest ways to improve your attitude.

5) Imagine that you are an independent contractor, You — Yourself Enterprises, with only one major client — your employer. Then allocate your time so that you not only meet the demands of your client but also have room to develop aspects of your business that you see as necessary for your own future growth.

6) Let's say you're working at a job that requires you to write reports and you find out you can produce nice phrases. That may not matter to the company executives, but you, as an independent contractor, should realize that your writing skills may open a whole new area of sales. So rather than turn in the ordinary verbiage expected in reports, you should make your sentences glow and thereby perfect your product for a broader market.

7) The most useful part of this concept is that it moves you from an outwardly controlled motivation of simply pleasing your boss to one where you recognize and improve your skills for your reasons.

8) Picture this: You invite a friend to stay at your place for a few days. The second day, his clothes are everywhere. On the third day, his Saint Bernard dog has taken up residence on your sofa. By the fourth day, you can't park in your garage because his car is there. Are you getting annoyed?

9) The same thing happens with some people and their careers. At first they work the odd extra hour or two in the evening. Then they start taking work home regularly during the week. Soon, weekends become nothing more than office hours. In effect, work becomes the ill-mannered guest that takes up more and more space and time. Suddenly people don't have a life apart from work, and they resent it.

10) This is not to say that taking work home is taboo. But doing it all the time is. If you do have a heavy workload, alternate evenings of intensive work and intensive leisure. On Monday, Wednesday and Friday evenings, for instance, do your work and try not to get side tracked. But on your leisure nights, don't even bother taking work home.

11) Take your hobbies and leisure activities as seriously as you do your work and take the same kind of pride in them. Too many people fall into the trap of getting their whole sense of identity from the office. This is great when things are going well, but if your self-esteem is a direct outcome of your work situation, you will feel humiliated when the going gets rough. If you can tie your self-esteem to your outside endeavours, you can maintain a

positive attitude even if the office forecast is calling for thunderstorms.

12）If you dread going to work each morning, it's probably partly because you're not getting along with those around you. You don't have to like the people you work with, but at least you should be able to interact positively with them.

13）When you smile in a lift, your fellow passengers respond with a smile. The same thing can happen in the office. Don't worry that suddenly striking up relationships with people you previously ignored will come across as insincerity. The fact is, you are being sincere in your efforts to improve work relations, and that will be felt by your co-workers.

14）Try to have more interactions. Step outside your office and join your co-workers' discussion about football. If you don't know much about the obscure film everybody's talking about, express an interest by asking someone who does know.

15）You can sit around bemoaning that you are underpaid, that you are not in the fast lane, that the corporate world is not treating you the way you'd like, but it won't do you any good. Cash, power and prestige must come to you from your employer. But self-esteem, pride in a job well done and a sense of importance are all bonuses you can give yourself. You've got nothing to lose and everything to gain by learning to find enjoyment in your work.

A：Change your attitude towards others
B：Dream a little, plan a lot
C：Look for success outside of work
D：Think of yourself as autonomous
E：Separate work and play

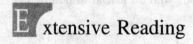

xtensive Reading

Passage One

The Disease of the Modern Era

艾尔斯顿·蔡斯（Alston Chase）是莱斯特大学（Macalaster College in Minnesota）哲学系教授,他撰写了畅销书《哈佛和邮包炸弹恐怖分子:一个美国恐怖分子所受的教育》（Harvard and the Unabomber）。他认为我们要担心的应该是卡可辛斯基成长背后的影响力。以下是《大西洋月刊》在线编辑斯道塞尔（Sage Stossel）就邮包爆炸案对艾尔斯顿·蔡斯的访谈。

Sage Stossel：
You emphasize that, as a man alienated（变孤独）by modern life, Kaczynski is "average"

of his time. Rather than an isolated case（孤立案例）. You seem to use him almost as tool through which to consider what went wrong with the society that produced him.

Alston Chase：

Right. The story of Kaczynski is something through which we can view（观察）recent American social, political, and intellectual history. That's what I think is instructive（有益的）about his story. His hatred to technology is a hatred to what he calls "technological society". More and more people are becoming fearful about the direction in which the modern society is going. At the core of that concern is an ethical crisis（伦理危机）. The message that the modern world carries is that we have no absolute standard on which to make moral judgments.

Sage Stossel：

You argue that in order to stop the development of future Ted Kaczynskis, we need to restore a broad liberal arts（人文教育）in the college curriculum, and "rethink（进行反思）the role of ideologies（思想信仰）in modern life." I was wondering what those measures would need to turn the tide（改变局面）.

Alston Chase：

There's a whole bundle of things here that concern me. Certainly high schools are the place for alienation. The high school was, during Kaczynski's growing up, just as it tends to be today（今天的中学和当初一样）, an anti-intellectual（反知识）place. If you are a young person with intellectual interests, you are almost automatically excluded or made to feel strange. Something we've seen in school killings is that kids who do it tend to be brighter than average. That's part of their problem.

Sage Stossel：

Those writings on the subject in the fifties and sixties seemed to have gotten a lot of attention. Did they not really change things?

Alston Chase：

No, they didn't. And on top of that, there was the culture of despair, which is still with us. It's something that kids are encountering even in grammar school. Back in the fifties there was a concern that modern society might destroy civilization and culture. By the sixties it had become a concern that technology and science would destroy nature. It's in the latter form that it's very much with us. You find grade school（小学）kids taught to worry about rainforest depletion（雨林消失）and global warming. I'm concerned about introducing kids to problems like that before they can understand the science. Being taught at such a young age that the world is coming to an end on the basis of scientific theories that may or may not be true I think is very damaging.

Ideology is the disease of the modern era. It's fine to have a political philosophy（政治信仰）, but when a person who holds a political philosophy reaches the point of such absolute certainty about it that he or she can't believe it could possibly be false and is not interested in debating its truth or falsity with others, it can become dangerous. They cause people to depersonalize those holding a different point of view.

Sage Stossel:

And you see education as one of the best ways to reverse this?

Alston Chase:

Education — true education — which would open minds rather than close them, is the solution. I remember a wonderful book by Bertrand Russell in which he discusses the philosophy of skepticism（质疑学说）. His case is that while skepticism may reduce ideas of what we know, it greatly expands our notions of what we *can* know. A healthy skepticism is a willingness to believe one is wrong. It goes back to the Greek notion（古希腊观念）that the greatest sin is arrogance（狂妄是最大的罪孽）.

I've found that there is a profound misunderstanding today of the role of science in modern life. Most people believe science has all the answers. But in fact, science is an ongoing debate. Different points of view — different theories — are put forward and tested. Over time, some of these theories are found wanting and are rejected, and others replace them. That is the history of science, and to me it's a very exciting process.

Sage Stossel:

I'd like to talk a little more about Kaczynski and what drove him to do what he did. It's clear from the painstaking efforts that he devoted to perfecting his bombs that he lavished extreme care（特别精心）on things that he considered important. But he seems to have been somewhat casual（漫不经心）about whom he sent his bombs to, and why? He randomly（随意）picked victims from academic department listings, addressed bombs to people who had since moved onto other institutions, misspelled names, and seems not to have looked all that deeply into the backgrounds of the people he targeted to make sure they embodied values he opposed.

Alston Chase:

That's a good point. I can't give you any insight（洞察、看透）into his thinking on that. But my own reading（解读）of it is that it represented his view that the nature of terrorism is to commit acts of violence at random, because that way everyone gets a little uneasy. If the acts were aimed very clearly at computer scientists, then I, as a philosopher, would feel safe. But if it's left ambiguous (不明确的), then a much wider range of people might feel fearful. He did believe, however, that all his victims represented ideas that promoted the technological society he hated and sought to destroy. He was like Raskolnikov in *Crime and Punishment*, (《罪与罚》中的拉斯柯尔尼科夫) who said, "I didn't kill an individual, I killed an idea. "(我并没有杀人,只是消灭了他的思想)

Sage Stossel：

I was wondering whether his carelessness might suggest that the act itself of striking out (出击) meant more to him than the intellectual theories he invoked to justify it (祈求为其行为辩护). After all, he was such an ineffectual (微弱) person that he must have found it gratifying (满足) to prove that he could have a physical (有形的) impact on the world and could interact (影响) confidently with others — even if only indirectly through bombs, letters, and riddles.

Alston Chase：

Oh, I think that's very much true. One shouldn't forget there are really two streams (两股思想) that came together in Kaczynski's mind to turn him into the Unabomber. One was the psychological stream — his personal anger. Another was the ideological stream, which allowed him to rationalize (合理化) his anger and make him feel that it was legitimate (合法) and that therefore he could act it out (付诸行动) without feeling guilty about it. Here's a fellow who knows he's very bright and yet he can't hold a job. He finds every job beneath him(不值他做). He feels insulted by his employers when they ask him to do things, so he doesn't do them or he doesn't do them well and he gets fired. That makes him all the more angry. And he's angry at his parents for emphasizing his studies too much and turning him into a socially isolated mathematician. All of these things converged and fueled his anger so that when he finally was able to summon up his courage to be bad, as he put it ineffect, and actually bomb people, he felt great relief. For once he didn't feel ineffectual, and finally there were people out there who were paying attention to him. But this relief was temporary. He was like an addict (瘾君子) who needed another fix (毒剂). One successful bombing wasn't enough — after a while, he would need to do it again. That's why I believe that if he had not been caught, he would have continued to bomb in spite of his promise to *The New York Times* and *The Washington Post* not to do so.

Sage Stossel：

But your description of his character struck me (给我的印象) as typical of mental disorder, symptoms include "marked deficiencies in social skills", "over-sensitivity to sounds, tastes, smells, and sights", a "rich vocabulary", but "difficulty using language in a social context. " I was wondering whether any consideration has been given to the possibility that he might suffer from that kind of disorder.

Alston Chase：

That was actually pointed out to me in another interview. I don't know much about that syndrome（病症）. But in fact, Kaczynski definitely has all of those symptoms you mentioned. So yes, he does form a psychological type. That's the nature of psychology. It can bundle up（归纳）a whole bunch of behavioral traits（特征）and give it a name, but it doesn't really explain anything. Maybe we feel better having a name for it. But that doesn't mean he couldn't help what he did. And it doesn't reduce the importance of noting that he used the arguments of logical positivism（逻辑实证主义）to assuage（减轻）his sense of guilt. It's not as if most people who have been diagnosed with the symptoms commit murder.

Sage Stossel：

Kaczynski has been sentenced to four consecutive life sentences with no possibility of parole. But you point out that he maintains a prodigious correspondence from his cell, that he has legions（大量）of anarchist（无政府主义）admirers, and that paperback editions of his manifesto have become best-sellers. It struck me that prison might actually afford him a kind of lifestyle that he would find congenial（适宜）. Have you been able to get a sense, through your correspondence with him, of what his morale is like these days?

Alston Chase：

That's a good question. I felt that during the time when I was corresponding with him, his morale was not particularly depressed. I was actually amused by the fact that he complained to me in his letters about being so busy. He is in a tiny cell for around twenty-three hours a day. He's not permitted to have, as I understand it, a television or a computer or anything but a pencil and a small amount of reading matter. And he's busy! His entire life he's been an inveterate（写作上瘾）writer, primarily a letter writer. Through letter writing he's had an enormous number of pen pals（笔友）. That's one way in which to say that Kaczynski was a loner who completely misses something. He had many friends. They were just people he didn't see, or didn't see often. When I wrote to him at the very beginning of my research he said that before he would be willing to correspond with me he wanted to see samples of my writing. So I sent him a whole bunch. And he wrote back, "Please don't send me so much at once. I'm too busy to read it all. "

I am inclined to believe that — much as he loved the wilderness — of all the people who might be put in these circumstances, he's probably psychically better able to survive than 99 out of a hundred of them, because he has such an active mind.

Sage Stossel：

Has he seen your book?

Alston Chase：

Not that I know of. I haven't heard one way or the other. But after my *Atlantic* article appeared, a network news producer who at that time thought of doing a piece on it called me up and said he'd contacted Kaczynski about my article. I said, "Oh, what did he think of it?" "Well, he didn't like it." That was all. But that didn't surprise me. I think Kaczynski would only like things written about him which he agrees with 100 percent. However, it was clear in our correspondence that we were both aware that we saw things very, very differently from each other. We carried on a debate on a lot of these issues. He's never been under any illusion that I would write exactly what he'd like to see.

Atlantic Unbound, May 20, 2003

I. Reading comprehension.

1. Chase seems to argue that _____

   A. American school and society were partly responsible for what Kaczynski did.

   B. the family of Kaczynski was largely responsible for his behavior.

   C. Kaczynski was indeed mentally unsound and therefore in no way should be held responsible for the consequences.

   D. Kaczynski was fighting to save the environment and therefore should be pardoned.

2. According to Chase, one factor playing a role in Kaczynski's behavior was the way he was taught in the grade school, _____

   A. which was largely about scientific theories.

   B. which was largely about civilization and culture.

   C. which was largely about introducing kids to problems well before they can understand them.

   D. which was largely about modern industrialization.

3. Chase mentioned Bertrand Russell in the interview _____

   A. for the fact that Bertrand Russell was a great philosopher.

   B. for the fact that Bertrand Russell encouraged healthy skepticism.

   C. for the fact that Bertrand Russell was against skepticism.

   D. for the fact that Bertrand Russell was a sceptic.

4. Kaczynski was casual about whom he sent his bomb _____

   A. so as to scare the whole general public.

   B. because he could not afford the time to pin down his target.

   C. because his intention is just to kill.

    D. because it's difficult to locate a target.

5. Kaczynski's morale was good in the prison _____

    A. due to the fact he enjoyed the food the prison provided.

    B. due to the fact he was happy to have escaped the death penalty.

    C. due to the fact that he changed and reformed himself.

    D. due to the fact that he enjoyed the freedom the prison provided to read, write and communicate with people outside.

II. Topics for further discussion.

1. Who do you think should be responsible for what Kaczynski did?

2. Do you think Kaczynski's behavior is just an over-reaction to the fear that modern way of life will ultimately destroy the environment that humans have to depend upon for survival?

3. Killing innocent people is 100 percent wrong, but do you think his worry about the direction the modern society is heading to can be justified?

4. Are you concerned about the present ongoing destruction of nature and the global warming? As a responsible individual, what do you think you can do in everyday life to help protect the environment?

Passage Two

Solitude (独处)

Henry Thoreau

This is a delicious evening, when the whole body is one sense, and imbibes delight through every pore. I go and come with a strange liberty in Nature, a part of herself. As I walk along the stony shore of the pond in my short-sleeves, though it is cool as well as cloudy and windy, and I see nothing special to attract me, all the elements are unusually congenial (适意的) to me. The bullfrogs trump to usher in the night, and the note of the whip-poor-will is borne on the rippling wind from over the water. Sympathy with the fluttering alder and poplar leaves almost takes away my breath; yet, like the lake, my serenity is rippled but not ruffled. These small waves raised by the evening wind are as remote from storm as the smooth reflecting surface. Though it is now dark, the mind still blows and roars in the wood, the waves still dash, and some creatures lull the rest with their notes. The repose (睡眠) is never complete. The wildest animals do not repose, but seek their prey now; the fox, and skunk, and rabbit, now roam the fields and woods without fear. They are Nature's watchmen-links which connect the days of animated life.

When I return to my house I find that visitors have been there and left their cards, either a bunch of flowers, or a wreath of evergreen, or a name in pencil on a yellow walnut leaf or a chip. They who come rarely to the woods take some little piece of the forest into their hands to play with by the way, which they leave, either intentionally or accidentally. One has peeled a willow wand, woven it into a ring, and dropped it on my table. I could always tell if visitors had called in my absence, either by the bended twigs or grass, or the print of their shoes, and generally of what sex or age or quality they were by some slight trace left, as a flower dropped, or a bunch of grass plucked and thrown away, even as far off as the railroad, half a mile distant, or by the lingering odor of a cigar or pipe. Nay, I was frequently notified of the passage of a traveller along the highway sixty rods off by the scent of his pipe.

Some of my pleasantest hours were during the long rain-storms in the spring or fall, which confined me to the house for the afternoon as well as the forenoon, soothed by their ceaseless roar and pelting（急降）; when an early twilight ushered in a long evening in which many thoughts had time to take root and unfold themselves. In those driving northeast rains which tried the village houses so, when the maids stood ready with mop and pail in front entries to keep the deluge out, I sat behind my door in my little house, which was all entry, and thoroughly enjoyed its protection. In one heavy thunder-shower the lightning struck a large pitch pine across the pond, making a very conspicuous and perfectly regular spiral groove from top to bottom, an inch or more deep, and four or five inches wide, as you would groove a walking-stick. I passed it again the other day, and was struck with awe on looking up and beholding that mark, now more distinct than ever, where a terrific and resistless bolt came down out of the harmless sky eight years ago. Men frequently say to me, "I should think you would feel lonesome down there, and want to be nearer to folks, rainy and snowy days and nights especially." I am tempted to reply to such — This whole earth which we inhabit is but a point in space. How far apart, think you, dwell the two most distant inhabitants of yonder star, the breadth of whose disk cannot be appreciated by our instruments? Why should I feel lonely? Is not our planet in the Milky Way? This which you put seems to me not to be the most important question. What sort of space is that which separates a man from his fellows and makes him solitary? I have found that no exertion of the legs can bring two minds much nearer to one another. What do we want most to dwell near to? Not to many men surely, the depot, the post-office, the bar-room, the meeting-house, the school-house, the grocery, Beacon Hill, or the Five Points, where men most congregate, but to the perennial source of our life, whence in all our experience we have found that to issue, as the willow stands near the water and sends out its roots in that direction. This will vary with different natures, but this is the place where a wise man will dig his cellar... I one evening overtook one of my townsmen, who has accumulated what is called "a handsome property" — though I never got a fair view of it — on the Walden road, driving a pair of cattle to market, who inquired of me how I could bring my mind to give up so many of the comforts of life. I answered that I was very sure I liked it passably well; I was not joking.

And so I went home to my bed, and left him to pick his way through the darkness and the mud to Brighton — or Bright — town — which place he would reach some time in the morning.

We are the subjects of an experiment which is not a little interesting to me. Can we not do without the society of our gossips a little while under these circumstances — have our own thoughts to cheer us? Confucius (孔子) says truly, "Virtue does not remain as an abandoned orphan; it must of necessity have neighbors ('德不孤,必有邻')."

With thinking we may be beside ourselves in a sane sense. By a conscious effort of the mind we can stand aloof from actions and their consequences; and all things, good and bad, go by us like a torrent. We are not wholly involved in Nature. I may be either the driftwood in the stream, or Indra in the sky looking down on it. I may be affected by a theatrical exhibition; on the other hand, I may not be affected by an actual event which appears to concern me much more. I only know myself as a human entity; the scene, so to speak, of thoughts and affections; and am sensible of a certain doubleness by which I can stand as remote from myself as from another. However intense my experience, I am conscious of the presence and criticism of a part of me, which, as it were, is not a part of me, but spectator, sharing no experience, but taking note of it, and that is no more I than it is you. When the play, it may be the tragedy, of life is over, the spectator goes his way. It was a kind of fiction, a work of the imagination only, so far as he was concerned. This doubleness may easily make us poor neighbors and friends sometimes.

I find it wholesome to be alone the greater part of the time. To be in company, even with the best, is soon wearisome and dissipating. I love to be alone. I never found the companion that was so companionable as solitude. We are for the most part more lonely when we go abroad among men than when we stay in our chambers. A man thinking or working is always alone, let him be where he will. Solitude is not measured by the miles of space that intervene between a man and his fellows. The really diligent student in one of the crowded hives of Cambridge College is as solitary as a dervish (苦修僧人) in the desert. The farmer can work alone in the field or the woods all day, hoeing or chopping, and not feel lonesome, because he is employed; but when he comes home at night he cannot sit down in a room alone, at the mercy of his thoughts, but must be where he can "see the folks," and recreate, and, as he thinks, remunerate (酬报) himself for his day's solitude; and hence he wonders how the student can sit alone in the house all night and most of the day without ennui (厌倦) and "the blues"; but he does not realize that the student, though in the house, is still at work in his field, and chopping in his woods, as the farmer in his, and in turn seeks the same recreation and society that the latter does, though it may be a more condensed form of it.

Society is commonly too cheap. We meet at very short intervals, not having had time to acquire any new value for each other. We meet at meals three times a day, and give each other a new taste of that old musty cheese that we are. We have had to agree on a certain set of rules, called etiquette and politeness, to make this frequent meeting tolerable and that we need not come to open war. We meet at the post-office, and at the sociable, and about the fireside every night; we live thick and are in each other's way, and stumble over one another, and I think that we thus lose some respect for one another. Certainly less frequency would suffice for all important and hearty communications. Consider the girls in a factory — never alone, hardly in their dreams. It would be better if there were but one inhabitant to a square mile, as where I live. The value of a man is not in his skin, that we should touch him.

I have heard of a man lost in the woods and dying of famine and exhaustion at the foot of a tree, whose loneliness was relieved by the grotesque visions with which, owing to bodily weakness, his diseased imagination surrounded him, and which he believed to be real. So also, owing to bodily and mental health and strength, we may be continually cheered by a like but more normal and natural society, and come to know that we are never alone.

I have a great deal of company in my house; especially in the morning, when nobody calls. Let me suggest a few comparisons, that some one may convey an idea of my situation. I am no more lonely than the loon in the pond that laughs so loud, or than Walden Pond itself. What company has that lonely lake, I pray? And yet it has not the blue devils, but the blue angels in it, in the azure tint of its waters. The sun is alone, except in thick weather, when there sometimes appear to be two, but one is a mock sun. God is alone — but the devil, he is far from being alone; he sees a great deal of company; he is legion. I am no more lonely than a single mullein or dandelion in a pasture, or a bean leaf, or sorrel, or a horse-fly, or a bumblebee. I am no more lonely than the Mill Brook, or a weathercock, or the north star, or the south wind, or an April shower, or a January thaw, or the first spider in a new house.

The indescribable innocence and beneficence of Nature — of sun and wind and rain, of summer and winter — such health, such cheer, they afford forever! and such sympathy have they ever with our race, that all Nature would be affected, and the sun's brightness fade, and the winds would sigh humanely, and the clouds rain tears, and the woods shed their leaves and put on mourning in midsummer, if any man should ever for a just cause grieve. Shall I not have intelligence with the earth? Am I not partly leaves and vegetable mould myself? What is the pill which will keep us well, serene, contented? Not my or thy great-grandfather's, but our great-grandmother Nature's universal, vegetable, botanic medicines, by which she has kept herself young always, outlived so many old Parrs in her day, and fed her health with their decaying fatness. For my panacea, instead of one of those quack vials of a mixture dipped from Acheron and the Dead Sea, which come out of those long shallow black-schooner looking wagons which we sometimes see made to carry bottles, let me have a draught of undiluted morning air. Morning air! If men will not drink of this at the fountainhead of the day, why, then, we must even bottle up some and sell it in the shops, for the benefit of those who have lost their subscription ticket to morning time in this world. But remember, it will not keep quite till noonday even in the coolest cellar, but drive out the stopples long ere that and follow westward the steps of Aurora. I am no worshipper of Hygeia, who was the daughter of that old herb-doctor Esculapius, and who is represented on monuments holding a serpent in one hand, and in the other a cup out of which the serpent sometimes drinks; but rather of Hebe, cup-bearer to Jupiter, who was the daughter of Juno and wild lettuce, and who had the power of restoring gods and men to the vigor of youth. She was probably the only thoroughly sound — conditioned, healthy, and robust young lady that ever walked the globe, and wherever she came it was spring.

Retrieved from *http : // eserver. org/ thoreau/ walden*05. *html*

Decide whether the following statements are True or False.

1. In a delicious serene evening, Thoreau felt himself identified with Nature. (　　)
2. Thoreau could always tell if visitors had called during his absence by some visible or invisible traces they left. (　　)
3. Thoreau felt lonely down in the wood cabin and wanted to be nearer to folks, on rainy and snowy days and nights especially. (　　)
4. When Thoreau says "No exertion of the legs can bring two minds much nearer to one another", he means people can be together and still feel lonely. (　　)
5. According to Thoreau, social etiquette and politeness make it possible for us to respect each other and thus enjoy our frequent meetings. (　　)

Unit 2

The Future of Science ... Is Art?

本单元课文综述

Text 精读 探讨未来科学的发现将如何取得突破？科学与艺术有什么关系？它们有相通之处吗？科学能否从艺术中得到启发？作者阐述隐喻（metaphor）——这一被传统认为属于文学艺术的表现手段——如何在科学家探索与认识物质世界的思维过程中发挥作用，进而阐明科学与艺术的融通之处。

Passage One 泛读 是 LiveScience 杂志与物理学家及小说家 Alan Lightman 就科学的未来发展问题进行的访谈。

Passage Two 泛读 论述科学的发展对社会产生了什么样的影响？是社会的繁荣，经济的全球化，还是暴力冲突与战争？科学家的责任是什么？科学精神起着什么样的作用？

ext

The Future of Science... Is Art?
JONAH LEHRER

In the early 1920s, **Niels Bohr** was struggling to reimagine the structure of matter. Previous generations of physicists had thought the inner space of an atom looked like a **miniature** solar system with the atomic nucleus as the sun and the **whirring** electrons as planets in orbit. This was the classical model.

But Bohr had spent time analyzing the radiation emitted by electrons, and he realized that science needed a new metaphor. The behavior of electrons seemed to **defy** every conventional explanation. As Bohr said, "When it comes to atoms, language can be used only as in poetry." Ordinary words couldn't capture the data.

Bohr had long been fascinated by cubist paintings. As the intellectual historian Arthur Miller notes, he later filled his study with abstract still life and enjoyed explaining his interpretation of the art to visitors. For Bohr, the **allure** of cubism was that it **shattered** the certainty of the object. The art revealed the **fissures** in everything, turning the **solidity** of matter into a **surreal blur**.

Bohr's **discerning conviction** was that the invisible world of the electron was essentially a cubist world. By 1923, De Broglie had already determined that electrons could exist as either particles or waves. What Bohr maintained was that the form they took depended on how you looked at them. Their very nature was a consequence of our observation. This meant that electrons weren't like little planets at all. Instead, they were like one of Picasso's **deconstructed** guitars, a blur of **brushstrokes** that only made sense once you stared at it. The art that looked so strange was actually telling the truth.

It's hard to believe that a work of abstract art might have actually affected the history of science. Cubism seems to have nothing in common with modern physics. When we think about the scientific process, a specific vocabulary comes to mind: objectivity, experiments, facts. In the passive tense of the scientific paper, we imagine a perfect reflection of the real world. Paintings can be profound, but they are always **pretend**.

This view of science as the sole **mediator** of everything depends upon one unstated assumption: While art cycles with the fashions, scientific knowledge is a **linear ascent**. The history of science is supposed to obey a simple equation: Time plus data equals understanding. One day, we believe, science will solve everything.

But the **trajectory** of science has proven to be a little more complicated. The more we know about reality — about its quantum mechanics and **neural** origins — the more **palpable** its paradoxes become. As Vladimir Nabokov, the novelist and **lepidopterist**, once put it, "The greater one's science, the deeper the sense of mystery."

Consider, for example, the history of physics. Once upon a time, and more than once, physicists thought they had the universe solved. Some obscure details remained, but the basic structure of the cosmos was understood. Out of this **naïveté**, relativity theory emerged, fundamentally altering classical notions about the relationship of time and space. Then came Heisenberg's uncertainty principle and the surreal **revelations** of quantum physics. String theorists, in their attempts to **reconcile** ever widening theoretical gaps, started talking about eleven dimensions. Dark matter still makes no sense. Modern physics knows so much more about the universe, but there is still so much it doesn't understand. For the first time, some scientists are openly wondering if we, in fact, are incapable of figuring out the cosmos.

I believe that understanding the world is a lot like seeing the world, and the visual illusions to which the eye **is prone** provide **exquisite** metaphors for the cognitive illusions to which the mind is prone. When you first look at a drawing such as Escher's *Relativity*, everything seems fine. But as you inspect it you suddenly realize that what you're seeing is impossible — each section of the canvas is coherent but all these possible parts add up to an impossible whole. Escher's work exposes the **masterful** fraud that our brains **perpetrate** upon us — the neural magic show that we call reality.

Relativity, 1953 M. C. ESCHER

Study for an angel's face from The Virgin of the Rocks,
ca. 1483 LEONARDO DA VINCI

This pencil study **stunningly** illustrates for me a key parallel between science and the arts: They strive for representation and expression, to capture some essential truth about a chosen subject with simplicity and economy. My equations and diagrams are no more the world I'm trying to describe than the artist's pencil strokes are the woman he drew. However, it shows what's possible, despite that limitation. The woman that emerges from the simple pencil strokes is so alive that she stares into your soul. In attempting to capture the universe, I mustn't confuse my equations with the real thing, but from them some essential truths about nature will spring forth, **transcending** the mathematics and coming to life.

At first glance, physics seems particularly remote from the subjective sphere of the arts. Its theories are **extracted from arcane** equations and the subatomic **debris** of **supercolliders**. This science continually insists that our most basic intuitions about reality are actually illusions, a sad myth of the senses. Artists rely on the imagination, but modern physics exceeds the imagination. To paraphrase Hamlet, there are more things in heaven and earth — dark matter, quarks, black holes — than could ever be dreamt up. A universe this strange could only be discovered.

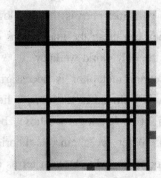

© Kimbell Art Museum/Corbis

Composition No. 8, 1939—1942 PIET MONDRIAN

Mondrian, in search of "the constant truths concerning forms," settled on the straight line as the major feature of his compositions. He believed that straight lines are **constituents** of all forms. Many years later, **physiologists** discovered orientation-selective cells, which respond selectively to straight lines, and are widely thought to be the physiological "**building blocks**" of form perception. Each cell responds increasingly more **grudgingly** when exposed to images that depart from the preferred orientation, until the response disappears altogether at the **orthogonal** orientation.

But the surreal nature of physics is precisely why it needs the help of artists. The science has progressed beyond our ability to understand it, at least in any literal sense. As Richard Feynman put it, "Our imagination is stretched to the utmost, not, as in fiction, to imagine things which are not really there, but just to comprehend those things which *are* there." It's a brute fact of psychology that the human mind cannot comprehend the double-digit dimensions of string theory, or the possibility of parallel universes. Our mind evolved in a simplified world, where matter is certain, time flows forward and there are only three dimensions. When we venture beyond these innate intuitions, we are forced to **resort to** *metaphor*. This is the irony of modern physics: It seeks reality in its most fundamental form, and yet we are utterly incapable of comprehending these fundaments beyond the math we use to represent them. The only way to know the universe is through analogy.

As a result, the history of physics is littered with metaphorical leaps. Einstein grasped relativity while thinking about moving trains. Arthur Eddington compared the expansion of the universe to an **inflated** balloon. James Clerk Maxwell thought of magnetic fields as little **whirlpools** in space, which he called **vortices**. The Big Bang was just a cosmic firecracker. Schrödinger's cat, trapped in a cosmic **purgatory**, helped illustrate the paradoxes of quantum mechanics. It's hard to imagine string theory without its garden hose.

These scientific similes might seem like **quaint** oversimplifications, but they actually perform a much more profound function. As the physicist and novelist Alan Lightman writes, "Metaphor in science serves not just as a **pedagogical** device, but also as an aid to scientific discovery. In doing science, even though words and equations are used with the intention of having precise meaning, it is almost impossible not to reason by physical analogy, not to form mental pictures, not to imagine balls bouncing and **pendulums** swinging." The power of a metaphor is that it allows scientists imagine the abstract concept in concrete terms, so that they can grasp the implications of their mathematical equations. The world of our ideas is framed by the only world we know.

But relying on metaphor can also be dangerous, since every metaphor is necessarily imperfect. (As Thomas Pynchon put it, "The act of metaphor is a **thrust** at truth and a lie, depending on where you are.") The strings of the universe might be *like* a garden hose, but they are *not* a garden hose. The cosmos isn't a plastic balloon. When we chain our theories to ordinary language, we are **trespassing on** the purity of the equation. To think in terms of analogies is to walk a **tightrope** of accuracy.

© The Bridgeman Art Library/Getty Images
A Couple in the Street, 1887 CHARLES ANGRAND

Human eyes are horizontally **offset** from each other, and the visual system uses that offset to calculate depth. When an object is **fixated upon**, images are **cast on** the same place on each **retina**. A view with many identical (or similar) objects casts multiple images on the eyes, which can either be correctly matched, giving a flat impression, or mismatched, so one image corresponds to the other, but at a different depth. I think that the artists from the impressionist and post-impressionist periods figured this out. They said they could paint air and managed to do so by creating false **stereopsis cues**, which manipulate depth perception. So Angrand's painting actually looks more three-dimensional when you view the painting with both eyes instead of with a single eye.

This is why modern physics needs the arts. Once we accept the importance of metaphor to the scientific process, we can start thinking about how we can make those metaphors *better*. Poets, of course, are masters of metaphor: The power of their art depends on the **compression** of meaning into meter; vague feelings are translated into **visceral** images. It's not a coincidence that many of the greatest physicists of the 20th century — eminent figures like Einstein, Feynman, and Bohr — were known for their distinctly romantic method of thinking. These eminent scientists depended on their ability to use metaphor to see what no one else had ever seen, so that the railroad became a metaphor for relativity, and a drop of liquid helped symbolize the atomic nucleus. Poets can speed this scientific process along, helping physicists to invent new metaphors and improve their old ones. Perhaps we can do better than a garden hose. Maybe a simile will help unlock the secret of dark matter. As the string theorist Brian Greene recently wrote, the arts have the ability to "give a vigorous shake to our sense of what's real," **jarring** the scientific imagination into imagining new things.

But there's another way that artists can bring something to the cosmic conversation: they can help make the scientific metaphors **tangible.** When the **metaphysical** equation is turned into a physical object, physicists can explore the meaning of the mathematics from a different perspective. Look, for example, at a Richard Serra sculpture. His **labyrinths** of bent metal let us participate in the theoretical, so that we might imagine the strange curves of space-time in an entirely new way. The fragmented shapes of cubism, which engaged in such a fruitful dialogue with the **avant-garde** physics of its time, served a similar purpose. Picasso never understood the equations — he picked up **non-Euclidean** geometry via the **zeitgeist** — but he was determined to represent this new way of thinking about space in his paintings. A century later, physicists are still using his shattered still **lifes** as a **potent** symbol of their science. Abstract art lets us comprehend, at least a little bit, the incomprehensible.

It's time for the dialogue between our two cultures to become a standard part of the scientific method. (Our universities could begin by offering a "Poetry for Physicists" class.) But it's also crucial to take our scientific metaphors beyond the realm of the metaphorical, so we can better understand the consequences of our theories. Art galleries should be filled with **disorienting evocations** of string theory and the EPR paradox. Every theoretical physics department should support an artist-in-residence. Too often, modern physics seems remote and irrelevant, its suppositions so strange that they're meaningless. The arts can help us reattach physics to the world we experience.

© Francis G. Mayer/Corbis
The Tragedy, 1903

PABLO PICASSO

Artists have known for a very long time that color and **luminance** can be treated independently. Our perception of depth, three-dimensionality, movement (or the lack of it), and **spatial** organization are all carried by a subdivision of our visual system that is essentially color-blind, and sees the world in shades of gray. This is an evolutionarily older part of our visual system. One cannot see depth or motion in the absence of luminance contrast. In Picasso's *The Tragedy*, one can appreciate the three-dimensionality of the scene because, despite the peculiar choice of colors, the luminance is just right.

Retrieved from *http://seedmagazine.com/news/2008/01/the_future_of_scienceis_art. php? page*

New Words and Phrases

miniature	adj.	being on a very small scale 小型的，微小的
whir	v.	作呼呼响
defy	v.	challenge 公然反抗，蔑视
allure	n.	the power to entice or attract 诱惑力，魅力
shatter	v.	to break into pieces; smash or burst 砸碎，粉碎
fissure	n.	a long narrow opening 裂缝或裂隙
solidity	n.	固体性
surreal	adj.	having an oddly dreamlike quality 超现实的
blur	n.	hazy 模糊
discerning	adj.	keen insight 有见识的
conviction	n.	坚定的信仰(主张)，深信，坚信
deconstructed	adj.	broken down into components; dismantled 解构的
brushstroke	n.	一笔，一画，笔法
pretend	adj.	informal imitation; make-believe 模仿的，仿制的
mediator	n.	a go-between 调停者
linear	adj.	of, relating to, or resembling a line 直线的，线性的
ascent	n.	a movement upward 上升
trajectory	n.	轨迹，轨道
neural	adj.	of or relating to the nervous system 神经的
palpable	adj.	easily perceived; obvious 明显的，明白的
lepidopterist	n.	鳞翅类学者
naivete	n.	innocence 天真，质朴
revelation	n.	an enlightening or astonishing disclosure 发现，揭露
exquisite	adj.	acutely perceptive or discriminating 敏感的，细致的

masterful	*adj.*	revealing supreme mastery or skill 大师的
perpetrate	*v.*	commit 犯（罪），作（恶）
stunningly	*adv.*	in a spectacular manner 惊人地，令人目瞪口呆地
arcane	*adj.*	secret or mysterious 神秘的，秘密的
debris	*n.*	ruins 碎片，残骸
supercollider	*n.*	a high-energy particle accelerator 超级对撞机
constituent	*n.*	component; element 成分，构成部分
physiologist	*n.*	a biologist specializing in physiology 生理学家
physiological	*adj.*	生理学的
building block		基本成分
grudgingly	*adv.*	in an unwilling manner 吝啬地
orthogonal	*adj.*	relating to or composed of right angles 直角的，直交的
inflate	*v.*	fill with gas or air 使充气（于轮胎、气球等）
whirlpool	*n.*	a magnetic, impelling force into which one may be pulled 漩涡
vortex	*n.*	漩涡（pl. vortices）
purgatory	*n.*	orment or suffering 炼狱
quaint	*adj.*	queer; odd; eccentric 少见的，古怪的
pedagogical	*adj.*	of or relating to pedagogy 教学法的
pendulum	*n.*	钟摆
thrust	*n.*	drive 驱动力
tightrope	*n.*	钢丝
retina	*n.*	视网膜
stereopsis	*n.*	立体观测，立体影像
cue	*n.*	evidence that helps to solve a problem; clue 线索
compression	*n.*	压缩
visceral	*adj.*	直觉的
jar	*v.*	to shake or shiver from impact 使震动
tangible	*adj.*	possible to understand or realize 明白的；有形的，可触摸的
metaphysical	*adj.*	highly abstract and overly theoretical 形而上学的
labyrinth	*n.*	maze 迷宫
avant-garde	*adj.*	radically new or original 先锋派
non-euclidean	*adj.*	非欧几里得的
zeitgeist	*n.*	时代精神，时代思潮
lifes	*n.*	活体模型，写真
potent	*adj.*	having great influence; powerful 强有力的
disorienting	*adj.*	使……迷惑的
evocation	*n.*	imaginative re-creation 再现，通过记忆和想象的力量再

创造

| luminance | n. | emitting or reflecting light 亮度 |
| spatial | adj. | 空间的 |

About the author：

Jonah Lehrer is an editor at large for Seed magazine. A graduate of Columbia University and a Rhodes scholar. He has written for the Boston Globe, Nature, NPR, and NOVA Science.

Notes to the text

1. **Niels Bohr**（尼尔斯·玻尔, 1885—1962）：A Denish physicist, Bohr made numerous contributions to our understanding of the structure of properties of atoms, for which he won the 1922 Nobel Prize for Physics. 丹麦物理学家, 1922 年, 由于在研究原子结构和由此产生的辐射所做出的贡献, 玻尔荣获诺贝尔物理学奖。

2. **Cubist painting**, **also Cubism**（立体绘画）：a nonobjective school of painting and sculpture developed in Paris in the early 20th century, characterized by the reduction and fragmentation of natural forms into abstract, often geometric structures usually rendered as a set of discrete planes.

3. **Arthur I. Miller**（阿瑟·米勒, 1915—2005）：Professor of History and Philosophy of Science at University College London.

   其代表作：*Einstein*, *Picasso*：*Space*, *Time*, *and the Beauty That Causes Havoc*

   《爱因斯坦和毕加索：空间、时间和动人心魄之美》

   Quote from Arthur I. Miller：

   "I am fascinated by the nature of creative thinking — the mind's ability to transform information from everyday experiences into the most sublime works of art, literature, music and science."

4. **De Broglie**（德布罗意, 1892—1987）：a French physicist and a Nobel laureate.

5. **Vladimir Nabokov**（弗拉基米尔·纳博科夫, 1899—1977）：a multilingual Russian-American novelist and short story writer. Nabokov wrote his first nine novels in Russian, then rose to international prominence as a master English prose stylist. He also made contributions to entomology and had an interest in chess problems. Nabokov's *Lolita*（1955）is frequently cited as his most important novel, exhibiting the love of intricate wordplay and descriptive detail that characterized all his works. 纳博科夫是二十世纪公认的杰出小说家和文体学家。1899 年 4 月 23 日, 纳博科夫出生于圣彼得堡, 1940 年移居美国。在威尔斯理、斯坦福、康奈尔和哈佛大学执教, 以小说家、诗人、批评家和翻译家身份享誉文坛, 著有《洛丽塔》、《微暗的

火》等长篇小说。

6. **Werner Karl Heisenberg**（海森伯，1901—1976）：a German theoretical physicist. He made contributions to quautum mechanics, nuclear physics, quantum field theory, and particle physics. Heisenberg, along with Max Born and Pascual Jordan, set forth the matrix formulation of quantum mechanics in 1925. Heisenberg was awarded the 1932 Noble Prize for Physics. 德国理论物理学家，量子力学第一种有效形式（矩阵力学）的创建者，1932 年获诺贝尔物理学奖。

7. **String theory**（线性理论）：a still-developing mathematical approach to theoretical physics, whose original building blocks are one-dimensional extended objects called strings. Unlike the point particles in quantum field like the standard model of particle physics, strings interact in a way that is almost uniquely specified by mathematical self-consistency, forming an apparently valid quantum theory of gravity. 线性理论即弦论，是理论物理学上的一门学说。弦论的一个基本观点就是，自然界的基本单元不是电子、光子、中微子和夸克之类的粒子。这些看起来像粒子的东西实际上都是很小的弦的闭合圈（称为闭合弦或闭弦），闭弦的不同振动和运动产生出各种不同的基本粒子。

8. **The Eleven Dimensions of Space/Time**（11 维时空）：All eleven dimensions have a common center; that is, the center of the line, the plane, and the sphere are the same, as is true with the subsequent dimensions. Time transforms the static into the dynamic, which is one reason for labeling it a transformation dimension. Time enables spatial movement (rotation) of the first three dimensions; this movement is measured along dimensions five, six, and seven.

9. **Maurits Cornelis Escher**（埃舍尔，1898—1972）：one of the world's most famous graphic artists. He is most famous for his so-called impossible structures, such as *Ascending and Descending*, *Relativity*.

10. **Quark**（构成原子的最小粒子）：(physics) hypothetical truly fundamental particle in mesons and baryons; there are supposed to be six flavors of quarks (and their antiquarks), which come in pairs; each has an electric charge of $+2/3$ or $-1/3$.

11. **Piet Mondrian**（蒙德里安，1872—1944）：a pioneering artist well-known for his abstract paintings from 1917 to 1944.

12. **Richard Feynman**（理查德·费曼，1918—1988）：an American physicist who won the Nebel Prize for Physics in 1965 for his contributions to the development of quantum electrodynamics.

13. **Authur Eddington**（阿瑟·爱丁顿，1882—1944）：an English physicist who was one of the first to appreciate the importance of Einstein's theories of special and general relativity, and published a treatise on the subject.

14. **James Clerk Maxwell**（詹姆斯·克拉克·麦克斯韦，1831—1879）：a Scottish mathematician and theoretical physicist most known for his classical electromagnetic theory. Maxwell's work in electromagnetism has been called the "*second great*

unification in physics", after the first one carried out by Newton.

15. **The Big Bang**(宇宙大爆炸理论)：the cosmological model of the universe that is best supported by all lines of scientific evidence and observation. The essential idea is that the universe has expanded from a primordial hot and dense initial condition at some finite time in the past and continues to expand to this day.

16. **Schrödinger's cat paradox**（薛丁格猫诡论）：a thought experiment, often described as a paradox, devised by Austrian physicist Erwin Schrödinger in 1935. It illustrated what he saw as the problem of the Copenhagen interpretation of quantum mechanics being applied to everyday objects, in the example of a cat that might be alive or dead, depending on an earlier random event（薛丁格猫诡论是一个诠释量子不确定性的思想实验）。

17. **Alan Lightman**(阿兰·莱特曼,1948—)：a physicist, novelist, and essayist born in Memphis, Tennessee in 1948. He is a professor at the Massachusetts Institute of Technology and the author of the international bestseller *Einstein's Dreams*《爱因斯坦之梦》。

18. **Thomas Ruggles Pynchon**, **Jr**(1937—)：an American writer based in New York City, noted for his dense and complex works of fiction. 托马斯·品钦是一名生于纽约的美国作家,以写晦涩复杂的小说著称。*Gravity's Rainbow*《万有引力之虹》是其代表作。

19. **Charles Théophile Angrand**（1854—1926）：a French neo-Impressionist painter and anarchist.

20. **Brian Greene**(布赖恩·格林)：a theoretical physicist（理论物理学家）and one of the best-known string theorists. He is known to a wider audience for his books：*The Elegant Universe*《高雅的宇宙》and *The Fabric of the Cosmos*《宇宙的结构》。

21. **Richard Serra**(理查德·塞拉)：an American minimalist（极简抽象派）sculptor and video artist known for working with large scale assemblies of sheet metal.

22. **EPR paradox**（EPR 悖论）：In quantum mechanics, EPR paradox is a thought experiment which challenged long-held ideas about the relation between the observed values of physical quantities and the values that can be accounted for by a physical theory. "EPR" stands for Einstein, Podolsky, and Rosen, who introduced the thought experiment in a 1935 paper to argue that quantum mechanics is not a complete physical theory（这三位物理学家为论证量子力学的不完备性而提出的一个悖论,又称 EPR 论证或 EPR 悖论。这个悖论涉及到如何理解微观物理存在的问题）。

Exercises

I. Answer the following questions based on Text 1, the words and expressions listed below are for your reference.

　1. **How do you understand the classical model of art**?

inner space / miniature solar system / nucleus / electron

2. Why did Bohr think that science needed a new metophor?

behavior / defy / language / capture data

3. Why does you author say that it is hard to believe that a work of abstract art might have actually affected the history of science?

have nothing in common / objectivity / experiment / fact / pretend

4. Why are scientists openly wondering if we are incapable of figuring out the cosmos?

physicist think / the basic structure of the cosmos / relativity theory / uncertainty principle / string theorist / dark matter / modern physics

5. How do you understand Escher's painting *Relativity*? What does it expose to us?

fine / inspect / impossible / coherent / impossible whole / masterful fraud

6. Why does the author say that the history of physics is littered with metaphorical leaps?

relativity / moving train / inflated balloon / magnetic / whirlpool / firecracker

7. What function does metaphor in science perform? Why does the author say that relying on metophor can also be dangerous?

abstract concept / concrete terms / grasp the implication / imperfect / trespass on the purity of equation / walk a tightrope of accuracy

8. Why does modern physics need the arts for help?

accept / metaphor / think about / use metaphor to see / speed scientific process / invent new metaphors and improve

9. In what other ways can artists bring something to the cosmic conversation?

help / make. . . tangible / physical object / explore / Richard Serra sculpture / the fragmented shapes of cubism / abstract art

10. What can we do to bring the dialogue between science and art in order to come up with a standard part of the scientific method?

offer. . . classes / art gallery / theoretical physics department

II. Further questions for discussion.

1. Do you believe that the future of science is art?

2. What is science? Why is science possible? How do scientists do their science?

3. How much do you know about the development of modern science?

4. What has science brought to us? Can you analyse the impact of science on society?

5. What is the relationship between knowledge and wisdom? Which is more important?

III. Vocabulary study.

1. Word in use.

1) **be prone to sth / to do sth**: having a tendency (to)易于……,倾向于……

Children of poor health are very prone to colds in winter.

People are more prone to make mistakes when they are tired.

Some plants are prone to a particular disease.

I am as suspicious and prone to take offence as a humpback or a dwarf.

2) **transcend**：go beyond 超越

She far transcends the others in beauty and intelligence.

When you are able to transcend them, you learn the lesson of limitlessness.

One never can see the thing in itself, because the mind does not transcend phenomena.

3) **extract ... from**：(好不容易)获得,取得

It took me a few days to extract the truth from her.

I had extracted a detailed account from him.

He looked up, for an instant at a time, when he was requested to do so; but, no persuasion would extract a word from him.

4) **resort to sth/doing sth**：fall back on someone or something in time of need 诉诸于……,求助于

It was after the failure of this attempt that he resorted to force.

You should have resorted to your parents.

If negotiations fail we shall have to resort to strike action.

5) **trespass on**：to infringe on the privacy, time, or attention of another 非法侵入

I don't want to trespass on your hospitality.

May I trespass on your valuable time?

He accused me of trespassing on his estate.

6) **offset**：make up for or compensate for or counterbalance 抵消

He raised his prices to offset the increased cost of materials.

Higher mortgage rates are partly offset by increased tax allowances.

Airlines will appeal for higher jet-fuel surcharges to help air carriers offset the rising prices of oil.

7) **fixate ... on / upon**：to focus the eyes or attention; pay attention to exclusively and obsessively 注视,凝视

An infant with normal vision will fixate on a light held before him.

He seems to be fixated on this idea of traveling around the world.

He is fixated on things that remind him of his childhood.

8) **cast ... on / over**：put or send forth 投射(光线,视线,影子)

The tree cast its shadow on the window.

The candles cast a warm glow on the table.

The grey evening light cast queer shadows on the floor.

Both leaders were repeatedly asked about Israel's continued settlement construction, an issue that has cast a shadow over Palestinian peace talks.

2. Word distinctions.

　1）**reconcile ... with , reconcile ... to**

　　课文中"String theoriests, in their attempts to reconcile ever widening theoretical gaps ..."其中 reconcile 的含义是"使一致,和解",其后可以加介词 with,即 reconcile ... with ...

　　但 reconcile ... to / reconcile oneself to 的含义是"使甘心,使接受"。

　　选择以上适当的词填空：

　　I can't _____ these figures _____ the statement you prepared.

　　Could you _____ a lifetime of unemployment?

　　She could never _____ his violent temper _____ his pacifist ideals.

　　We watch the character as he tries to _____ the idea of his own death.

　　After 20 years of silence, he was finally _____ his family.

　　The struggle to _____ personal fulfillment _____ familial obligation is common in this generation of immigrant daughters.

　2）**identify 辨认, identify with 认同**

　　选择以上适当的词填空：

　　I found it hard to _____ any of the characters in the film.

　　Could you _____ your umbrella among a hundred others?

　　They, in turn, are loyal and _____ the company's goals.

　　So some schools are using response to intervention as a way to _____ problems much earlier.

　　We must then _____ our dreams and establish financial goals so we can turn our dreams into reality.

　　Having read *The Tales of Two Cities*, we _____ the main characters' struggle.

3. Decide the meanings of the following words from the context by matching each word in Column A with the word or expression in Column B that is similar in meaning.

A	B
1）labyrinth	a. attract
2）defy	b. counterbalance
3）allure	c. a movement upward
4）discerning	d. go beyond
5）ascent	e. perceptive
6）inflate	f. maze
7）vortex	g. whirlpool
8）offset	h. instinctive
9）visceral	i. challenge

10) transcend   j. blow up

4. Try to write a brief story or a conversation with the following words and phrases.

science, art, society, impact, progress, harm, scientific spirit, ethics, scientific method, have ... in common

IV. Translation.

1. Put the following Chinese expressions into English.

1）物质结构　　2）量子物理学　　3）科学想象　　4）原子的内部空间

5）抽象概念　　6）古典模式　　7）科学隐喻　　8）加速科学进程

2. Put the following Chinese sentences into English with the words or phrases in the brackets.

1）任何与上古神话传说有关的东西都会使我着迷。(fascinate)

2）由于这些困难,有些妇女选择接受现实,而这可能会导致未来更严重的家庭暴力。(reconcile)

3）日本是世界上最易发生地震的国家,每年经历数以千计的小地震。(prone)

4）他们的设计绝大部分符合实际需要和有关环境要求的条例。(correspond to)

5）为找到一份合适的工作, 有些大学毕业生求教于就业顾问。(resort to)

6）他退休前一天正好将是他执教满 40 年的日子,这真是奇妙的巧合。(coincidence)

7）亨利无意干预我所负责的领域,但他觉得必须指出我的报告中的一两处疏漏。(trespass on)

8）更重要的是要花时间给您的家人或给自己,而不是只关注整理家务。(fixate on)

3. Put the following Chinese paragraph into English.

爱伯·爱伯斯费尔塔(Eibl·bibesfeldt)说:"艺术探索人的情感的深度,进而主要是表达信念和其他价值,而科学的目的是传达客观知识。这似乎是艺术与科学的基本差异。"科学与艺术的基本出发点的不同,导致了科学与艺术对客体的基本态度和方式的不同。概括地讲,科学是以数学原理为基础,以抽象简化的方式描述对自然对象的认识,数学公式是它给予自然的最终图像;艺术是以生命——情感原理为基础,以具体感性的方式表达对自然对象的感受,艺术形象是它给予自然的主要表象。

4. Put the following quotes into Chinese.

1）True science teaches, above all, to doubt and be ignorant.

—— Miguel de Unamuno

2）Truth has no special time of it's own. Its hour is now always.

—— A. Schweitzer

3）That is the essence of science: ask an impertinent question, and you are on the way to the pertinent answer.

—— Jacob Bronowski

4) Love alone can release the power of the atom so it will work for man and not
against him.   —— W. A. Peterson

5) I want to bring out the secrets of nature and apply them for the happiness of man.
I don't know of any better service to offer for the short time we are in the world.
                                                        —— Thomas Edison

5. Translate the following passage into Chinese.

　　But putting parables aside, I am unable to understand how any one with a
knowledge of mankind can imagine that the growth of science can threaten the
development of art in any of its forms. If I understand the matter at all, science and
art are the obverse and reverse of Nature's medal; the one expressing the eternal order
of things, in terms of feeling, the other in terms of thought. When men no longer
love nor hate; when suffering causes no pity, and the tale of great deeds ceases to
thrill, when the lily of the field shall seem no longer more beautifully arrayed than
Solomon in all his glory, and the awe has vanished from the snow-capped peak and
deep ravine, then indeed science may have the world to itself, but it will not be
because the monster has devoured art, but because one side of human nature is dead,
and because men have lost the half of their ancient and present attributes.

V. Comment on the structure of the text.

This text is a piece of expository writing（论说文）

　　The title of the text *The Future of Science . . . Is Art?* is question-marked after a
statement; obviously therefore, the writer does not intend to provoke argument.
Traditional theory deems science and art as two fields of clear-cut difference: while
science is based on logic and reasoning, art belongs to the realm of imagination and
romance. Is art irrelevant to science? The writer proceeds from how we perceive the
world by quoting Physicist Bohr. "When it comes to atoms, language can be used only
as in poetry. Ordinary words couldn't capture the data." Bohr realised "science needs a
new metaphor". This perception diminishes the boundary between art and science.
Metaphor has been thought to be of a distinctive feature of art and literature, and amply
employed by artists, but in the text, the writer notes that metaphor is an important means
in our perception of the world, as he puts it: "When we venture beyond these innate
intuitions, we are forced to resort to *metaphor*." This is where art joins science and hence
the gist of this expository writing.

　　And this explains why "Bohr had long been fascinated by cubist paintings. ... For
Bohr, the allure of cubism was that it shattered the certainty of the object. The art
revealed the fissures in everything（立体绘画揭示了物质裂变）, turning the solidity of
matter into a surreal blur."

There have been studies on the relationship between metaphor and the perception of the material world, among them "*Metaphor We Live By*" by Lakoff & Johnson published in 1980 sums up the gist: metaphor partakes our perception of the world and is the basic mode of human existence.

Extended Exercises

1. In the following article, some paragraphs have been removed. Choose the most suitable paragraph from the list A — G to fit into each of the numbered gaps. There are TWO paragraphs which do not fit in any of the gaps.

Researchers have found that genes play a large role in shaping a child's emotional makeup, but a child's personality traits are also profoundly affected by his or her environment. Genetic and environmental factors combine in complex ways to shape a child's psychological development.

The wizards of genetics keep closing in on the biological roots of personality. It's not your imagination that one baby seems born cheerful and another morose. But that's not the complete picture. 1) _____.

In the last few years scientists have identified genes that appear to predict all sorts of emotional behavior, from happiness to aggressiveness to risk-taking. 2) _____. But the answer may not be so simple after all. Scientists are beginning to discover that genetics and environment work together to determine personality as intricately as Astaire and Rogers danced. Nature affects nurture and back and forth. Each step influences the next.

3) _____. An aggressive toddler, under the tight circumstances, can essentially be rewired to channel his energy more constructively. A child can overcome his shyness — forever. No child need be held captive to her genetic blueprint. The implications for child rearing — and social policy — are profound.

While Gregor Mendel's pea plants did wonders to explain how humans inherit blue eyes or a bald spot, they turn out to be an inferior model for analyzing something as complex as the brain. 4) _____. Genes control the brain's neurotransmitters and receptors, which deliver and accept mental messages like so many cars headed for their assigned parking spaces. But there are billions of roads to each parking lot, and those paths are highly susceptible to environmental factors.

5) _____.

Children conceived during a three-month famine in the Netherlands during a Nazi blockade in 1945 were later found to have twice the rate of schizophrenia as did Dutch children born to parents who were spared the trauma of famine. "Twenty years ago, you couldn't get your research funded if you were looking for a genetic basis for schizophrenia, because everyone knew it was what your mother did to you in the first few years of life, as Freud said," says Robert Plomin, a geneticist at London's Institute of Psychiatry. "Now you can't get funded unless you're looking for a genetic basis. Neither extreme is right, and the data show why. There's only a 50 percent concordance between genetics and the development of schizophrenia."

A: Many scientists now believe that some experiences can actually alter the structure of the brain.

B: Meanwhile, genetic claims are being made for a host of ordinary and abnormal behaviors, from addiction to shyness and even to political views and divorce. If who we are is determined from conception, then our efforts to change or to influence our children may be futile. There may also be no basis for insisting that people behave themselves and conform to laws. Thus, the revolution in thinking about genes has monumental consequences for how we view ourselves as human beings.

C: DNA is not destiny; experience plays a powerful role, too.

D: A gene is only a probability for a given trait, not a guarantee. For that trait to be expressed, a gene often must be "turned on" by an outside force before it does its job. High levels of stress apparently activate a variety of genes, including those suspected of being involved in fear, shyness and some mental illnesses.

E: The human body contains about 100,000 genes, of which 50,000 to 70,000 are involved in brain function.

F: The inextricable interplay between genes and environment is evident in disorders like alcoholism, anorexia, or overeating that are characterized by abnormal behaviors. Scientists spiritedly debate whether such syndromes are more or less biologically driven. If they are mainly biological — rather than psychological, social, and cultural — then there may be a genetic basis for them.

G: The age-old question of whether nature or nurture determines temperament seems finally to have been decided in favor of Mother Nature and her ever-deepening gene pool.

2. **The following paragraphs are given in the wrong order. Try to reorganize them into a coherent article.**

1) This time the creationists' proposals are "far more radical and much more dangerous", says Keith Miller of Kansas State University, a leading pro-evolution campaigner. "They redefine science itself to include non-natural or supernatural explanations for natural phenomena." The Kansas standards now state that science finds "natural" explanations for things. But conservatives on the board want that changed to "adequate". They also want to define evolution as being based on an atheistic religious viewpoint. "Then they can argue that intelligent design must be included as 'balance'," Miller says.

2) These moves are part of numerous recent efforts by fundamentalist Christians, emboldened by a permissive political climate, to discredit evolution. "As of January this year 18 pieces of legislation had been introduced in 13 states," says Eugenie Scott, head of the National Center for Science Education in Oakland, California, which helps oppose creationist campaigns. That is twice the typical number in recent years, and it stretched from Texas and South Carolina to Ohio and New York. The legislation seeks mainly to force the teaching of ID, or at least "evidence against evolution", in science classes.

3) Also in June, a publicly funded zoo in Tulsa, Oklahoma, voted to install a display showing the six-day creation described in Genesis. The science museum in Fort Worth, Texas, decided in March not to show an IMAX film entitled *Volcanoes of the Deep Sea* after negative reaction to its acceptance of evolution from a trial audience.

4) The fight is being waged on other fronts as well. Scott counts 39 creationist "incidents" other than legislative efforts in 20 states so far this year. In June, for example, the august Smithsonian Institution in Washington DC allowed the showing of an ID film on its premises and with its unwitting endorsement. After an outcry, the endorsement was withdrawn and officials insisted that it was all a mistake, although the screening did go ahead.

5) On 10 July 1925, a drama was played out in a small courtroom in a Tennessee town that touched off a far-reaching ideological battle. John Thomas Scopes, who was a school teacher, was found guilty of teaching evolution. Despite the verdict, Scopes, and the wider scientific project he sought to promote, seemed at the time to have been vindicated by the backlash in the rugan press against his creationist opponents.

6) In the US, Kansas has long been a focus of creationist activity. In 1999 creationists on the Kansas school board had all mention of evolution deleted from its state school standards. Their decision was reversed after conservative Christian board members were defeated in elections in 2002. But more elections brought a conservative majority in November 2004, and the standards are under threat again.

7) Yet 80 years on, creationist ideas have a powerful hold in the US, and science is still under attack. US Supreme Court decisions have made it impossible to teach divine creation as science in state-funded schools. But, in response, creationists have invented "intelligent design" (ID) which, they say, is a scientific alternative to Darwinism. ID has already affected the way science is taught and perceived in schools, museums, zoos and national parks across the US.

8) In January in Dover, Pennsylvania, 9th-grade biology students were read a statement from the school board that said state standards "require students to learn about Darwin's theory of evolution. The theory is not a fact. Gaps in the theory exist for which there is no evidence". Intelligent design, it went on, "is an explanation for the origin of life that differs from Darwin's view". Fifty donated copies of an ID textbook would be kept in

each science classroom. Although ID was not formally taught, students were "encouraged to keep an open mind".

Extensive Reading

Passage One

The Future of Science:
A Conversation with Alan Lightman

Sara Goudarzi

阿兰·莱特曼（Alan Lightman）是名物理学教授，任教于麻省理工学院，同时从事科学研究与写作，著有《爱因斯坦的梦》等小说和科幻作品。在接受 LiveScience 杂志记者的访谈中，他谈了自己对未来科学发现、科学与艺术的关系以及未来科学研究方法等问题的看法。

LiveScience:

What do you think the next great discoveries will be? What fields?

Alan Lightman:

It's hard to know what the next great discoveries will be. In 1900, for example, I don't think it would have been possible to predict that in the next 25 years that both relativity and quantum physics would have been discovered. It's easier to say where the frontiers are for each science.

For example, in physics the frontiers are at string theory, which is a theory of the smallest elements of matter, an explanation of why particles have the masses that they do. Why the proton has the mass that it does.

In astronomy and also in physics the frontiers are in finding the nature of dark energy, which is this anti-gravitational force discovered in the last 5 years [it makes up the bulk of the total mass-energy budget of the universe].

In biology, I think understanding why stem cells begin specializing with some becoming liver cells and some becoming heart cells and some becoming brain cells. We don't know why cells specialize. They all start out the same yet during the cell division process, they start going in different directions. We don't understand that.

I think biotechnology is a tremendous field for growth and new discoveries, combining inanimate matter with animate matter. I think in the next 100 years we will have some organisms that are half human and half machine.

LiveScience:

Do you have any idea who these people might be (the discoverers)?

Alan Lightman:

No. I know some of the great scientists of today but don't know who the great scientists of tomorrow will be. In string theory for example, one of the areas I mentioned, we know that a great genius is Edward Whitten who works for the Institute for Advance Studies in Princeton, and he seems to be the most brilliant of the physicists working in string theory. So it may be that either something that he's already done or something that he will do in the next few years will be a great discovery.

LiveScience:

All these great discoverers sit on the shoulders of little discoverers, right?

Alan Lightman:

Yes, that's right. One of the problems of writing a book of this type where you focus on the great discoveries is that it tends to give the impression that all science depends upon a small number of geniuses and that's not really true.

There are many people who work in science and whose works, although not necessarily of monumental (非常的) importance by themselves, are all part of the great tapestry of science. And it's true that all the great discoveries depend upon previous discoveries both big and small.

LiveScience:

Some people say science is under assault(攻击), with intelligent design, nonbelievers of global warming, lack of support for stem cell research, etc. Do you really think it is really under assault compared to 100 years ago, 200 years ago?

Alan Lightman:

I think science has always been under assault to some extent. I think there are fashions in cycles in which science is attacked for a period of time and is embraced for a period of time and it's attacked again. Generally attack against science is part of a greater attack against intellectualism in general. I think right now we're in an anti-intellectual period in the United States, but I think the pendulum (钟摆) will swing back in the other direction again. I agree with you that we're not seeing anything now that hasn't happened in earlier centuries.

LiveScience:

Do you think it's just human nature because we want to know, and science only takes us to a certain boundary and people have this need to explain how things work?

Alan Lightman:

Yes, human beings have always had a need to find meaning in their personal lives and meaning in the world at large. If you look at the Cro-Magnon paintings (法国克鲁麦农洞穴绘画) and caves in Lascaux in France (法国拉斯科洞窟) you could see that these people 100,000 years ago were searching for meaning.

There are a lot of different ways of searching for meaning. You can search for it in religion; you can search for it in philosophy, you can search for it in science. And science will never fully satisfy most people because science has limitations. Science will never be able to explain why the universe is as it is. Science will never be able to explain what is right and what is wrong and moral and ethical behavior.

LiveScience:

But you always need a skeptic to come by later and push the boundaries of science.

Alan Lightman:

Science is essentially a skeptical (怀疑论者) endeavor, and over the long run the way science proceeds is to be skeptical of received knowledge, to be skeptical of authority. But there are many interesting questions that don't lie in the realm of science. For example, is there a God? Or what is the nature of love? Or would we be happier if we lived to be 1,000 years old?

These are extremely interesting questions. They are important questions. They are questions that provoke us and stimulate us and express our humanity but they are not scientific questions. They cannot be falsified (篡改,伪造). They are questions that you cannot test definitively with experiment. So science has its limitations and there's a great deal of life and human longing that lies outside of science. It's a mistake to try to lump (归并在一起考虑) these questions in with science. Science is very powerful but it has its limitations.

LiveScience:

In your books and interviews and essays, you constantly make the distinction between art and science and their intersection. I wonder if there is a distinction. When you want to cross a scientific boundary, it's often an art to push it, especially in theoretical fields.

Alan Lightman:

Well, you have to be creative, just as you have to be creative in the arts. I think that science and the arts have many things in common but they also have some things that are different, and I think the differences are important and we should not try to obscure the differences. There are many different ways of being in the world just as there are many different cultures.

And just as we lose the richness of human existence by trying to homogenize（同化）the different cultures and ethnicities（种族关系）, we lose the richness of being human by trying to merge（混合，合并）all the different disciplines including science and art.

I think scientists and artists are both searching for truth but they're not the same kind of truth. The scientist is looking for the truth in the world of mass and force, a truth that exists outside of our human existence, a truth about the inanimate physical world. Whereas the artist is looking for an emotional truth, a truth that is inherently rooted in our human existence. The scientist is always at any one moment working on questions that have answers.

LiveScience:

If you could have discovered one of the great discoveries you name in your book, which would you pick?

Alan Lightman:

Special relativity.

LiveScience:

Why?

Alan Lightman:

Because I think that there is nothing more fundamental in human existence than time. I think we begin having experience with time before we're born, in the womb. It's fundamental. It's primary, and to re-conceive the nature of time seems to me an exquisite（极好的）experience.

LiveScience:

What novels / literature books would you recommend to scientists and vice versa?

Alan Lightman:

Great question. ［To the scientists］ I would recommend "*Invisible Cities*" by Italo Calvino, "*Blindness*" by Jose Saramago, "*The Metamorphosis*" by Franz Kafka, and "*The Rubaiyyat of Omar Khayyam.*"

And for works of science for non scientists, I would recommend first of all "*The Origin of Species*" by Charles Darwin, "*The Character of Physical Law*" by Richard Feynman, and "*A Mathematician's Apology*" by G. H. Hardy, the great Cambridge mathematician.

Although that's mathematics and not science, it's a stunning (极好的) book.

LiveScience:

Do you generally have your writing students read old or current literature?

Alan Lightman:

Both. One of the mistakes that a lot of the American English departments make is that they don't have their students read contemporary literature, and I would say this is a problem with high schools also, that you often in high school English classes read only the great classics and the great problem with this is that it gives students the impression that great literature is something that happened in the past, and in fact great literature is being created all the time. Even now, there is some writer working away right now as we speak, writing great literature. And it's important for students to understand that literature is a living thing and is being produced every minute.

LiveScience:

But there was a time known for its flowering of literature with an appreciation of writing and music that may not be as prevalent right now. So there's a reason they go back to work from that period.

Alan Lightman:

We have great literature that's being written now and I think that we need to emphasize that it is being written now. I think that Gabriel Garcia Marquez is a great writer. I think that JM Coetze, the South African writer that moved to Australia is a great writer. I think Don DeLillo and Phillip Roth in the United States are great writers, , and of course there are many European writers and great Iranian writers who I just don't know.

LiveScience:

Do you think there's a lot of self-censorship with scientists?

Alan Lightman:

I don't think that scientists are censoring (审查) themselves. No. I think that you look at the frontiers of any pure science and people are following it wherever it leads. There was a censoring of bio-engineering, genetic engineering in the early 1970's because people thought that maybe with genetic engineering they were unleashing (解除…的束缚,释放, 发泄) new forms of life that could cause great damage. But since then, there's been no censoring. Scientists are very independent-minded. They are very anti-authority and they really bristle (发怒) at the idea of censorship.

LiveScience:

If you could live to see one great upcoming discovery, what would you like to see?

Alan Lightman:

I would like to see an understanding of the nature of dark energy, which is a cosmic force that accounts for most of the material of the universe and I am certain that when we find that it will be a revolution in physics.

LiveScience:

Do you really think that there is a dark energy?

Alan Lightman:

Yes, I do. There's something very significant about the behavior of the universe that we don't understand. Our experiments and observations show us that the expansion of the universe is accelerating, and that can't happen with the traditional gravitational force. It would take some anti-gravitational force.

Whenever we try to calculate what would be expected of such a force we get wildly incorrect answers, so there's a great disparity (不同) between theory and experiment. And in the past, in all the previous centuries in science when there's a great disparity between theory and experiment you were on the verge of a revolution of a new conception. That happened with relativity theory, it happened with quantum theory.

LiveScience:

Some scientists say it's not dark energy, but rather modifications in gravity.

Alan Lightman:

Even if that were true it would be extremely interesting.

LiveScience:

So you just want the acceleration puzzle solved?

Alan Lightman:

I want to see whatever it is. If it's a modification (改变) in the law of gravity, I want to see that. But even that would be a great learning experience. It's something that we don't understand and scientists are always excited at things they don't understand. It means they're on the verge of discovery.

Retrieved from *http://www.livescience.com/strangenews/060215_alan_lightman.html*

Reading comprehension.

1. What can be learned from the text?

   A. Researches in the areas of stem cell and global warming are facing inedequate financial support due to opposition from believers of Intelligence Design.

   B. What Edward Whitten has been doing may lead to great discoveries in the near future.

   C. The next great discovery will be in the field of biotechnology, which is a tremendous field for growth and new discoveries.

   D. All great discoveries sit on the shoulders of little discoveries, and all science depends upon a small number of geniuses.

2. Which of the following is not true according to the text?

   A. Human beings have always had a need to find meaning in their personal lives and meaning in the world at large, and science is to satisfy their need.

   B. Science has its limitations and can never fully satisfy the need of human beings.

   C. There are many questions that don't lie in the realm of science and they cannot be tested by experiement.

   D. Those questions that challenge us and stimulate us and express our humanity are more important than their answers.

3. How do you understand the statement "When you want to cross a scientific boundary, it's often an art to push it, especially in theoretical fields."?

   A. Scientists have to be creative in science, just as an artist has to be creative in the arts.

   B. Scientists and artists are both searching for truth.

   C. Science and the arts have many things in common but they also have some things that are in difference.

   D. A scientist has to be creative, just as an artist has to be creative in the arts.

4. The phrase "on the verge" most probably means _____

   A. be on the edge or border of a road or path.

   B. be very close to.

   C. to move in a certain direction.

   D. be on an edge or rim.

5. What can you infer from the text?

   A. Great literature is something that happened in the past, so students should read the great classics.

   B. As literature is a living thing, students should read only contemporary literature.

   C. Students should read not only classics but also contemporary literature.

   D. American high schools do not have courses of contemporary literature available for their students.

Passage Two

The Impact of Science on Society（科学对社会的影响）

Prof. P. Krishna

Though modern science is of relatively recent origin, having started with Galileo about 350 years ago, it has made very rapid progress and completely transformed outwardly the manner of our living. It is said that our life outwardly has changed more in the last one hundred years than it did in thousands of years earlier, because of the scientific knowledge accumulated over the last three centuries, and its application in the form of technology. So the impact of science on society is very visible; progress in agriculture, medicine and health care, telecommunications, transportation, computerization and so on, is part of our daily living.

In spite of all this progress, the consequent development of technology and industry, and the conveniences, comforts and power we have got through this knowledge, in no part of the world are human beings happy, at peace with themselves, living without violence. It was hoped that the development of science would usher in（开创）an era of peace and prosperity, but that has been belied（使被误解）. On the contrary, if we look at the level of violence throughout the world during a ten-year period, from 1900 to 1910, or 1910 to 1920 and so on, in every decade, in every country, the graph is going up. So, on the one hand, greater prosperity and so-called globalization; but, on the other, greater violence, sorrow, tension, and newer diseases.

Krishnamurti raised the question: Has there been psychological evolution at all in the last two or five thousand years? Have we progressed at all in wisdom, or the quest for truth, inwardly in our consciousness? Science has generated tremendous power; knowledge always gives power and is useful because it increases our abilities. But when we do not have wisdom and love, compassion or brotherhood, which are all by-products of wisdom, then power can be used destructively. Sixty-five percent of all the scientific research being done currently is directly or indirectly meant for developing weapons, and supported by the Defence Ministry in every nation. In the last one century, 208 million people have been killed in wars, which is without precedent in any previous century.

So, does humanity deserve to have the knowledge which science is generating? We do not let children play with fire, for they might set the whole house on fire or burn themselves. And is not humanity in that state, without wisdom? There is hatred in our motivations; we are badly divided into groups-caste（社会等级）, national, linguistic, religious and other groups. Is it then responsible for scientists to generate knowledge, giving more and more power, without the wisdom to use it rightly? Responsibility from a theosophical（神智学的）point of view is universal responsibility. It means not saying: I am only responsible for generating scientific knowledge? You are also responsible for the whole of society, all of humankind, and even the earth. We are living in a scientific age, but what is so great about the scientific age? Have we used the discoveries of science to be more protective, kind and gentle, to bring about greater prosperity and peace?

We have been at war for thousands of years, but we now have nuclear weapons. Joy Mills in her talk said: It is important to watch your next step, but before you take the next step, make sure that you have a long vision, which gives the direction to that step. Is the new knowledge, which is a new step, in the right direction? Through genetic engineering we might develop new power, but can we ensure that we will use that power for the benefit of mankind and for the earth at large? We cannot ensure that. If we cannot, is it responsible? Yet, all the nations of the world are spending huge amounts in developing scientific knowledge, as if that is our priority. Are the problems of humanity today caused by not having sufficiently fast aeroplanes or computers? Of course not. The problems exist because of lack of understanding of life and the psychologically primitive state in which we find ourselves.

Einstein is on record saying that had he known that his equation $E = mc^2$, which stated a great truth about Nature, that mass is just another form of energy, will be used to make atomic bombs and kill large numbers of people in Japan, he would never have done that research or published the findings. That is something which has already happened in the last century. So, why do science?

Of course, we should distinguish between science and technology. Science is the quest for truth about Nature. Its aim is not to produce technology, but to understand how Nature works and discover the tremendous order and intelligence operating around us. If Nature were chaotic, if sometimes a stone went up and sometimes down, then there would be no science. But definite causes produce definite effects, and that is why science is possible. The scientist does not create order, he merely studies it. We are living in a very intelligent universe. A million things take place in perfect order within our body without any conscious voluntary effort on our part, but we have not discovered order in consciousness, which is virtue, peace of mind, love, happiness, compassion, freedom from conflict, non-violence. Socrates wrote that there is only one virtue, that is order in consciousness, though we may describe it in different words in different situations. And the quest for truth, and wisdom, which is the essence of Theosophy (接神论), is the quest for order in consciousness, and coming upon virtue.

So humanity has succeeded in the quest for science, because there is order already there. Newton only discovered gravitation, which existed a million years before Newton and will exist a million years hence. The laws of Nature are independent of the scientist. If you ask why Nature is ordered, the scientist cannot answer. He can only say: I am a student of Nature. I observe and find that order there and I am studying the laws that govern that order? The technologist takes the knowledge which the scientist discovers and uses it to make guns, or a motorcar, or generate electricity. Technology is a by-product of science, but science itself is the quest for truth about Nature.

Human beings use the knowledge gained by science and decide what kind of application to make of it. If there is wisdom, we will not use knowledge for destructive purposes. And if there is no wisdom, we are violent and selfish, and use knowledge in a destructive way. History shows that man has used it and is still using it primarily for destruction rather than for construction, bringing our planet and our lives to a level of danger which never existed before. Scientists are pointing out that the third world war would be the last, if it takes place. So is there anything we can learn from science as Theosophists interested in wisdom, in coming upon a deeper understanding of life and of ourselves? Science, or scientific knowledge, does not deal with values per se (本身), with what is right and what is wrong? It does not say that you should be kind. Scientific knowledge is said to be value-neutral. But one must discover what is called the scientific spirit, for the spirit is always more important than the technique, the knowledge or the method in any activity.

Although in society we have valued scientific knowledge and its application as technology, we have not really valued the scientific spirit, without which it is wrong to call ours a scientific society. We are an unscientific society. Science says that the whole earth is one, that we are all citizens of this planet, but it is we who divide ourselves and say, this is my culture and this is my country and I will work only for this? For the benefit of our nation we have armies to exploit other nations. All this is not scientific. War is not scientific in spirit.

So what is this scientific spirit? What can we learn from science which is precious? To understand this, let me take the example of the particular science I am familiar with, which is fairly basic to all science, that is, physics. It begins with observation, for understanding any phenomenon in Nature calls for careful observation, honest documentation and measurement, and recording. Then having collected a lot of data about the phenomenon, you look for correlations among them. From empirically (以经验为主地) found data, correlations between two variables (变量) are established, and then guessing what is the underlying reality which would cause those correlations. That is what the physicist calls the model, that is where his insight or his genius manifests (显示,证明), for he has to guess what is unknown.

Whenever scientists talk about theory, about reality, they are talking about an imaginary model of the underlying reality. Nobody has seen electrons actually going around a nucleus inside an atom. That is a conjecture (推测), a model about the underlying reality. To this model they apply logic, using the existing known laws determined from previous work and the peculiar form of logic called mathematics, which is a product of the human mind. And then they deduce a theory, and try to explain all observed facts and also predict new facts which have not been observed until then. Then again the scientists go back to observation and do experiments to check if their predictions are correct. If the experimental values do not tally with (吻合) the theoretically predicted values, they either modify the model, or they discard it altogether and start all over again. It is a deep quest because they are not accepting the reality as they see it. They are saying there is an underlying reality which is not visible, and we are going to find it. But since it is not visible, we have to guess, to imagine it, and that is the model.

Usually the model gives approximately correct results, and they have only to modify it and make successive models closer and closer approximations (接近) to reality. It is fortunate that the logic called mathematics has an application in Nature. Somehow, Nature follows mathematics, which is really a mystery. Galileo wrote that mathematics is the language in which God wrote the universe, and this seems to be true. Mathematics, evolved by the human mind, actually applies. Einstein could do two hundred pages of mathematics, starting from certain hypotheses, using the known laws of Nature, and then deduce that when light goes near a star it must bend, and calculate how much it must bend. When twenty years later they are able to do the experiment because technology has got refined (完善) to that point, they find that indeed it bends by exactly the amount he has calculated, which means that those two hundred pages of mathematics applies in Nature. But if you ask: Why does it apply, we do not know. If you ask why there are laws, we do not know. If you ask why Nature is ordered, we do not know.

So the spirit of science is one of great humility. It begins with saying, we do not know the truth about Nature. I am making a conjecture, and I have found a method by which I can test whether this conjecture is correct or not, and to what extent it is correct. And that is how science has progressed, without accepting authority. Science demands proof, observation, testing with experiments; and the truth must be something which is universal, which everybody can be convinced of. Of course, they limit themselves to studying phenomena which are measurable.

There is also much in life which is not measurable, which is the field of religion. But there are a number of values which are inherent (内在的,固有的), which we can learn from science. One, as we said, is humility. Scientists are not humble, science is humble. It encourages observation, testing what is observed, questioning, doubt; and the truth is the same for everybody. There is no such thing as American truth and Indian truth. There is no Indian mathematics and American mathematics. Either a stone is attracted by the earth and gravitation exists, or it does not exist; it cannot exist for Indians and not for Americans. So, it is a global activity, a dialogue among thousands of people who have never met, because that experiment is then repeated in another country by another group of scientists. And they write the results, and publish them, and everybody reads them. There is a process of dialogue and constant correction.

So truth is global, universal; it is not the private property of any individual. It is the same for everybody. These are values constituting the scientific spirit. In order to settle a dispute, violence is not used, nor authority. So the spirit is one of non-violence, of dialogue. It is also a truly democratic endeavour, based on cooperation, humility, and mutual respect. All scientists may not be true scientists if they do not work with that spirit, but science is done in that way. Unfortunately, the scientist adopts that policy in the laboratory but not at home nor in his life.

Retrieved from *http://www.pkrishna.org/*

Decide whether the following statements are True or False.

1. The development of science has brought about peace and prosperity to our era. (   )
2. Genetic engineering helps us develop new power, which will be used for the benefit of mankind. (   )
3. Scientists study order hanging around us in the material world, but they haven't discovered order in human consciousness. (   )
4. If an experimental value doesn't tally with the theoretically predicted value, a scientist either modify the model, or discard it altogether and start all over again. This is an accepted scientific practice. (   )
5. The purpose of science is to produce more advanced technology so that we can enjoy better life. (   )

Topics for further discussion.

1. How do you understand the statement "Scientists are not humble, science is humble."?
2. What is the scientific spirit? Why is it necessary?
3. Do you agree that science has become a servant of society?

Unit 3

Ronald Reagan: Remarks on the 40th Anniversary of D-Day

本单元课文综述

Text 精读　1984 年 6 月 6 日, 时任美国总统罗纳德·里根在可以俯瞰诺曼底奥马哈海滩的二战英雄纪念碑前发表了怀念登陆勇士及纪念诺曼底登陆 40 周年的著名演讲。

Passage One 泛读　罗马天主教第 264 任教宗, 梵蒂冈城国国家元首约翰·保罗二世在欧洲第二次世界大战结束五十周年纪念日发表演讲, 对二战进行诸方面的反思。

Passage Two 泛读　Marshall Plan Speech: 1947 年 6 月 5 日, 美国国务卿乔治·马歇尔在哈佛大学发表演说, 首先提出援助欧洲经济复兴的方案。"马歇尔计划", 通称《欧洲复兴计划》, 是第二次世界大战后美国争夺全球战略重点的欧洲扩张计划。

Reagan Delivered the Speech on the 6th of June 1984 in Pointe Du Hoc, Normandy, France

ext　　　　Ronald Reagan: Remarks on the 40th
Anniversary of D-Day

This was an emotional day.

The ceremonies honoring the fortieth anniversary of D-Day became more than

commemorations.

They became celebrations of heroism and sacrifice.

This place, **Pointe du Hoc**, in itself was moving and **majestic**. I stood there on that **windswept** point with the ocean behind me. Before me were the boys who forty years before had fought their way up from the ocean. Some rested under the white crosses and **Stars of David** that stretched out across the landscape. Others sat right in front of me. They looked like elderly businessmen, yet these were the kids who climbed the cliffs.

We're here to mark that day in history when the Allied armies joined in battle to **reclaim** this continent to **liberty**. For four long years, much of Europe had been under a terrible shadow. Free nations had fallen, Jews cried out in the camps, millions cried out for liberation. Europe was **enslaved** and the world prayed for its rescue. Here, in Normandy, the rescue began. Here, the Allies stood and fought against **tyranny**, in a giant **undertaking unparalleled** in human history.

We stand on a lonely, windswept point on the northern shore of France. The air is soft, but forty years ago at this moment, the air was dense with smoke and the cries of men, and the air was filled with the crack of rifle fire and the roar of cannon. At dawn, on the morning of the 6th of June, 1944, two hundred and twenty-five **Rangers** jumped off the British landing craft and ran to the bottom of these cliffs.

Their mission was one of the most difficult and **daring** of the invasion: to climb these **sheer** and **desolate** cliffs and take out the enemy guns. The Allies had been told that some of the **mightiest** of these guns were here, and they would be trained on the beaches to stop the Allied advance.

The Rangers looked up and saw the enemy soldiers at the edge of the cliffs, shooting down at them with **machine guns** and throwing **grenades**. And the American Rangers began to climb. They shot **rope ladders** over the face of these cliffs and began to pull themselves up. When one Ranger fell, another would take his place. When one rope was cut, a Ranger would **grab** another and begin his climb again. They climbed, shot back, and **held their footing**. Soon, one by one, the Rangers pulled themselves over the top, and in seizing the firm land at the top of these cliffs, they began to seize back the continent of Europe. Two hundred and twenty-five came here. After two days of fighting, only ninety could still **bear arms**.

And behind me is a **memorial** that symbolizes the Ranger **daggers** that were thrust into the top of these cliffs. And before me are the men who put them there. These are the boys of Pointe du Hoc. These are the men who took the cliffs. These are the champions who helped free a continent. And these are the heroes who helped end a war. Gentlemen, I look at you and I think of the words of **Stephen Spender**'s poem. You are men who in your "lives fought for life and left the vivid air signed with your honor."

I think I know what you may be thinking right now — thinking "we were just part of a bigger effort; everyone was brave that day." Well, everyone was. Do you remember the story of Bill Millin of the 51st Highlanders? Forty years ago today, British troops were **pinned down** near a bridge, waiting desperately for help. Suddenly, they heard the sound of **bagpipes**, and some thought they were dreaming. Well, they weren't. They looked up and saw Bill Millin with his bagpipes, leading the **reinforcements** and ignoring the **smack** of the bullets into the ground around him.

Lord Lovat was with him — Lord Lovat of Scotland, who calmly announced when he got to the bridge, "Sorry, I'm a few minutes late," as if he'd been delayed by a traffic jam, when in truth he'd just come from the bloody fighting on Sword Beach, which he and his men had just taken.

There was the impossible **valor** of the **Poles**, who threw themselves between the enemy and the rest of Europe as the invasion **took hold**; and the **unsurpassed** courage of the Canadians who had already seen the horrors of war on this coast. They knew what awaited them there, but they would not be **deterred**. And once they hit Juno Beach, they never looked back.

All of these men were part of a **roll call** of honor with names that spoke of a pride as bright as the colors they bore; **The Royal Winnipeg Rifles, Poland's 24th Lancers, the Royal Scots' Fusiliers, the Screaming Eagles, the Yeomen of England's armored divisions, the forces of Free France, the Coast Guard's "Matchbox Fleet,"** and you, the American Rangers.

Forty summers have passed since the battle that you fought here. You were young the day you took these cliffs; some of you were hardly more than boys, with the deepest joys of life before you. Yet you risked everything here. Why? Why did you do it? What **impelled** you to put aside the **instinct** for **self-preservation** and risk your lives to take these cliffs? What inspired all the men of the armies that met here? We look at you, and somehow we know the answer. It was faith and belief. It was loyalty and love.

The men of Normandy had faith that what they were doing was right, faith that they fought for all humanity, faith that a just God would grant them mercy on this **beachhead**, or on the next. It was the deep knowledge — and pray God we have not lost it — that there is a **profound** moral difference between the use of force for liberation and the use of force for conquest. You were here to liberate, not to conquer, and so you and those others did not doubt your cause. And you were right not to doubt.

You all knew that some things are worth dying for. One's country is worth dying for, and democracy is worth dying for, because it's the most deeply honorable form of government ever devised by man. All of you loved liberty. All of you were willing to fight tyranny, and you knew the people of your countries were behind you.

The Americans who fought here that morning knew word of the invasion was spreading through the darkness back home. They thought — or felt in their hearts, though they couldn't know in fact, that in Georgia they were filling the churches at 4:00 am. In Kansas they were kneeling on their porches and praying. And in Philadelphia they were ringing **the Liberty Bell**.

Something else helped the men of D-Day; their **rock-hard** belief that **Providence** would **have a** great **hand in** the events that would **unfold** here; that God was an ally in this great cause. And so, the night before the invasion, when **Colonel Wolverton** asked his **parachute troops** to kneel with him in prayer, he told them: "Do not bow your heads, but look up so you can see God and ask His blessing in what we're about to do. " Also, that night, **General Matthew Ridgway** on his **cot**, listening in the darkness for the promise God made to **Joshua**: "I will not fail thee nor **forsake** thee. "

These are the things that impelled them; these are the things that shaped the unity of the Allies.

When the war was over, there were lives to be rebuilt and governments to be returned to the people. There were nations to be reborn. Above all, there was a new peace to be assured. These were huge and **daunting** tasks. But the Allies **summoned** strength from the faith, belief, loyalty, and love of those who fell here. They rebuilt a new Europe together. There was first a great **reconciliation** among those who had been enemies, all of whom had suffered so greatly. The United States did its part, creating **the Marshall Plan** to help rebuild our allies and our former enemies. The Marshall Plan led to the Atlantic alliance — a great **alliance** that serves to this day as our shield for freedom, for prosperity, and for peace.

In spite of our great efforts and successes, not all that followed the end of the war was happy or planned. Some liberated countries were lost. The great sadness of this loss **echoes** down to our own time in the streets of **Warsaw**, **Prague**, and **East Berlin**. The Soviet troops that came to the center of this continent did not leave when peace came. They're still there, uninvited, unwanted, **unyielding**, almost forty years after the war. Because of this, allied forces still stand on this continent. Today, as forty years ago, our armies are here for only one purpose: to protect and defend democracy. The only territories we hold are memorials like this one and graveyards where our heroes rest.

We in America have learned bitter lessons from two world wars. It is better to be here ready to protect the peace, than to take blind shelter across the sea, rushing to respond only after freedom is lost. We've learned that **isolationism** never was and never will be an acceptable response to tyrannical governments with an expansionist **intent**. But we try always to be prepared for peace, prepared to deter aggression, prepared to negotiate the reduction of arms, and yes, prepared to reach out again **in the spirit of** reconciliation. In truth, there is no reconciliation we would welcome more than a reconciliation with the Soviet Union, so, together, we can lessen the risks of war, now and forever.

It's **fitting** to remember here the great losses also suffered by the Russian people during World War II. 20 million **perished**, a terrible price that **testifies** to all the world the necessity of ending war. I tell you from my heart that we in the United States do not want war. We want to wipe from the face of the earth the terrible weapons that man now has in his hands. And I tell you, we are ready to seize that beachhead. We look for some sign from the Soviet Union that they are willing to move forward, that they share our desire and love for peace, and that they will give up the ways of conquest. There must be a changing there that will allow us to turn our hope into action.

We will pray forever that someday that changing will come. But for now, particularly today, it is good and fitting to renew our **commitment** to each other, to our freedom, and to the alliance that protects it.

We're bound today by what bound us 40 years ago, the same loyalties, traditions, and beliefs. We're bound by reality. The strength of America's allies is vital to the United States, and the American security guarantee is essential to the continued freedom of Europe's democracies. We were with you then; we're with you now. Your hopes are our hopes, and your destiny is our **destiny**.

Here, in this place where the West held together, let us **make a vow to** our dead. Let us show them by our actions that we understand what they died for. Let our actions say to them the words for which Matthew Ridgway listened: "I will not fail thee nor forsake thee."

Strengthened by their courage and **heartened** by their valor and borne by their memory, let us continue to stand for the ideals for which they lived and died.

Thank you very much, and God bless you all.

Retrieved from *http://www.reaganfoundation.org/reagan/speeches/dday_pdh.asp*

New Words and Phrases

commemoration	*n.*	to keep in memory by ceremony 纪念、纪念会
majestic	*adj.*	imposing 雄伟的、庄严的、崇高的
windswept	*adj.*	exposed to high winds 当风的、被强风吹光的
reclaim	*v.*	seek return of (one' property) 收复、回收、开垦
liberty	*n.*	freedom from captivity 自由、自由权
enslave	*v.*	make (person) a slave 奴役、使作奴隶
tyranny	*n.*	government of a cruel ruler 暴政、苛政、专制
undertaking	*n.*	work 事业、任务
unparalleled	*a.*	having no parallel or equal 无比的、无双的、空前未有的
daring	*a.*	bold; courageous 大胆的、勇敢的
sheer	*a.*	steep 陡峭的、垂直的
desolate	*a.*	deserted, uninhabited, barren 荒芜的、荒凉的、孤

寂的

mighty	*a.*	powerful, massive 强大的、强有力的、巨大的
machine gun		机(关)枪
grenade	*n.*	small bomb thrown by hand 手榴弹
rope ladder		绳梯
grab	*v.*	seize suddenly 抓取、强夺
hold one's footing		to stand firmly 站稳脚跟
bear arms		to carry weapons 手持武器
memorial	*n. a.*	纪念物、纪念碑、纪念的
dagger	*n.*	short pointed stabbing weapon 匕首、短剑
pin down		restrict actions of 阻止、约束、压住
bagpipe	*n.*	（苏格兰人用的）风笛
reinforcement	*n.*	增援、援军
smack	*n.*	sharp slap or blow, sharp sound 拍击声、噼啪作响
valor	*n.*	courage esp. in battle 勇猛、英勇
take hold		become established 站稳
unsurpassed	*a.*	not exceeded by 未被超越的、卓绝的
deter	*v.*	prevent (from) through fear 威慑、吓住
roll .call		calling of a list of names 点名
impel	*v.*	drive, urge, propel 激励、驱使、迫使
instinct	*n.*	innate propensity 本能、直觉
self-preservation		自我保护
beachhead	*n.*	滩头堡、登陆场
profound	*a.*	far-reaching 意义深远的、深刻的
rock-hard	*a.*	as hard as rock 坚硬的
Providence	*n.*	God 天公、上帝
have a hand in		intervene, interfere, get involved in 插手、介入
unfold	*v.*	spread out, reveal 展开、打开、呈现
parachute troops		伞兵部队
cot	*n.*	small light bed 帆布床、吊床
forsake	*v.*	give up, renounce 抛弃、遗弃
daunt	*v.*	discourage, intimidate 威吓、使胆怯、使气馁
summon	*v.*	call in 召集、鼓起（勇气等）
reconciliation	*n.*	和解、（重新）和好
alliance	*n.*	union or agreement to co-operate 联盟、同盟、联合
echo	*v.*	reflection of sound-waves 回声、重复、共鸣
unyielding	*a.*	firm 不屈的
isolationism	*n.*	孤立主义

intent	*n.*	intention, purpose 意图、目的、意义
in the spirit of		本着……的精神
fitting	*a.*	proper 合适的、恰当的
perish	*v.*	be destroyed, suffer death or ruin 灭亡、消灭、枯萎
testify	*v.*	bear witness, give evidence 证实、作证
commitment	*n.*	承担义务、许诺、约定
destiny	*n.*	fate 命运
make a vow to		to swear 向……发誓
hearten	*v.*	cheer 振作、鼓励、激励
Pointe du Hoc		奥克角海滩
Star of David		（犹太教）大卫王之星
Poles		波兰人
The Royal Winnipeg Rifles		皇家温尼伯来复枪团
Poland's 24ᵗʰ Lancers		波兰的第 24 重装枪骑兵团
The Royal Scots' Fusiliers		皇家苏格兰燧发枪手团
The Screaming Eagles		第 101 空击师"尖叫鹰"
The Yeomen of England's Armored Divisions		英格兰装甲师的义勇骑兵队
The Forces of Free France		自由法国军队
Coast Guard's Matchbox Fleet		海岸警卫队的"火柴盒"舰队
The Liberty Bell		独立钟（1776 年 7 月 4 日鸣此钟宣布美国独立）
Colonel Wolverton		沃尔夫顿中校
Joshua		约书亚（基督教《圣经》中的人物）
Warsaw		（波兰首都）华沙
Prague		（捷克首都）布拉格
East Berlin		东柏林（苏军在 1945 年设立的柏林占领区，至 1990 年）

About the speaker：罗纳德·威尔逊·里根（Ronald Wilson Reagan,1911—2004），美国第 40 任总统，是历任总统之中就职年龄最大，又是历任总统中唯一的一位演员出身的总统。大学毕业后,里根成为一名电台体育播音员,后进入好莱坞华纳兄弟电影公司当影视演员。第二次世界大战期间他应征入伍,在空军服役,退伍后重返好莱坞,共参加了 53 部电影的演出。1962 年、1976 年两次争取共和党提名总统候选人,均未成功。1980 年再次争取,被提名,并在竞选中击败卡特而获胜。1984 年谋求连任成功。里根执政期间,提出一项旨在压缩政府开支、减少国营事业、降低通货膨胀率的政治改革计划,收效甚微。在他任职末期,是美国历史上持续时间最长的、没有经济衰退和经济萧条的和平时期。对外,对苏联等社会主义国家采取强硬立场,并提出了"星球大战计划"。他是中美两国建交后首位在任时访华的美国总统。1989 年 1 月里根任期届满。2004 年 6 月 5 日,93 岁的

里根去世。

About the author：皮基·诺南(Peggy Noonan)和安东尼·多南(Antonio Donen)是这场著名演讲的撰稿人。

Notes to the text

1. **D-Day**：行动开始预定日的缩写，这里指诺曼底登陆日。

2. **Allied armies**：同盟国军队。参与该联盟的国家主要有美国、英国、法国、苏联、中国、加拿大、朝鲜、澳大利亚、埃塞俄比亚等数十个国家。与其对立的是轴心国，成员国为德国、日本、意大利，并有少数国家拥护，如罗马尼亚、匈牙利和芬兰等。

3. **Ranger**：A member of a group of U. S. soldiers specially trained for making raids either on foot, in ground vehicles, or by airlift. 在美国众多的特种部队中，游骑兵（又称突击兵或特攻队）是一支历史悠久、武力强悍的精锐部队。拥有光荣历史与优秀传统的游骑兵，凭着不畏不惧的精神和毅力在各地执行世界警察的角色，并获得国际上的认同与赞扬。基本上游骑兵属于轻型步兵，和骑兵并无任何关联。它可以运用各式交通工具迅速进入战区执行任务，因此往往在其它特种部队抵达之前，游骑兵就已经完成任务。就如同代表游骑兵精神的座右铭"游骑兵，做前锋（Rangers, lead the way）"和绣着 RANGER 字样的黑色贝雷帽及飘带型臂章，一直是游骑兵荣耀与尊严的象征。

4. **Stephen Spender**：Sir Stephen Harold Spender (1909 — 1995) was an English poet, novelist and essayist who concentrated on themes of social injustice and the class struggle in his works. The original lines are as follows：

The names of those who in their lives fought for life,

Who wore at their hearts the fire's centre.

Born of the sun they traveled a short while towards the sun,

And left the vivid air signed with their honour.

5. **Bill Millin**：the Piper of the 1st Special Service Brigade, and was amongst the more noticeable men to land on the Normandy Beaches on the 6th June as he played the Brigade ashore with his bagpipes.

6. **Lord Lovat**：洛瓦特勋爵，曾率领第一特种旅的突击队员登滩。

7. **Sword Beach**：二次世界大战盟军为开辟第二战场，选定 1944 年 6 月 6 日作为登陆日（D-Day）。盟军集结 39 个师共 288 万人，飞机约 15 700 架，各种船只 6 000 多艘，在 6 日拂晓对诺曼底发起猛烈攻击。登陆的五个海滩由西向东分别是犹他滩（Utah Beach）、奥马哈滩（Omaha Beach）、金滩（Gold Beach）、朱诺滩（Juno Beach）、斯沃德滩（Sword Beach）。现在沿诺曼底登陆海滩建有无数的纪念碑，烈士墓及博物馆。卡昂郊外的纪念馆（Memorial Caen Normandie）1988 年开放，这里有介绍二次世界大战的图片和实物及反映登陆场景的电影资料。

8. **General Matthew Ridgway**：美国将领马修·李奇微上将（1895 年 3 月 3 日—1993 年

7 月 26 日),1917 年毕业于西点军校。1943 年 7—9 月参加西西里和萨勒诺登陆战,12 月参加阿登战役。1951 年 4 月接替麦克阿瑟任"联合国军"总司令。1952 年 4 月出任北大西洋公约组织武装部队最高司令。1955 年退役。著有《朝鲜战争》等书。

9. **Marshall Plan**:"马歇尔计划"是《欧洲复兴计划》的通称,即第二次世界大战后美国争夺全球战略的重点——欧洲的扩张计划。1947 年 6 月 5 日,国务卿乔治·马歇尔在哈佛大学发表演说,首先提出援助欧洲经济复兴的方案,故名。马歇尔计划是战后美国对外经济技术援助最成功的计划,它为北大西洋公约组织和欧洲经济共同体的建立奠定了基础,对西欧的联合和经济的恢复起到了促进作用,同时也缓和了美国国内即将发生的经济危机。

10. **The Atlantic alliance**:The North Atlantic Treaty Organization(NATO,北大西洋公约组织,简称北约组织或北约)。1949 年 3 月 18 日美国和西欧国家公开组建北大西洋公约组织,于同年 4 月 4 日在美国华盛顿签署《北大西洋公约》后正式成立,为与以前苏联为首的东欧集团国成员相抗衡。成员国一旦受到攻击时,其他成员国可以作出即时反应。但这一条款在九一一事件之前,一直都未被动用过。前苏联解体以后,华沙公约组织宣告解散,北约也就成为一个地区性防卫协作组织。北约的最高决策机构是北约理事会。理事会由成员国国家元首及政府首脑、外长、国防部长组成。总部设在布鲁塞尔。

Exercises

I. **Answer the following questions based on Text. The words and expressions listed below are for your reference.**

1. **Why did the ceremonies honoring the fortieth anniversary of D-Day become more than commemorations?**

   Celebration / heroism / sacrifice

2. **What inspired the armymen to risk their lives to fight against the Nazi troops?**

   Faith / belief / loyalty / love

3. **Why was June 6 named the D-Day?**

   Military term / H for hour / D for day / two letters to indicate / time for particular operation or mission / highly confidential / first found in WWI

4. **Why did Ronald Reagan address the veterans as boys?**

   Young at that time / nickname for men of all ages / shorten distance between speaker and audience

5. **Name a few of the countries that joined the Allied army.**

   America / Britain / France / China / the Soviet Union / Canada / Australia, etc.

6. **What adjectives were employed by the speaker to describe the Rangers' mission to climb the cliffs and take out the enemy guns?**

   Most difficult / daring / sheer / desolate / mightiest

7. **What were the casualties for the Rangers after two days of fighting**?

225 came / 90 could still bear arms / 135 Rangers died or got seriously injured

8. **Did the Rangers thrust the enemies with daggers**?

The shape of the memorial symbolizes daggers / dagger is metaphor here / Rangers are compared to daggers

9. **What did the British troops pinned down near a bridge find when they heard the sound of bagpipes**?

First thought they were dreaming / then looked up and saw Bill Milin with his bagpipes / Led reinforcements and ignored smack of bullets

10. **Name some of the glorious troops mentioned by Ronald Reagan**:

Royal Winnipeg Rifles / Poland's 24th Lancers / Royal Scots' Fusiliers / Screaming Eagles / Yeomen of England's Armored Divisions / Forces of Free France / Coast Guard's "Matchbox Fleet" / American Rangers

II. Further questions for discussion.

1. Who is Ronald Reagan?
2. How much do you know about WWII?
3. Why did Ronald Reagan say that the Allied armymen were right not to doubt their cause?
4. How did Ronald Reagan view the relationship between America and the Europe's democracies?
5. What do you think of Ronald Reagan's accusation of the Soviet Union's occupation of the center of Europe? Is he justified?

III. Vocabulary study.

1. Word in use.

1) **stretch out**: to lie with one's legs and body in a straight line; to reach out; to extend 伸展;伸长

She **stretched herself out** after sitting for hours on end.

He was about to **stretch out** to grab me when the rope yielded.

The rescuers had the stretcher **stretched out** for the earthquake victim.

2) **mark**: *vt.* to show a sign that sth. different is about to happen; to remember 标志;纪念

The city held festivities to **mark** the 20th anniversary of its founding.

The city held festivities to **mark** the 20th anniversary of its founding.

Devotion to the revolution **marks** the youth of our era.

The announcement **marks** the end of an extraordinary period in European history.

3) **advance**: *vt. vi.* to move forward, often in order to attack; to make progress; to lend 提升;借贷

The passionate speech **advanced** the movement to a new stage.

Now that medical technology has **advanced** to its present state, more people are aware of how long one can be kept alive.

I **advanced** him some money, which he would repay on our way home.

4) **hold one's footing**: to stand firmly and steadily 站稳

She grabbed the rail in order to **hold her footing** in the gale.

No sooner had he **held his footing** in the city than he picked up his family in the remote village.

The way up to the mountain top was so steep that we found it difficult to find a place to **hold our footing**.

5) **thrust**: *vt.* to push or move sth. quickly with a lot of force 塞;推

The messenger **thrust** a letter into the mailbox.

The courageous soldier **thrust** a dagger into the enemy's heart.

She grabs a stack of baby photos and **thrusts** them into my hands.

6) **pin down**: to curb; to check; to contain 扣牢;牵制

The earthquake victim **was pinned down** by a fallen roof.

A battalion was stationed to **pin down** the enemy troops.

Our men had been **pinned down** by the enemy fire for days before the reinforcements arrived.

7) **have a hand in**: intervene, get involved in 插手

He thanked all who **had a hand in** his release from the jail.

The matter could have been settled earlier if his parents had not **had a hand in** it.

China will not allow any other countries to **have a hand in** its internal affairs.

8) **unfold**: *vt.* appear 呈现;展开

Little by little, the story **unfolds** itself before the reader.

Mr. Wills **unfolds** his story with evident enjoyment and enthusiasm.

The landscape **unfolds** before us after we got off the coach.

9) **echo**: *vt.* to repeat; to reflect off a surface and can be heard again after the original sound has stopped 回声;反射

The sound of gongs and drums **echoed** in the great hall.

Life and death is the theme which **echoes** throughout the play.

Mother asked Mike not to **echo** his elder sister's nonsense.

10) **testify**: *vt.* to formally prove 作证

The fingerprints left on the victim **testified** to his innocence.

Acts **testify** intent.

He **testifies** under oath that what he provides is authentic.

2. Word distinctions.

1) **await, wait** (await 是及物动词,多用于书面语,如:On arriving at the guest house, he

found a telegram awaiting him；而 wait 是不及物动词,多用于口语,后要带介词 for 才可跟一般表示人或事物的宾语,之后也可接动词不定式。)

选择以上适当的词填空:

I will _____ your answer with patience.

I have been _____ for the ambulance for nearly half an hour.

_____,I did not get what you say just now.

A warm welcome _____ you when you get to the kindergarten.

This is exactly the person for whom he is _____.

The judge _____ the coroner's inquest before giving a verdict.

2) **change, changing** (change *vt. n.* 名词强调变化最后的结果;changing *adj. n.* 名词强调变化过程的渐变性,常用在 there be 结构中。)

选择以上适当的词填空:

Great _____ have taken place in my hometown after I left it 20 years ago.

Some people find it hard to follow such a rapidly _____ world.

I've _____ my mind after his repeated persuasions.

The experiments reported no _____ in the color of the sample.

Scientists believe that there must be a _____ in the matter's physical properties.

3) **intent, intention** (intent *n.* 意图、目的、意向,多为法律用语,有更强的故意的含义 *a.* 专心的、决心的、热心的;intention *n.* 仅仅指想要采取的行动。)

选择以上适当的词填空:

He is notorious for his murderous _____ behind his smiles.

He has no _____ of renewing his contract with his company where he has been working for really a long time.

A letter of _____ should be signed before we proceed to the agreement next month.

We should be on guard against those who harbor ill _____.

He is _____ on the extinction of dinosaur.

3. **Decide the meanings of the following words from the context by matching each word in Column A with the word or expression in Column B that is similar in meaning.**

A	B
1) majestic	a. freedom
2) unparalleled	b. abandon
3) mark	c. encourage
4) valor	d. eliminate
5) liberty	e. spectacular
6) forsake	f. compromise
7) reconciliation	g. bare
8) hearten	h. celebrate

9) wipe   i. unsurpassed

10) desolate   j. courage

4. Try to write a brief story with as many following war-related words and phrases as possible.

sacrifice, reclaim, crack of rifle fire, landing craft, invasion, hold one's footing, thrust a dagger at sb., bloody fighting, deter, instinct for self-preservation, liberate, unyielding

IV. Translation.

1. Put the following Chinese expressions into English.

1）手持武器   2）把匕首刺向   3）反抗暴政   4）伞兵部队

5）本着……的精神   6）自我保护的天性   7）荣誉册   8）从……中吸取力量

2. Put the following Chinese sentences into English with the words or phrases in the brackets.

1）画轴展开,观众眼前展示出一幅壮观的场景。(stretch out)

2）成千上万的人走上街头纪念自己国家的独立。(mark)

3）八路军士兵向敌人的驻地进击。(advance)

4）你在攻击对手之前总得先站稳脚跟。(hold the footing)

5）绑架者把孩子推进小车,然后就急驰而去。(thrust)

6）这位著名电影演员被他的影迷和一批批的狗仔队所围困。(pin down)

7）肯定有一个犯罪集团在幕后操纵这次的毒品交易。(have a hand in)

8）一幅悉心耕作的农场美景在访客眼前展开。(unfold)

9）最后两章中有很多是在重复前面段落的词汇。(echo)

10）法庭上约翰证明看到皮特持枪上了楼梯。(testify)

3. Put the following Chinese paragraphs into English.

　　我来到贵国时是个小女孩,我生命中成长的岁月是和贵国人民一起度过的。我现在使用你们的语言,和你们一样地思维。今天我来到这里,感觉好象回到家里。

　　不过,我相信不只是我回到了家,我觉得,如果中国人民会用你们的语言与你们说话,或者你们能了解我们的语言,他们会告诉你们,实际上,我们都在为相同的理念奋战;我们有一致的理想;亦即贵国总统所揭示的"四个自由"。

　　中国人民渴望和贵国合作以实现这些理想,使我们的子孙能够享有自由带来的新生活。

　　　　　　　　　　　　　　　　——节选自宋美龄1943年在美国参议院的演讲

4. Put the following quotes into Chinese.

1) A Farewell to Arms.   —— Ernest Hemingway, American writer

2) All delays are dangerous in war.   —— John Drydon, British poet

3) In war, there is no second prize for the runner-up.

　　　　　　　　　　　　　　　　—— Omar Bradley, American general

4) In war, whichever side may call itself the victor, there are no winners, but all are

losers.   —— Nerille Chamberlain, British Prime Minister

5) Cowards die many times before their deaths; the valiant never taste of death but once.   —— William Shakespeare

5. Translate the following passage into Chinese.

Evening had now come, the last of Adolf Hitler's life. He instructed Mrs. Junge, one of his secretaries, to destroy the remaining papers in his files, and he sent out word that no one in the bunker was to go to bed until further orders. This was interpreted by all as meaning that he judged the time had come to make his farewells. But it was not until long after midnight, at about 2:30 AM of April 30, as several witnesses recall, that the Fuehrer emerged from his private quarters and appeared in the general dining passage where some 20 persons, mostly the women members of his group of associates, were assembled. He walked down the line shaking hands with each and mumbling a few words that were inaudible. There was a heavy film of moisture on his eyes and, as Mrs. Junge remembered, "They seemed to be looking far away, beyond the walls of the bunker."

V. Comment on the structure of the text.

Remarks on the 40th Anniversary of D-Day by Ronald Reagan is a powerful speech. Although the address was delivered orally, it was read from a written text composed with great care.

The text could be divided into four parts. The first part (Para. 1 — Para. 12) reviews the victorious history and names of honor of D-Day. The second part (Para. 13 — Para. 18) points out that faith, belief, loyalty and love was what inspired the armymen to risk their lives. The third part (Para. 19. — Para. 22) depicts the post-war status of the European Continent. And finally the fourth part (Para. 23 — Para. 27) reiterates America's resolution to hang together with its allies.

Here are some of the rhetorical devices employed in the speech to inspire and persuade.

1. **Repetition:** Throughout the speech, Reagan repeats words and phrases. Repetition not only makes it easy for the audience to follow what he is saying, but also gives a strong rhythmic quality to the speech and renders it more memorable. For example:

1) Para. 4: Free nations had fallen, Jews **cried out** in the camps, millions **cried out** for liberation.

2) Para. 14: ... there is a profound moral difference between the **use of force** for **liberation** and the **use of force** for **conquest**. You were here to **liberate**, not to **conquer**, and so you and those others did not **doubt** your cause. And you were right not to **doubt**.

3) Para. 24: We are **bound** today by what **bound** us 40 years ago, the same

loyalties, traditions, and beliefs. We're **bound** by reality.

We were **with you** then; we're **with you** now. Your **hopes** are our **hopes**, and your **destiny** is our **destiny**.

2. **contrast**: Another rhetorical device that effectively adds to the persuasive power of the speech is contrast. In Para. 5, for example:

The air is soft, but forty years ago at this moment, **the air was dense** with smoke and the cries of men, and the air was filled with the crack of rifle fire and the roar of cannon. (The present and the past are juxtaposed to show that the victory is hard-earned. The word "air" is repeated.)

3. **metaphor**: metaphors are comparisons that show similarities in things that are basically different. For example:

Para. 8: And behind me is the memorial that symbolizes the Ranger **daggers** that were thrust into the top of these cliffs.

4. **Parallelism**: parallelism means the balancing of sentence elements that are grammatically equal. To make them parallel, balance nouns with nouns, verbs with verbs, prepositional phrases with prepositional phrases, clauses with clauses, and so forth. In his speech, Ronald Reagan uses parallelism to create a strong rhythm to help the audience line up his ideas, here are a few examples:

1) Para. 8: **These are** the boys of Pointe du Hoc. **These are** the men who took the cliffs. **These are** the champions who helped free a continent. And **these are** the heroes who helped end a war.

2) Para. 14: The men of Normandy had **faith that** what they were doing was right, **faith that** they fought for all humanity, **faith that** a just God would grant them mercy on this beachhead, or on the next.

3) Para. 16: ... **in** Georgia **they were** filling the churches at 4:00 am. **In** Kansas **they were** kneeling on their porches and praying. And **in** Philadelphia **they were** ringing the Liberty Bell.

4) Para. 19: When the war was over, **there were** lives to be rebuilt and governments to be returned to the people. **There were** nations to be reborn. Above all, **there was** a new peace to be assured.

... a great alliance that serves to this day as our shield **for** freedom, **for** prosperity, and **for** peace.

5) Para. 20: They're still there, **un**invited, **un**wanted, **un**yielding, almost forty years after the war.

6) Para. 21: But we try always to be **prepared** for peace, **prepared** to deter aggression, **prepared** to negotiate the reduction of arms, and yes, **prepared** to reach out again in the spirit of reconciliation.

7) Para. 23: But for now, particularly today, it is good and fitting to renew our

commitment to each other, **to** our freedom, and **to** the alliance that protects it.

8) Para. 26: Strengthened **by their** courage and heartened **by their** valor and borne **by their** memory, let us continue to stand for the ideals for which they lived and died.

Extended Exercises

1. **In the following speech given by Winston Churchill, some paragraphs have been removed. Choose the most suitable paragraph from the list A — F to fit into each of the numbered gaps. There is ONE paragraph which does not fit in any of the gaps.**

Never Give In, Never, Never, Never
October 29, 1941   Harrow School

When Churchill visited Harrow on October 29 to hear the traditional songs again, he discovered that an additional verse had been added to one of them. It ran:

1) _____

Almost a year has passed since I came down here at your Head Master's kind invitation in order to cheer myself and cheer the hearts of a few of my friends by singing some of our own songs. The ten months that have passed have seen very terrible catastrophic events in the world — ups and downs, misfortunes — but can anyone sitting here this afternoon, this October afternoon, not feel deeply thankful for what has happened in the time that has passed and for the very great improvement in the position of our country and of our home? Why, when I was here last time we were quite alone, desperately alone, and we had been so for five or six months. We were poorly armed. We are not so poorly armed today; but then we were very poorly armed. We had the unmeasured menace of the enemy and their air attack still beating upon us, and you yourselves had had experience of this attack; and I expect you are beginning to feel impatient that there has been this long lull with nothing particular turning up!

2) _____

Another lesson I think we may take, just throwing our minds back to our meeting here ten months ago and now, is that appearances are often very deceptive, and as Kipling well says, we must "... meet with Triumph and Disaster and treat those two impostors just the same."

3) _____

Very different is the mood today. Britain, other nations thought, had drawn a sponge across her slate. But instead our country stood in the gap. There was no flinching and no thought of giving in; and by what seemed almost a miracle to those outside these Islands, though we ourselves never doubted it, we now find ourselves in a position where I say that we can be sure that we have only to persevere to conquer.

4)　_____

I have obtained the Head Master's permission to alter darker to sterner. "Not less we praise in sterner days."

5)　_____

A: You cannot tell from appearances how things will go. Sometimes imagination makes things out far worse than they are; yet without imagination not much can be done. Those people who are imaginative see many more dangers than perhaps exist; certainly many more than will happen; but then they must also pray to be given that extra courage to carry this far-reaching imagination. But for everyone, surely, what we have gone through in this period — I am addressing myself to the School — surely from this period of ten months this is the lesson: never give in, never give in, never, never, never, never — in nothing, great or small, large or petty — never give in except to convictions of honour and good sense. Never yield to force; never yield to the apparently overwhelming might of the enemy. We stood all alone a year ago, and to many countries it seemed that our account was closed, we were finished. All this tradition of ours, our songs, our School history, this part of the history of this country, were gone and finished and liquidated.

B: You sang here a verse of a School Song: you sang that extra verse written in my honour, which I was very greatly complimented by and which you have repeated today. But there is one word in it I want to alter — I wanted to do so last year, but I did not venture to. It is the line — "Not less we praise in darker days."

C: "Not less we praise in darker days
The leader of our nation,
And Churchill's name shall win acclaim.
From each new generation.
For you have power in danger's hour
Our freedom to defend, Sir!
Though long the fight we know that right
Will triumph in the end, Sir!

D: Do not let us speak of darker days: let us speak rather of sterner days. These are not dark days; these are great days — the greatest days our country has ever lived; and we must all thank God that we have been allowed, each of us according to our stations, to play a part in making these days memorable in the history of our race.

E: But we must learn to be equally good at what is short and sharp and what is long and tough. It is generally said that the British are often better at the last. They do not expect to move from crisis to crisis; they do not always expect that each day will bring up some noble chance of war; but when they very slowly make up their minds that the thing has to be done and the job put through and finished, then, even if it takes months — if it takes years — they do it.

F: To form an Administration of this scale and complexity is a serious undertaking in itself, but it must be remembered that we are in the preliminary stage of one of the greatest battles in history, that we are in action at many other points in Norway and in Holland, that we have to be prepared in the Mediterranean, that the air battle is continuous and that many preparations, such as have been indicated by my hon. Friend below the Gangway, have to be made here at home. In this crisis I hope I may be pardoned if I do not address the House at any length today. I hope that any of my friends and colleagues, or former colleagues, who are affected by the political reconstruction, will make allowance, all allowance, for any lack of ceremony with which it has been necessary to act. I would say to the House, as I said to those who have joined this government: "I have nothing to offer but blood, toil, tears and sweat."

2. **Group the following numbered paragraphs into effective sections and choose the most suitable subheading from the list A-E for each section.**

The Long March
A Long Way to Go for Chinese Entrepreneurs

1) "Made in China" lost its novelty long ago. The label has become widespread in much of the world, affixed to shoes, toys, apparel and a host of other items produced for global companies. What is novelty, however, are China-made goods sold under Chinese brand names? Only a handful of Chinese firms so far have the money and the management expertise to establish international brands. Most of the vast remainders are struggling to get even national recognition. But the pioneering companies which have started exploring overseas market might be regarded as on the threshold of something big.

2) Some believe that individually, with the help of enterprising local management or eager national partners wanting to add new products to their stable, Chinese brands could become a global phenomenon within a decade, marketed on quality and foreign appeal, as well as competitive pricing. Says Viveca Chan, Hong Kong based managing director at Grey China, an advertising agency: "If there's one country in the world that has ample potential for taking brands global, it's China."

3) The concept of Chinese brands has been evolving through the 1990s, but is now getting greater attention at home. Although the domestic market is still robust, a handful of state-owned enterprises, or SOEs, including listed Chinese companies, are now looking to establish international brands because they believe the quality of both their products and their management has improved. Chinese joint ventures think their

products can compete on quality with foreign brands anywhere, while enjoying the advantage of being perceived as exotic.

4) Besides bringing in additional revenues, a global brand also burnishes a company's image in China, stimulating sales among status-conscious domestic consumers. For example, state-owned soft-drinks maker Jianlibao has developed its overseas market in part to "establish a good image", which in turn enhances consumption at home, says Chief Executive Han Weixian.

5) But building a brand takes time, money and marketing wisdom. Many Chinese brands have nudged into the international market on the back of competitive pricing and only a few have utilized other strategies. Jianlibao has highlighted its Asian appeal, presenting itself as the preferred sports-drink of China's athletes. Others like Haier, one of China's leading home-appliance producers, have pointedly avoided pricing strategy, competing instead on product quality and an efficient distribution and after-sales service.

6) Of course, global sales don't mean global brands, as Grey China's Chan points out. And it's still early days for Chinese companies. For a start, investment funds for brand promotion are hard to obtain, says Chu Liangjin, the Qingdao-based director of the overseas division of China's Tsingtao Brewery. "No more than 5% of our total export sales can be reinvested in promoting our brand overseas," explains Chu, adding that Tsingdao is trying to persuade the foreign-currency authorities to change this standard practice for SOEs. With the government's emphasis on preventing the outflow of foreign currency, the chances of the restrictions being lifted are small.

7) Although targeted only at SOEs, the 5% limit is bound to hamper Chinese brands. Jianlibao, for example, has invested about $10 million to sell its brand in the U. S. market, but Li Jingwei, the company' general manager, knows that's just a drop in the bucket. He believes that to successfully generate brand recognition among Americans, the company needs to spend at least $50 million to $100 million on marketing. He has no doubt that consumers will like Jianlibao's range of sports and soft drinks, but explains that "we need money to invest in promoting ourselves".

8) Indeed, Jianlibao will need a great deal more money and years before it can be considered a serious player abroad. Although it has funded a host of promotional events, its marketing efforts pale in comparison with those of Coca-Cola.

9) In the short term, the strongest promise is in Chinese medicine, herbs and specialty food, as well as goods that play to the romantic foreignness of China — whether in cosmetics, fashion or music. Kevin Tan, general manager for China of market-research firm Taylor Nelson Sofres in Shanghai, says: "There's still a lot of mystique associated with China. If you're taking something like cosmetics, which is image-driven ... suddenly you've got a strong player. " Also making a bid to go global are a few trendsetting Chinese beverage and beer brands. Further down the road there is

brand-potential for products such as home appliances that can offer quality at a competitive price.

10) Some of these brands will eventually go broad via joint ventures or merges and acquisitions. For their foreign owners, the brands will provide speedier access to China's consumer market and distribution channels, while at the same time serving to complement the owners' premium brands in global markets.

11) Specifically, one promising area for Chinese brands in the global market is goods of low-to-mid-technology. By some estimates, Chinese brands have roughly 90% of the domestic market for refrigerators and washing machines, 70%—80% of the market for air-conditioners and 60% for color televisions. "In many areas the quality of products has improved to the point where they are quite marketable," says Philip Day, a vice president at consulting firm A. T. Kearney in Hong Kong. "What we're now seeing is Chinese companies getting their act together in terms of marketing."

12) Another example might be cosmetics industry. In 1996, a New York-based cosmetics maker formed a venture in China with Yue-Sai Kan Cosmetics. Yue-Sai Kan is a household name and face in the country of her birth. Although technically owned by an American company, Yue-Sai Kan Cosmetics is considered one of China's leading brands of color cosmetics.

13) This blend of East and West may not catch all consumers, but a lot of smart people are betting it will be enough to help launch Chinese brands into global markets.

A: Promising industries

B: Difficulties on the way

C: Short-term prospects

D: Prospects of a new direction

E: Why going abroad?

Extensive Reading

Passage One

On the 50th Anniversary of the End
of the World War II in Europe

JOHN PAUL II

罗马天主教教宗,梵蒂冈城国国家元首约翰·保罗二世在欧洲第二次世界大战结束五十周年纪念日发表演讲,对二战进行方方面面的反思。他指出战争给世界人民带来的巨大危害并提醒大家警惕未来的战争倾向。

教皇保罗二世

1. Fifty years ago, on 8 May 1945, the Second World War ended in Europe. The conclusion of that terrible calamity (灾难) not only led people to hope for the return of the prisoners, deportees (被放逐者) and refugees (难民); it also awakened a desire to build a better Europe. The Continent could begin once more to hope in a future of peace and democracy. Half a century later, individuals, families and peoples still retain memories of those six terrible years: memories of fear, violence, extreme poverty, death; tragic experiences of painful separation, endured in the absence of all security and freedom; recurring traumas (创伤) brought about by the incessant (不停的) bloodshed (流血).

With the passing of time its meaning becomes clearer

2. It was not easy at the time to comprehend fully the many tragic dimensions of the conflict. But the passage of time has brought an increased awareness of the effect of that event on the 20th century and on the future of the world. The Second World War was not only an historical event of the first order; it also marked a turning-point for humanity in our time. As the years go by, the memories of the War must not grow dim; rather, they ought to become a stern (严厉的) lesson for our generation and for generations yet to come.

An incredibly (难以置信地) destructive war

3. The consequences of the Second World War for the life of nations and of continents were enormous. Military cemeteries are memorials to Christians and believers of other religions alike, to soldiers and civilians from Europe and other areas of the world. In fact, soldiers from non-European countries also came to fight on the soil of the Old Continent: many fell in the field, while for others 8 May marked the end of a terrible nightmare. Tens of millions of men and women were killed, not counting the wounded and the missing. Great masses of families found themselves forced to abandon lands to which they had been attached for centuries. Communities and monuments rich in history were devastated (破坏); cities and countries were thrown into turmoil (混乱) and reduced to ruins. In no earlier conflict had the civilian population, particularly women and children, ever paid such a high toll (伤亡人数) in deaths.

The marshalling (集结) of hatred

4. Still more grave was the spread of the "culture of war" with its bleak (冷酷的) consequences of death, hatred and violence. It led to an unprecedented marshalling of

hatred, which in turn trampled (践踏) on man and on everything that is human, all in the name of an imperialistic (帝国主义的) ideology. It can never be sufficiently repeated that the Second World War changed the life of so many individuals and peoples for the worse. The point was reached where hellish death camps were built, where millions of Jews and hundreds of thousands of gypsies (吉普赛人) and other human beings met their death in atrocious (糟透的) conditions; their only fault was that they belonged to another people.

Auschwitz: a monument to the effects of totalitarianism

5. Auschwitz (纳粹德国奥斯威辛集中营), along with so many other concentration camps, remains the horribly eloquent symbol of the effects of totalitarianism (极权主义). It is our duty to make a pilgrimage (朝圣) to these places, in mind and heart, on this 50th anniversary.

6. This meditation (冥思) raises questions which humanity needs to ask. Why did things come to the point where man himself and whole peoples were brought so low? Why, once the War was over, was there a failure to draw from its bitter lesson the necessary conclusions for the whole continent of Europe? At the time, unfortunately, people failed to understand that when freedoms are trampled on, the foundations are laid for a dangerous decline into violence and hatred, the harbingers (先兆,预兆) of the "culture of war".

A humane society is not built on violence

7. The Second World War was the direct result of this process of degeneration; but were the necessary lessons learned in the following decades? Sadly, the end of the War did not lead to the disappearance of the policies and ideologies which were its cause or contributed to its outbreak. It was not by chance that a number of wise statesmen in Western Europe desired to forge (锻造) a common bond between their countries. That pact developed in subsequent decades, making clear the will of the nations no longer to be alone in facing their future. They understood that in addition to the common good of individual peoples there is a common good of humanity which is violently trampled on by war. This reflection on a terrible experience convinced them that the interests of any one nation cannot be fittingly pursued except in the context of amicable interdependence with other peoples.

The Church listens to the plea of the victims

8. Many are the voices raised on this 50th anniversary of the end of the Second World War in an effort to overcome the divisions between victors and the vanquished (征服). There are commemorations of the courage and sacrifice of millions of men and women. For her part, the Church wishes to listen in particular to the plea of all the victims. It is a plea

which helps us understand better the scandal of those six years of conflict. It is a plea which asks us to reflect on what the War meant for all humanity. In the face of every war, we are all called to ponder (沉思) our responsibilities, to forgive and to ask forgiveness. We feel bitter regret, as Christians, when we consider that "the horrors of that war took place on a continent which could claim a remarkable flowering of culture and civilization."

War is incapable of bringing about justice

9. The divisions caused by the Second World War make us realize that force in the service of the "will to power" is an inadequate means for building true justice. Instead, it sets in motion a sinister process with unforeseeable consequences for men, women and whole peoples, who risk the complete loss of their dignity, together with their property and life itself. We can still appreciate the stern warning which Pope Pius XII (教宗比约十二世) voiced in August 1939, on the very eve of that tragic conflict, in a last-minute attempt to prevent recourse (求助) to arms: "The danger is imminent (逼近的), but there is yet time. Nothing is lost with peace; all may be lost with war. Let men return to mutual understanding. Let them begin negotiations anew". I do so especially by reason of the haunting memory of the *atomic explosions* which struck first Hiroshima and then Nagasaki in August 1945. "To remember the past is to commit oneself to the future. To remember Hiroshima is to abhor nuclear war. To remember Hiroshima is to commit oneself to peace. To remember what the people of this city suffered is to renew our faith in man, in his capacity to do what is good, in his freedom to choose what is right, in his determination to turn disaster into a new beginning". Fifty years after that tragic conflict, it appears ever more clearly as "a self-destruction of mankind". War is in fact, if we look at it clearly, as much a tragedy for the victors as for the vanquished.

The Propaganda Machine

10. A further reflection is called for. During the Second World War, in addition to conventional, chemical, biological and nuclear weapons, there was widespread use of another deadly instrument of war: propaganda (宣传). Before striking the enemy with weapons aimed at his physical destruction, efforts were made to annihilate (歼灭) him morally by defamation (诽谤), false accusations and the inculcation (教诲) of an irrational intolerance, by means of a thorough programme of indoctrination (灌输), directed especially to the young. The perverse (背理的) techniques of propaganda do not stop at falsifying (歪曲) reality; they also distort information about where responsibility lies, thus making an informed moral and political judgment extremely difficult. War gives rise to a propaganda which leaves no room for different

interpretations, critical analysis of the causes of conflict, and the attribution of real responsibility.

War has not disappeared

11. After 1945, wars unfortunately did not come to an end. Violence, terrorism and armed attacks have continued to darken these last decades. We have witnessed the so-called "Cold War". Today too many conflicts are still raging in different parts of the world. Public opinion, shaken by the horrible pictures which enter homes each day via television, reacts emotionally but all too quickly grows accustomed to these conflicts and comes to accept their inevitability. Besides being unjust, this attitude is extremely dangerous. We must never forget what happened in the past and what is still happening today. We cannot and must not yield to the logic of arms!

A school for all believers

12. War never again! Yes to peace! These were the sentiments commonly expressed after the historic date of 8 May 1945. The six horrible years of conflict provided everyone with an opportunity to grow in the school of suffering. Christians too were able to draw closer together and question their own responsibilities for their disunity. They also discovered anew the solidarity of a destiny which they share in common and with all men and women of whatever nation.

13. The wave of suffering with which the War engulfed the earth has impelled believers belonging to all religions to put their spiritual resources at the service of peace. As I said in 1989 for the 50th anniversary of the beginning of the war: "From the heart of our various religious traditions flows the testimony (证明) of compassionate (有同情心的) sharing in the sorrows of mankind, of respect for the sacredness of life. This is a great spiritual force which makes us more confident for the future of humanity."

Some are still preparing for war

14. During these days, in many parts of Europe, celebrations and commemorations are taking place. As I join in this commemoration of the sacrifice made by the many victims of the war, I wish to invite all men and women of good will to reflect seriously on the connection that must exist between the memory of that terrible world conflict and the aims which should inspire national and international policies. In particular, it will be necessary to ensure effective means of controlling the international arms market and to make joint efforts to set up adequate structures for intervention in case of crises, in order to persuade all those involved to prefer negotiations to violent confrontation. Sadly, while we are celebrating the return of peace, is it not a fact that there are people who continue to prepare for war, both by promoting a culture of hatred and by distributing

sophisticated（精密的）weapons of war?

A special significance for youth

15. My thoughts now turn to the young people who have had no personal experience of the horrors of that War. To them I say: dear young people, I have great confidence in your ability to be authentic witnesses to the Gospel. Make a personal commitment to serve life and peace. The victims, the combatants and the martyrs（烈士）of the Second World War were for the most part young people like you. For this reason I ask you, the young people of the 21st century, to be particularly alert to the signs that the culture of hatred and death is growing. Reject sterile（枯燥乏味的）and violent ideologies. Renounce（宣布放弃）every form of extreme nationalism and intolerance. It is along these paths that the temptation to violence and war slowly but surely appears. May Mary be ever watchful and concerned for all her children, obtain for all humanity the precious gift of harmony and peace.

Retrieved from *http://www. vatican. va/holy_father/john_paul_ii/speeches/*1995

I. Reading comprehension.

1. The major purpose of John Paul II in delivering such a speech was to _____.
   A. condemn the atrocity committed by the Nazi fascists
   B. commemorate an event of the world significance
   C. reflect on the nature of the war
   D. tell people how destructive wars could be

2. The word "incessant" in Line 8 of Paragraph 1 is closest in meaning to _____.
   A. continuous
   B. sporadic
   C. tremendous
   D. cruel

3. The speech implied that millions of Jews and gypsies were killed because of _____.
   A. their disobedience under the fascist rule
   B. their noted intelligence
   C. feud and hatred passed down from history
   D. racial differences and discrimination

4. The speaker asked the youths of today to do the following except _____.
   A. to be on guard against the growth of cultural hatred
   B. to remember victims, combatants and martyrs of the Second World War
   C. to exercise internationalism and tolerance

D. to abandon violence

5. In "it is along these paths that the temptation to violence and war slowly but surely appears" in Line 8 of Paragraph 15, the word "paths" refers to _____.

  A. militarism practised by the Japanese imperialists

  B. expansionism of the German fascists

  C. extreme nationalism and intolerance

  D. totalitarianism

II. Topics for further discussion.

1. How much do you know about John Paul II?

2. What negative impact did the Propaganda Machine in WWII bring?

3. What conflicts do you think the speaker may have in mind when he says "today too many conflicts are still raging in different parts of the world."?

4. Who is Mary and why did John Paul II say "May Mary be ever watchful and concerned for all her children, obtain for all humanity the precious gift of harmony and peace."?

Passage Two

Marshall Plan Speech

1947 年 6 月 5 日马歇尔在哈佛大学发表演说。他首先提出援助欧洲经济复兴的方案,呼吁欧洲国家采取主动,共同制订一项经济复兴计划,美国则用其生产过剩的物资援助欧洲国家。

Mr. President, Dr. Conant, members of the board of overseers (监督员), ladies and gentlemen:

乔治·马歇尔进入哈佛大学发表本篇著名演说

I'm profoundly grateful and touched by the great distinction and honor and great compliment (褒奖) accorded me by the authorities of Harvard this morning. I'm overwhelmed, as a matter of fact, and I'm rather fearful of my inability to maintain such a high rating as you've been generous enough to accord to me. In these historic and lovely surroundings, this perfect day, and this very wonderful assembly, it is a tremendously (极大地) impressive thing to an individual in my position.

But to speak more seriously, I need not tell you that the world situation is very serious. That must be apparent to all intelligent people. I think one difficulty is that the problem is one of such enormous complexity that the very mass of facts presented to the public by press and radio make it exceedingly（极度地）difficult for the man in the street to reach a clear appraisement of the situation. Furthermore, the people of this country are distant from the troubled areas of the earth and it is hard for them to comprehend the plight（困境）and consequent reactions of the long-suffering peoples, and the effect of those reactions on their governments in connection with our efforts to promote peace in the world.

In considering the requirements for the rehabilitation（复兴）of Europe, the physical loss of life, the visible destruction of cities, factories, mines, and railroads was correctly estimated, but it has become obvious during recent months that this visible destruction was probably less serious than the dislocation（打乱）of the entire fabric（结构）of European economy. For the past ten years conditions have been abnormal. The feverish（狂热的）preparation for war and the more feverish maintenance of the war effort engulfed all aspects of national economies. Machinery has fallen into disrepair or is entirely obsolete（过时的）. Under the arbitrary and destructive Nazi rule, virtually every possible enterprise was geared into the German war machine. Long-standing commercial ties, private institutions, banks, insurance companies, and shipping companies disappeared through loss of capital, absorption through nationalization, or by simple destruction. In many countries, confidence in the local currency has been severely shaken. The breakdown of the business structure of Europe during the war was complete. Recovery has been seriously retarded（妨碍）by the fact that two years after the close of hostilities（敌对状态）a peace settlement with Germany and Austria has not been agreed upon. But even given a more prompt solution of these difficult problems, the rehabilitation of the economic structure of Europe quite evidently will require a much longer time and greater effort than has been foreseen.

There is a phase of this matter which is both interesting and serious. The farmer has always produced the foodstuffs to exchange with the city dweller for the other necessities of life. This division of labor is the basis of modern civilization. At the present time it is threatened with breakdown. The town and city industries are not producing adequate goods to exchange with the food-producing farmer. Raw materials and fuel are in short supply. Machinery, as I have said, is lacking or worn out. The farmer or the peasant cannot find the goods for sale which he desires to purchase. So the sale of his farm produce for money which he cannot use seems to him an unprofitable transaction（交易）. He, therefore, has withdrawn many fields from crop cultivation and is using them for grazing（放牧）. He feeds more grain to stock and finds for himself and his family an ample（充分的）supply of food, however short he may be on clothing and the other ordinary gadgets（小玩意儿）of civilization. Meanwhile, people in the cities are short of food and fuel, and in some places approaching the starvation levels. So the governments are forced to use their foreign money and credits to procure these necessities abroad. This process exhausts funds which are urgently needed for reconstruction. Thus a very serious situation is rapidly developing which bodes（预兆）no good for the world. The modern system of the division of labor upon which the exchange of products is based is in danger of breaking down.

The truth of the matter is that Europe's requirements for the next three or four years of foreign food and other essential products — principally from America — are so much greater than her present ability to pay that she must have substantial additional help or face economic, social, and political deterioration (恶化) of a very grave character.

The remedy (补救措施) seems to lie in breaking the vicious circle and restoring the confidence of the European people in the economic future of their own countries and of Europe as a whole. The manufacturer and the farmer throughout wide areas must be able and willing to exchange their product for currencies, the continuing value of which is not open to question.

Aside from the demoralizing (使陷入混乱的) effect on the world at large and the possibilities of disturbances arising as a result of the desperation of the people concerned, the consequences to the economy of the United States should be apparent to all. It is logical that the United States should do whatever it is able to do to assist in the return of normal economic health in the world, without which there can be no political stability and no assured peace.

Our policy is directed not against any country or doctrine (主义) but against hunger, poverty, desperation, and chaos. Its purpose should be the revival of a working economy in the world so as to permit the emergence of political and social conditions in which free institutions can exist. Such assistance, I am convinced, must not be on a piecemeal (零碎的) basis as various crises develop. Any assistance that this Government may render in the future should provide a cure rather than a mere palliative (姑息剂). Any government that is willing to assist in the task of recovery will find full cooperation, I am sure, on the part of the United States Government. Any government which maneuvers (耍花招) to block the recovery of other countries cannot expect help from us.

Furthermore, governments, political parties or groups which seek to perpetuate (使永久存在) human misery in order to profit therefrom politically or otherwise will encounter the opposition of the United States.

It is already evident that, before the United States Government can proceed much further in its efforts to alleviate (缓和) the situation and help start the European world on its way to recovery, there must be some agreement among the countries of Europe as to the requirements of the situation and the part those countries themselves will take in order to give proper effect to whatever action might be undertaken by this Government. It would be neither fitting nor efficacious (灵验的) for our Government to undertake to draw up unilaterally (单边地) a program designed to place Europe on its feet economically. This is the business of the Europeans. The initiative, I think, must come from Europe. The role of this country should consist of friendly aid in the drafting (起草) of a European program and of later support of such a program so far as it may be practical for us to do so. The program should be a joint one, agreed to by a number of, if not all, European nations.

An essential part of any successful action on the part of the United States is an understanding on the part of the people of America of the character of the problem and the remedies to be applied. Political passion and prejudice should have no part. With foresight, and a willingness on the part of our people to face up to the vast responsibility which history has clearly placed upon our country, the difficulties I have outlined can and will be overcome.

I am sorry that on each occasion I have said something publicly in regard to our international situation. I've been forced by the necessities of the case to enter into rather technical discussions. But to my mind, it is of vast importance that our people reach some general understanding of what the complications (复杂情况) really are, rather than react from a passion or a prejudice or an emotion of the moment. As I said more formally a moment ago, we are remote from the scene of these troubles. It is virtually impossible at this distance merely by reading, or listening, or even seeing photographs and motion pictures, to grasp at all the real significance of the situation. And yet the whole world of the future hangs on a proper judgment. It hangs, I think, to a large extent on the realization of the American people, of just what are the various dominant factors. What are the reactions of the people? What are the justifications of those reactions? What are the sufferings? What is needed? What can best be done? What must be done?

Thank you very much.

Retrieved from *http://www.historyplace.com/speeches/marshall.htm*

Decide whether the following statements are True or False.

1. There is nothing more serious than the physical loss of life and the visible destruction of cities, factories, mines and railways. (   )

2. People in most European countries still had confidence in the local currency after the war ended. (   )

3. A peace agreement with Germany and Austria was reached immediately after the war. (   )

4. Farmers were unwilling to sell their farm produce because they found that it was unprofitable. (   )

5. American policy was overtly aimed at a certain country which was viewed as a latent threat to security in Europe. (   )

Unit 4

Caught Between Places

本单元课文综述

Text 精读　对弃医从文的约翰·默里（John Murray）的访谈录的节选。从医生到作家的转型是否一帆风顺呢？他是如何走上创作的道路的？他的小说的主题是什么？他能否在医务工作和文学创作中寻找到二者的平衡点呢？在接受美国女作家克蒂丝．希坦菲的访谈中，约翰·默里为我们娓娓道来故事的前因后果。

Passage One 泛读　丘吉尔在伦敦作家协会上发表的关于写作乐趣的演说。生动形象的语言和大量修辞手法的运用，使得整篇演说幽默而且睿智。

Passage Two 泛读　在文中作者以挑选银勺为例，诠释艺术创作的简约之美。

ext　　　　　　　　　**Caught Between Places**

John Murray, a doctor-turned-writer, was born in Australia in 1963. Murray received his medical degree and moved to the United States to get a master degree from Johns Hopkins University. Yet by 1999, Murray said, "I'd reached a point where I'd accumulated so much uncertainty about the purpose of what I was doing that I had to write fiction to **figure** it **out**."

Curtis Sittenfeld:

What was it like to go from being a doctor to being a writer?

John Murray:

I was very conflicted. I didn't dislike what I was doing as a doctor. I liked it. I believed in it. And I'd actually spent some fifteen years of my life training for it and had just gotten to the point where I was a junior **faculty** member at Hopkins. I wasn't leaving that career entirely, as it turned out. At Hopkins, I was in an academic setting with people who aspired to make what I was doing their career as well. A lot of them thought I was absolutely crazy, because I was giving up things which they valued, including security. The interesting thing was that people who were my contemporaries told me I was crazy, but when I talked to people who were many years my **senior**, they were usually the ones who said that I should pursue my interests and my **inclination** and not feel like I had to stick at a career for the career's sake.

Curtis Sittenfeld:
Given all the potential **drawbacks**, what made the switch worth it?

John Murray:
I really wanted to write. The **bottom line** is, I had a **drive** to do it. It was something in me that I didn't quite understand, and I still don't quite understand it. I think writing is fundamentally irrational. You sit alone in a room with your **subconscious**, and to some degree your **conscious**, with no external **reinforcement** for long periods of time and with absolutely no guarantee that you will ever earn an income from it. I think for a lot of writers it's not a rational decision. What I had to do was give myself over to that feeling that I just had to do it.
Medicine is a good preparation for writing because both require a lot of discipline — sticking to a task and working every day without question.

Curtis Sittenfeld:
Had the impulse to write existed for your whole life or had it been building in recent years?

John Murray:
It had existed all my life — I've written all my life one way or the other, and I've always probably had more of an artistic side than a scientific side. But I couldn't get to the point where I was able to follow my artistic side. I went into medical school really because I was pushed by my family.
All my family were sheep farmers, and my father was the first Murray to go to university. He did agricultural science as a degree because he thought he would get a bit more education than most of his family had but then go back on the land. What he found when he was taking a class in biochemistry was that he just loved it. He had this instinctive feel for biochemistry, of all things, which was completely unexpected and **out of the blue**. When he told his father that he'd decided he was going to do a Ph. D. in biochemistry and be a biochemist, his father didn't talk to him for a year.
Nevertheless, when it came to what I was going to do, my father wasn't as different from his family as you might have thought. He was a scientist, and he saw no value at all in the arts. He saw no value in writing.

Curtis Sittenfeld:

So how had your early interest in writing developed?

John Murray:

I tried to imitate books that I read when I was six or seven. We grew up with all the British books — Agatha Christie, Rudyard Kipling. I spent a lot of time out on my grandparents' farm, which is this enormous 6,000-acre sheep station in the mid-north of south Australia. They've got a 150-year-old stone house which sits out there in the middle of absolutely **nowhere**. You can look out through the living-room window and you know there's nothing for 2,000 miles in that direction. We used to go there to help with the **shearing**. When you're a kid, you love doing things you don't normally do.

At night, we'd come back to this big old stone house, and it was just dead quiet, so quiet it feels as if it's sucking up sound. We used to sit up in a room with big old leather chairs and leather couches and these bookcases **stacked** to the ceiling with books. That's when I really started reading. I spent nights **poring over** these books. I have fond memories of that, and I think it started me on a pathway to writing.

Curtis Sittenfeld:

Yet you **ended up** entering medical school.

John Murray:

In a way, medical school was the only acceptable course for my family, given the grades that I got and the obvious inclination that I had to do something that was a little more academic. Medicine seemed to my family practical and sensible because they knew family doctors. They could see that it was something you could do, and it could have a value and give you a stable income and a status in society.

I started in medical school without really thinking about it. I was sixteen and I was twenty-two when I graduated and, I had no idea what I was doing. When I think back, it's laughable how little I understood about the world, about why I was doing it.

Curtis Sittenfeld:

How did you decide you wanted to work in other countries?

John Murray:

I loved the study of medicine. The process of learning I liked, but it was the practice of it I didn't like. The study is fascinating — you learn so much about how things work. The practice is **grueling**, repetitive, stressful, and highly **bureaucratic**. Although I really liked people, I didn't enjoy the clinical side. I needed to do something I could believe in and see as useful. I didn't see working in these systems in hospitals, where there was so much paper work and you were rushed all the time and you didn't have time to spend with people properly, as being something that suited me.

In my training, we had worked with Australian **Aborigines** who were really a developing-country population in the middle of a highly developed country. It was a **revelation** to me that they were there at all, and I found they had what seemed to be real problems. They get infectious diseases that you don't see anymore in the West, and it felt as if these problems weren't being properly addressed. That opened my eyes to more developing-country type work. It was something I could get my hands on and something that was fascinating to me, partly because of seeing how people very different from me lived, seeing other cultures and other languages.

Curtis Sittenfeld:

Did you ever feel afraid during the trips?

John Murray:

When you're in the midst of something, you often don't quite **appreciate** the level of risk, and when you're engaged in doing something actively, you get on with it. I found that appreciating your situation tends to happen later, though I've had a couple of occasions when I really felt scared at the time.

Curtis Sittenfeld:

Why do you think you're so interested in the immigrant experience?

John Murray:

Partly because I *am* an immigrant. And I feel as if there are a lot of **displaced people** in the world — I feel almost as if the century we're living in is the century of displacement. Living in the States, there are more foreign-born nationals than ever before.

A lot of people whom I see and meet are caught between places. They've come from somewhere else, they have a past, and they're trying to make a present. These were the sorts of issues I was trying to explore in these stories — people who have to reconcile their past with their present, who may want to go back to the past but can't. And also people who go to developing countries from developed countries to try and help. They have to **reconcile** their view of what they thought those places were like with the way they really are.

Curtis Sittenfeld:

One of the debates across your stories is about how much of a difference one person can make. What do you think about the individual's ability to **make a difference**?

John Murray:

When I started working, I thought I understood everything. I thought that the technical knowledge that I had would make a difference. What I found is that a lot of my work came to nothing, partly because the sort of places where I was working ended up being destroyed by war or political change.

I was writing to try and find what gave my characters a purpose and how they saw the world in the face of quite a lot of uncertainty. Underneath, I'm an **idealist** because I'd like to believe that an individual *can* make a difference. You may make a difference but not be aware of it — you may make tiny **incremental** changes that ultimately lead to something you will never see or understand.

Curtis Sittenfeld:

What is it about fiction, as opposed to essays or articles, that allows you to address these issues?

John Murray:

More fact-based articles don't quite convey the true essence of what's going on. It's a paradox, because we have more information available to us now than perhaps we ever have, but this **barrage** of information tends to **numb** you to the reality behind it. The more we see and know, the less we really understand what it means for people. If it's done reasonably well, fiction can convey better than anything else the emotional reality of a situation.

Curtis Sittenfeld:

How much is your writing affected by the current conditions of the world — for example, by the fact that we're now at war?

John Murray:

I think it's indirect. Most of the information that most people get is highly processed from big networks, and I don't think it's real. That does **motivate** me to get to the **heart** of the matter a bit more. A lot of media uses very particular words to describe the war, clinical language which is removed from reality. "The liberation of Iraq" or "the **disarmament**", for example, is used to describe what is in fact the killing of people. "**Collateral** damage" is often used to describe the killing of innocent civilians.

The truth that lies behind these images is the truth for each individual. What does it mean to a person to not be able to go outside if there are bombs dropping, or to be **on the run**, having left all your possessions and some members of your family? More than that, what does it mean in the **context** of your entire life, in terms of your family and the people you've left behind and your past and the places you grew up and all the sounds and **sensations** you remember? There's a weight to all of this that you don't get from most of the images in the media. Part of the motivation to write fiction, to try and write about characters, is to get to that weight.

Curtis Sittenfeld:

But do you ever feel guilty for spending most of your time now writing rather than doing work that helps people in more obvious, practical ways?

John Murray:

I **grapple** with that issue all the time. All the time, I feel like I should be living in Africa and working on HIV, which is possibly Africans' biggest health and social problem ever and will be for the next several years. I feel like I should be using the training I have.
But you can't escape your natural inclination. If you have a chance to do so you should follow the inclination that you feel is right for you and that you can do your best at. Ultimately, I hope if you follow your inclination, then you will contribute in some way. I don't think you should be miserable and feel that you're **squandering** your life doing something you believe in only intellectually. What I'm trying to find is a balance between sitting in my own room, writing symbols on pieces of paper, and making a difference in a broader sense.

From *Atlantic Unbound April* 2, 2003

New Words and Phrases

figure out		come to understand sb / sth by thinking 弄明白
faculty	*n.*	全体教员
senior	*n.*	an older person 年长者
inclination	*n.*	a liking or preference 爱好,癖好
given	*prep.*	taking something into account 考虑到
drawback	*n.*	disadvantage 缺点
bottom line	*n.*	essential point, crucial factor 决定性因素
drive	*n.*	an inner urge or desire 冲动,动力
subconscious	*n.*	潜意识心理活动
conscious	*n.*	意识
reinforcement	*n.*	the act of strengthening 加强

out of the blue		unexpected 突然的,意外的
nowhere	*n.*	an unknown and remote place 不知名的地方,一片荒芜的地区
shearing	*n.*	removing by cutting off or clipping 剪毛,修剪,剪切
stack	*v.*	to pile, arrange or place in a stack 把……叠成堆……
pore over		专心阅读
end up		最后,最终,结果
grueling	*adj.*	exhausting, very tiring 累垮人的
bureaucratic	*adj.*	arbitrary or routine 机械刻板的
aborigine	*n.*	native 土著居民;(常做 Aborigines)澳大利亚土著居民
revelation	*n.*	被揭示的真相
appreciate	*v.*	be fully conscious of, be aware of 领会
displace	*v.*	compel a person to leave home, country etc. 迫使某人离开家或者祖国
displaced people	*n.*	失去家园者
reconcile	*v.*	bring into agreement or harmony 调和,使一致
make a difference :		have an effect on sb / sth 对……有作用,有影响
idealist	*n.*	理想主义者
incremental	*adj.*	increasing gradually 递增的
barrage	*n.*	an overwhelming quantity or explosion 大量
numb	*v.*	使麻木不仁,使失去知觉
motivate	*v.*	stimulate the interest of 激起……的兴趣
heart	*n.*	core, the vital or essential part 中心,要点
collateral	*adj.*	additional, accompanying 伴随的
on the run		fleeing from pursuit or capture 逃跑
context	*n.*	the circumstances in which an event occurs 背景
sensation	*n.*	知觉;轰动
grapple	*v.*	work hard to overcome (a difficulty) 努力解决,对付
squander	*v.*	use sth wastefully 挥霍(时间、金钱等)

About the author:

John Murray was born in Australia in 1963. During most of the 90's he worked as an epidemiologist for the Center of Disease Control in Atlanta after earning his master's in public health from Johns Hopkins University. This position allowed him to travel to many developing countries in Africa, the Middle East and Central Asia, and those travels helped enrich many of the themes in his debut collection. In 1999, John and his family moved to Iowa where he enrolled in the Iowa Writer's Workshop on a teacher-writer fellowship. He spent the next two years writing *A Few Short Notes on Tropical Butterflies*: long, elegant narratives that jump from continent to continent, exploring ideas about family, national identity, memory, loss, love, science, and medicine. Vivid and alive, these stories reveal whole lives — characters caught between the past and the present, between different cultures, and between their intellects and emotions. And they are often searching to reconcile their new lives with the ones they've left behind. In beautiful language, with both frankness and compassion, Murray often highlights the disparities between developing and developed countries and depicts people's struggles to understand their lives and find meaning in a world that is often brutal and senseless. And yet, knowing that real life must somehow be lived, Murray's characters push forward, both burdened and comforted by their memories and obsessions. A short story from this volume, "The Hill Station" won the Prairie Lights Short Fiction Award, and the title story of the collection was selected by Joyce Carol Oates for the Best New American Voices 2002 anthology of short fiction.

Notes to the text

1. **The Johns Hopkins University**, commonly referred to as Hopkins, is a private American university based in Baltimore, Maryland. It also maintains full-time campuses elsewhere in Maryland, Washington, D. C. , Italy and China. It is particularly esteemed for its medical, health, scientific, music, and international studies programs. The undergraduate studies program is one of the top ranked in the world.

2. **Agatha Christie** (1890—1976) was a prolific English writer of detective novels and plays. Her works, particularly featuring detectives Hercule Poirot or Miss Jane Marple, have given her the title the "Queen of Crime". Her major works include *The Murder of Roger Acroyd*, *Murder on the Orient Express*, *Death on the Nile* and a stage play *The Mousetrap*.

3. **Joseph Rudyard Kipling** (1865—1936) was an English author of novels and poetry who was born in India. His major works, including the short story *The Man Who Would Be King*, a collection of children's stories, *The Jungle Book*, and the novel *Kim*, are set in British-occupied India. He won the 1907 Nobel Prize for literature.

4. **Aborigines** is a common name to refer to all indigenous Australians, who live in many different communities with their individual languages and unique cultures. Some of the issues facing them are health, education, unemployment, poverty and crime. For instance, about 70% of Aboriginal population lives in rural towns or remote areas. They have poor access to medical facilities and health services, and sometimes cultural differences may result in poor communication between them and health workers. Accordingly, they are more likely to have health problems.

5. **HIV**, an acronym from "human immunodeficiency virus," is a variable retrovirus that invades and inactivates helper T cells of the immune system. It is a cause of AIDS and AIDS-related complex.

Exercises

I. Answer the following questions based on Text. The words and expressions listed below are for your reference.

1. **Why did John Murray decide to become a writer?**

   pursue his interests and inclination / like his job as a doctor

   uncertainty about the purpose of medical work

   the impulse to write / give himself over to that feeling

2. **What are the potential drawbacks of writing as a profession?**

   no external support / no guarantee of earning an income from it

   people around question his crazy switch from a doctor to a writer

3. **How did John Murray's family view his choice and shift of profession?**

   medicine: seemed practical and sensible / have a value / a stable income / a status in society

   writing: no values / no value in the arts / as a scientist

4. **What did John Murray learn from his working abroad?**

   Australian Aborigines / problems facing developing countries

   within his reach / fascinating / different ways of living, different cultures and languages

5. **What's John Murray's attitude towards immigrant experience?**

   a lot of displaced people / live in the century of displacement / caught between places / reconcile the past with the present

6. **What are some of the issues John Murray deals with in his fiction?**

   problems facing developing countries / immigrant experience / individual's ability to make a difference

7. **Why do media not often seem to reveal the whole truth of the current events?**

   highly processed information / not real / removed from reality / numb people to the reality behind it

8. **What kind of conflict does John Murray encounter in his life?**

   a conflict between medical work and writing

   a conflict between working on HIV and contributing in a broader sense

II. Further questions for discussion.

1. What are the similarities and differences between being a writer and being a doctor?

2. Should people follow their inclination and pursue their interests regardless of all the objections from their family and friends?

3. Why are many people caught between places? What problems will they face in a different place?

4. Can fiction better convey the emotional reality of a situation?

5. How does John Murray portray the life of a doctor as a medical professional?

III. Vocabulary study.

1. Word in Use.

1) **figure sb / sth out**: come to understand sb / sth by thinking 理解,弄明白

I've never been able to figure him out.

Have you figured out what's wrong with your car?

I can't figure out a way to settle the problem.

2) **drawback**: ~ (of / to doing sth) disadvantage, problem 缺点,障碍,不利条件

The great drawback to living on a main road is the constant noise.

Living in a large house has its drawbacks as well as its advantages.

The major drawback to studying English is that we don't have the proper language environment.

3) **give oneself over to sth**: sink into (the specified state), devote oneself completely to sth 沉溺于（某种状态）,完全献身于……

After his wife's death, he seemed to give himself over to despair.

She gave herself over to laughter before she could go on.

Unable to succeed in this competitive society, he gave himself over to drink for a very long time.

4) **pore over**: study sth by looking at it or thinking about it very carefully 钻研,审察,审视,专心阅读

The child spends hours poring over her books.

A scholar was poring over a rare old manuscript.

He would pore over the major newspapers.

5) **end up**: reach or come to a certain place, state or action, esp. by a lengthy route or process 最后,最终,结果

He ended up head of the firm.

Wasteful people usually end up in debt.

At first he refused to accept any responsibility but he ended up apologizing.

6) **revelation**: a (surprising) fact that is made known （尤指出人意料的）被揭示的真相,惊人的新发现

Life would be only a series of such sorry revelations for him.

The ease with which he drives was quite a revelation to me.

His Hamlet was a revelation to the critics.

7) **reconcile**：make（aims, statements, ideas, etc.）agree when they seem to conflict 使（似有分歧的目标、说法、意见等）一致,调和

They did their best to reconcile religion and science.

Can eating fish be reconciled with vegetarianism?

I will reconcile my way of thinking with yours.

8) **barrage**：a large number（of questions, criticisms, etc. delivered quickly, one after the other） 大量,连珠炮似的一大堆（问题、批评等）

He had to face a barrage of angry complaints.

He directed a heavy propaganda barrage against his opponent.

The famous musician was under a barrage of questions.

9) **numb**：make（sb）emotionally incapable of thinking or acting 使麻木不仁,使麻痹,使失去知觉

She was completely numbed by the shock of her father's death.

His mind has been numbed by half a lifetime of hardship.

He lay there, numbed with grief.

10) **grapple**：work hard to overcome（a difficulty）努力克服,努力解决,对付,斗争

He has been grappling with this difficulty for a long time.

He grappled with the problem for an hour before he solved it.

The new president had to grapple with a grave economic crisis when taking office.

11) **squander**：waste（time, money, etc.）; use sth wastefully 浪费,挥霍（时间、金钱等）

He squandered all his savings on drink.

Don't squander your affection on him. He'll never love you.

Those who squander natural resources should be punished.

2. Word Distinctions.

1) **sit, sit up**（stay up）熬夜

Never stand when you can _____.

I shall get back late, so don't _____ for me.

The nurse _____ with the patient all night.

He _____ in an armchair and fell asleep.

2) **end, end up**（ususally doing sth）最终,结果

If you continue to steal you'll _____ in prison.

How does the story _____?

They _____ the play with a song.

He _____ designing the whole car and putting it into production.

3. Decide the meanings of the following words by matching each word in Column A with the word or expression in Column B that is similar in meaning.

A	B
1）inclination	a. waste（time, money, etc.）
2）drawback	b. very tiring, exhausting
3）appreciate	c. state of great surprise, excitement
4）grueling	d. a remote or unknown place
5）barrage	e. disadvantage
6）make a difference	f. to be fully conscious of; be aware of
7）sensation	g. a liking or preference
8）nowhere	h. have an effect
9）bottom line	i. deciding or crucial factor
10）squander	j. a large number

4. Try to write a brief story with the following words and phrases.

conflict, inclination, impulse, work abroad, themes, developing countries, immigrant experience, displaced people, make a difference,

IV. Translation.

1. Put the following Chinese expressions into English.

1）应用文　　2）文学批评　　3）人物塑造　　4）故事的高潮

5）构思小说　　6）修辞手段　　7）作品的主题　　8）诗中有画,画中有诗

2. Put the following Chinese sentences into English with the words or phrases in the bracket.

1）我琢磨不透他为什么要辞职。(figure out)

2）该计划实施的惟一障碍是经费问题。(drawback)

3）她晚年专事写作。(give oneself over to)

4）她正在仔细阅读该地区的旧地图。(pore over)

5）我们反复商量到国外度假的事情,最后决定去新加坡。(end up)

6）他无法作出符合事实的陈述。(reconcile)

7）他的意见招来了一连串的批评。(barrage)

8）那个破了产的前百万富翁不得不忍住挥霍的欲望。(squander)

3. Put the following Chinese paragraph into English.

　　我笑她十年的笔耕生涯,没能磨掉敏而好动的演员气质,又不由暗暗佩服她的记忆力,为她的回忆和有真知灼见的议论所感染。渐渐,眼前娓娓而谈的作家,幻化成了她的作品,一一浮现出来。真是"文如其人"啊! 一面是冷静的观察、深沉的思考,一面又含有孩提般的天真、诚挚、顽皮、严肃的题材,深刻的开掘,新鲜巧妙的艺术想像,不拘成规的语法修辞;这一切,在她的作品中熔于一炉,形成了她自己特有的风格。这正是她的作品魅力之所在。

4. Put the following quotes into Chinese.

1) Reading makes a full man, conference a ready man, and writing an exact man.

—— Bacon

2) One hates an author that's all author. —— Byron

3) A writer is someone who can make a riddle out of an answer. —— Karl Kraus

4) Fill your paper with the breathings of your heart. —— William Wordsworth

5) Writing is both mask and unveiling. —— E. B. White

5. Translate the following passage into Chinese.

The writer must find a technique that will let him describe anybody, anything, any situation — a technique that will permit him to use all his experience of living, tragic, comic, embarrassing, cruel, beautiful.

Few writers are born with this technique. They must search until they find it. Actually it is a little difficult to separate the technique of writing from the technique of living — which is another way of saying the style is the man. I have no patience with that view of writing, which looks on style and techniques of writing as a trick.

Writing is not apart from living. Writing is a kind of double living. The writer experiences everything twice. Once in reality and once in that mirror which waits always before or behind him.

However, I happen to think a writer's life is the most privileged there is in our society. It is a life exciting, varied. If success comes, it is a life that lends itself to expansion both materially and spiritually.

V. Comment on the structure of the text.

An interview is a form of asking and answering questions. In this text, the interviewee is a doctor-turned-writer, so the interview is centered on his writing: the switch from a doctor to a writer, his writing experience, the themes of his fiction and so on.

In this text, most of the words are easy-to-understand everyday vocabulary. The combination of short and long sentences along with the use of simple, compound and complex sentences contributes to the variety and variation of the talk. The story-telling now and then makes the serious interview appealing and convincing. On the whole, the text is well organized and coherent.

Extended Exercises

1. Arrange the following paragraphs in a logical order.

1) Professional success has allowed some women to rid their homes of menfolk whose presence they once tolerated out of material necessity.

2) The rise of divorce extends this exclusion, since mothers win custody in most instances; in one in three cases in America, fathers get no visitation rights at all. Human beings are returning to "the mammalian default mode": in most primate species, the family unit consists of a mother and her offspring.

3) Ever since the feminist revolution, we are told, men have felt under threat. And though the sound of masculine complaint has risen and fallen, it has rarely been as loud as it is today.

4) The growth of births out of wedlock, usually treated as a problem for children, is also a disaster for men. It excludes men from traditional family bonds.

5) Women's pay goes up, we read, while men's pay goes down; women are free to behave vampishly as men are sued for sexual harassment; feminism has destroyed men's traditional role without creating a replacement; men do not know whether to be new-men or he-men, lovely fathers or corporate warriors. It is all enough to disturb even sunny, feministical men who believe in the equality of the sexes.

6) Moreover, public policy tends to reinforce men's new exclusion. Divorce law, for example, makes it easier for women to drive dad out: not only can they usually count on retaining the children, they can expect financial support from him as well.

7) Emotionally and financially upset, some men refuse to pay. But, in America and increasingly in Britain, the state is growing ruthless in tracking down "deadbeat dads". When you renew your driver's licence in New York, you must provide your social-security number so that the state can check you are not a delinquent father. If your are, prison beckons.

8) Relations between the sexes have changed in western society over the past generation and some men at least have watched women draw equal with them at work while not abandoning their female primacy in the home.

2. In the following article, some paragraphs have been removed. Choose the most suitable paragraph from the list A-E to fit into each of the numbered gaps. There is ONE paragraph which does not fit in any of the gaps.

Feminists have harped on about the position of women in modern societies. But what about the men?

The radical changes in sexual mores, patterns of employment, and domestic life have turned their lives upside down.

1) _____

And in the private sphere, where an ancient division of labor once gave guidance to those who crossed its threshold, there is no knowing what strategy will be most effective.

Manly gestures — holding open a door for a woman, handing her into an automobile, taking charge of her bags — can spark insulted rejection.

2) _____.

And the disappearance of female modesty and sexual restraint has made it hard for a man to believe, when a woman yields to his advances, that her doing so is a special tribute to his masculine powers, rather than a day-to-day transaction, in which he is dispensable.

3) _____.

Social, political, and legal changes have shrunk the all-male sphere to the vanishing point, redefining every activity in which men once proved that they were indispensable, so that now women can do the job, too — or at any rate appear to do it.

Feminists have sniffed out male pride wherever it has grown and ruthlessly uprooted it.

4) _____.

The advent of in vitro fertilization and the promise of cloning create the impression that men are not even necessary for human reproduction, while the growth of the single-parent household — in which the mother is the only adult — has made fatherless childhood into an increasingly common option.

5) _____.

A: The sexual revolution is not the only cause of men's confusion.

B: This is the core idea of feminism — that "gender roles" are not natural but cultural, and that by changing them we can overthrow old power structures and achieve new and more creative ways of being.

C: Displays of wealth, power, or influence are likely to seem ridiculous to a woman who herself has more of them.

D: These changes threaten to make manhood redundant.

E: Under their pressure, modern culture has downgraded or rejected such masculine virtues as courage, tenacity, and military prowess in favor of more gentle, more 'socially inclusive' habits.

F: Men now encounter women not as "the weaker sex" but as equal competitors in the public sphere.

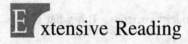xtensive Reading

Passage One

The Joys of Writing

Winston Churchill

作为英国杰出的演说家,丘吉尔认为写作是一种乐趣,作家享有多数人不能感受到的

自由与安全感;但是同时作家也面临机遇和挑战:他们必须能够以简单、正确、练达的英语为媒介表达自己的思想感情,尽自己最大的努力把最好的作品呈现给读者。

The fortunate people in the world — the only really fortunate people in the world, in my mind, — are those whose work is also their pleasure. The class is not a large one, not nearly so large as it is often represented to be; and authors are perhaps one of the most important elements in its composition. They enjoy in this respect at least a real harmony of life. To my mind, to be able to make your work your pleasure is the one class distinction in the world worth striving for; and I do not wonder that others are inclined to envy those happy human beings who find their livelihood in the gay effusions (作品、谈话中思想感情的倾泻,迸发) of their fancy, to whom every hour of labour is an hour of enjoyment, to whom repose (休息,歇息), however necessary, is a tiresome interlude (插曲) and even a holiday is almost deprivation (丧失,损失). Whether a man writes well or ill, has much to say or little, if he cares about writing at all, he will appreciate the pleasures of composition. To sit at one's table on a sunny morning, with four clear hours of uninterruptible security, plenty of nice white paper, and a Squeezer pen that is true happiness. The complete absorption of the mind upon an agreeable occupation — what more is there than that to desire? What does it matter what happens outside? The House of Commons may do what it likes, and so may the House of Lords. The heathen (异教徒) may rage furiously in every part of the globe. The bottom may be knocked clean out of the American market. Consols may fall and suffragettes (主张妇女参政权或者选举权的女子) may rise. Never mind, for four hours, at any rate, we will withdraw ourselves from a common, ill-governed, and disorderly world, and with the key of fancy unlock that cupboard where all the good things of the infinite are put away.

And speaking of freedom, is not the author free, as few men are free? Is he not secure, as few men are secure? The tools of his industry are so common and so cheap that they have almost ceased to have commercial value. He needs no bulky pile of raw material, no elaborate apparatus, no service of men or animals. He is dependent for his occupation upon no one but himself, and nothing outside him that matters. He is the sovereign (君主,元首) of an empire, self-supporting, self-contained (自立的). No one can sequestrate (没收,接收) his estates. No one can deprive him of his stock in trade; no one can force him to exercise his faculty against his will; no one can prevent him exercising it as he chooses. The pen is the great liberator of men and nations. No chains can bind, no poverty can choke (压制,阻挡), no tariff (关税) can restrict the free play of his mind, and even the "Times" Book Club can only exert a moderately depressing influence upon his rewards. Whether his work is good or bad, so long as he does his best he is happy. I often fortify (增强) myself amid the uncertainties and vexations (伤脑筋的事情) of political life by believing that I possess a line of retreat into a peaceful and fertile country where no rascal (流氓,无赖) can pursue and where one need never be dull or idle or even wholly without power. It is then, indeed, that I feel devoutly thankful to have been born fond of writing. It is then, indeed, that I feel grateful to all the brave and generous spirits who, in every age and in every land, have fought to establish the now unquestioned freedom of the pen.

And what a noble medium the English language is. It is not possible to write a page without experiencing positive pleasure at the richness and variety, the flexibility and the profoundness of our mother-tongue. If an English writer cannot say what he has to say in English, and in simple English, you may depend upon it, it is probably not worth saying. What a pity it is that English is not more generally studied. I am not going to attack classical education. No one who has the slightest pretension to literary tastes can be insensible to the attraction of Greece and Rome. But I confess our present educational system excites in my mind grave misgivings (疑虑,担忧). I cannot believe that a system is good, or even reasonable, which thrusts upon reluctant and uncomprehending multitudes (民众) treasures which can only be appreciated by the privileged and gifted few. To the vast majority of boys who attend our public schools, a classical education is from beginning to end one long useless, meaningless rigmarole (胡言乱语,冗长的废话). If I am told that classics are the best preparation for the study of English, I reply that by far the greater number of students finish their education while this preparatory stage is still incomplete and without deriving any of the benefits which are promised as its result.

And even of those who, without being great scholars, attain a certain general acquaintance with the ancient writers, can it really be said that they have also obtained the mastery of English? How many young gentlemen there are from the universities and public schools who can turn a Latin verse with a facility which would make the old Romans squirm (蠕动,扭动) in their tombs. How few there are who can construct a few good sentences, or still less a few good paragraphs of plain, correct, and straight forward English. Now, I am a great admirer of the Greeks, although, of course, I have to depend upon what others tell me about them, — and I would like to see our educationists imitate in one respect, at least, the Greek example. How is it that the Greeks made their language the most graceful and compendious mode of expression ever known among men? Did they spend all their time studying the languages which had preceded theirs? Did they explore with tireless persistency the ancient root dialects of the vanished world? Not at all. They studied Greek. They studied their own language. They loved it, they cherished it, they adorned (装饰) it, they expanded it, and that is why it survives a model and delight to all posterity (后代,后世). Surely we, whose mother-tongue has already won for itself such an unequalled empire over the modern world, can learn this lesson at least from the ancient Greeks and bestow a little care and some proportion of the years of education to the study of a language which is perhaps to play a predominant part in the future progress of mankind.

Let us remember the author can always do his best. There is no excuse for him. The great cricketer (板球运动员) may be out of form. The general may on the day of decisive battle have a bad toothache or a bad army. The admiral may be seasick — as a sufferer I reflect with satisfaction upon that contingency (偶然性,意外). Caruso may be afflicted with catarrh (黏膜炎), or Hacken-schmidt with influenza. As for an orator, it is not enough for him to be able to think well and truly. He must think quickly. Speed is vital to him. Spontaneity (自然,自发) is more than ever the hallmark (标志,特征) of good speaking. All these varied forces of activity require from the performer the command of the best that is in him at a particular moment which may be fixed by circumstances utterly beyond his control. It is not so with the author. He need never appear in public until he is ready. He can always realise the best that is in him. He is not dependent upon his best moment in any one day. He may group together the best moments of twenty days. There is no excuse for him if he does not do his best. Great is his opportunity; great also his responsibility. Someone I forget who has said: "Words are the only things which last for ever." That is, to my mind, always a wonderful thought. The most durable structures raised in stone by the strength of man, the mightiest monuments of his power, crumble (消失,瓦解) into dust, while the words spoken with fleeting breath, the passing expression of the unstable fancies of his mind, endure not as echoes of the past, not as mere archaeological curiosities or venerable (珍贵的) relics, but with a force and life as new and strong, and sometimes far stronger than when they were first spoken, and leaping across the gulf (巨大的差距,不可逾越的鸿沟) of three thousand years, they light the world for us today.

Retrieved from http://zhidao.baidu.com/question/19852968.html

I. Reading comprehension.

1. According to the text, who considers work and pleasure to be one? _____
   a) Ordinary people.
   b) Writers.
   c) Labourers.
   d) Housewives.

2. Which of the following is not **true** about writers? _____
   a) Writers find their livelihood in the gay effusions of their fancy.
   b) Writers love taking a holiday now and then.
   c) Writers enjoy their work all the time.
   d) Writers think rest is a tiresome interlude.

3. What can be said of classical education? _____
   a) Classical education would cultivate a literary taste for people.
   b) The vast majority of boys in public schools believe classical education is useful.
   c) Classic works are the basic foundation for your good English.
   d) A large number of students finish their education with little acquaintance of classical literature.

4. According to the text, the best way to learn good English is _____
   a) to read more of modern English literature.
   b) to read more of old English.
   c) to write poetry regularly .
   d) to devote more time and have more patience in the course of learning English.

5. According to the text, which of the following is the most enduring? _____
   a) The mightiest monuments.
   b) The most durable stone structure.
   c) Archaeological curiosities and venerable relics.
   d) Words spoken.

II. Topics for further discussion.

1. Would you personally consider writing as a plesure?
2. To what extent does the author enjoy the freedom and security of writing?
3. What opportunities and responsibilities do you think there would possibly be for a professional writer?

Passage Two

Simplicity in Art (简约的艺术)

Frank Norris

Once upon a time I had occasion to buy so uninteresting a thing as a silver soup-ladle (汤勺). The salesman at the silversmith's (银器店) was obliging and for my inspection brought forth quite an array of ladles. But my purse was flaccid (松弛的), anemic (无力的), and I must pick and choose with all the discrimination in the world. I wanted to make a brave showing with my gift — to get a great deal for my money. I went through a world of soup-ladles — ladles with gilded (镀金的) bowls, with embossed (浮雕图案的) handles, with chased arabesques (阿拉伯式雕花图案), but there were none to my taste. "Or perhaps," says the salesman, "you would care to look at something like this," and he brought out a ladle that was as plain and as unadorned as the unclouded sky — and about as beautiful. Of all the others this was the most to my liking. But the price! Ah, that anemic purse; and I must put it from me! It was nearly double the cost of any of the rest. And when I asked why, the salesman said:

"You see, in this highly ornamental ware the flaws of the material don't show, and you can cover up a blow-hole (瑕疵) or the like by wreaths (环形瑕疵) and beading (小珠镶边). But this plain ware has got to be the very best. Every defect is apparent."

And there, if you please, is a conclusive comment upon the whole business — a final basis of comparison of all things whether commercial or artistic; the bare dignity of the unadorned that may stand before the world all unashamed, panoplied (盛装的) rather than clothed in consciousness of perfection. We of this latter day, we painters and poets and writers — artists — must labour with all the wits of us, all the strength of us, and with all that we have of ingenuity (心灵手巧) and perseverance to attain simplicity. But it has not always been so. At the very earliest, men — forgotten, ordinary men — were born with an easy, unblurred vision that today we would hail as marvelous genius. Suppose, for instance, the New Testament was all unwritten and one of us were called upon to tell the world that Christ was born, to tell of how we had seen His, that this was the Messiah (救世主耶稣). How the adjectives would marshall (排列成形) upon the page, how the exclamatory phrases would cry out, how we would elaborate and elaborate, and how our rhetoric would flare and blazon till — so we should imagine — the ear would ring and the very eye would be dazzled; and even then we would believe that our words were all so few and feeble. It is beyond words, we should vociferate (大声说). So it would be. That is very true — words of ours. Can you not see how we should dramatize it? We would make a point of the transcendent (超然的) stillness of the hour, of the deep blue of the Judean (犹太人的) midnight, of the liplapping of Galilee (地名), the murmur of Jordan, the peacefulness of sleeping Jerusalem. Then the stars, the descent of the angel, the shepherds — all the accessories. And our narrative would be as commensurate with the subject as the flippant (灵活的) smartness of a "bright" reporter in the Sistine chapel (西斯廷教堂). We would be striving to cover up our innate incompetence, our impotence to do justice to the mighty theme by elaborateness of design and arabesque intricacy of rhetoric.

But on the other hand — listen：

"The days were accomplished that she should be delivered, and she brought forth her first born son and wrapped him in swaddling clothes (襁褓用长布条) and laid him in a manger, because there was no room for them in the inn."

From *Writing Prose*：*Techniques and Purpose Oxford University Press* 1969

Decide whether the following statements are True or False.

1. Frank Norris was very wealthy and so he decided to buy the most expensive soup-ladle at the silversmith's. (　　)

2. The ladles with embossed handles were to Frank Norris' taste. (　　)

3. The plain and unadorned ladle was the cheapest at the silversmith's. (　　)

4. Frank Norris believed that the highest degree of excellence in writing is simplicity and therefore writers should strive for perfection by mastering the art of simplicity. (　　)

5. Some writers tended to cover up their incompetence and impotence with intricacy of rhetoric. (　　)

Unit 5

Marco Polo's Legacy

本单元课文综述

Text 精读　节选自美国 Macalester College 教授 John Hubbard 的文章 Marco Polo's Asia。对 13 世纪意大利旅行家马可·波罗所著《马可·波罗游记》一书的历史背景以及马可·波罗介绍中国文化所持的视角作了评述,肯定了该书是研究蒙古统治时期中国社会文化的重要依据。

Passage One 泛读　介绍了意大利北部城市佛罗伦萨在 14 世纪如何从一个纺织商业中心发展成欧洲文艺复兴的发源地。

Passage Two 泛读　讲述了宗教统治一切社会生活的欧洲中世纪是如何在各种社会矛盾和冲突中分崩离析,从而开始了一个伟大的文艺复兴的新时代。

ext　　　　　　　　**Marco Polo's Legacy**

John Hubbard

The Middle Ages represents a **unique** period in world history. An advanced Chinese civilization had been flourishing for many centuries, but at the time was under Mongol rule. Although many records of Chinese history exist from within the culture, an outsider's perspective on Chinese civilization would yield further information. Fortunately, there is one historical document that offers such an account: the text of Marco Polo's journeys in

Asia. This book serves as an important work on Chinese civilization during Mongol rule.

In the year 1295 A. D., after an absence of twenty-four years, Maffeo, Nicolo, and Marco Polo returned to their hometown of Venice, Italy. The Polo trio looked like strangers to their fellow citizens: they wore **bizarre** and ragged clothes and spoke in an accented tongue. It is said that their own family neither recognized nor acknowledged them due to their foreign appearance.

Marco, having left Venice as a young man of 17, was now 41 years old. He had spent most of his life traveling in Asia. Having spent so much of his life in the Orient, Marco must have experienced an extreme culture shock upon returning to his homeland. While in Asia during the voyages to and from China, Marco Polo saw vast numbers of different lands and lifestyles. His Venetian upbringing gave him a **unique perspective** on Asian civilization.

A few years after his return to Venice in 1295, Marco found himself aboard a Venetian ship under the post of gentleman-commander during a regional war between Venice and Genoa. The ship was captured by the Genoese fleet and Marco consequently spent the next few years, until May of 1299, in a Genoa prison. It was during this period that Marco found the time to dictate, possibly with the help of notes taken during his voyage, the story of his years abroad. Rustigielo, a citizen of Pisa and fellow prisoner of Marco, took down Marco's story. The book was dictated in prison and copied by hand, as the technology of mass printing had not yet immigrated to Europe from China. As a consequence, there exist today many versions, translations, and reconstructions of the Rustigielo transcript.

Polo's book, entitled The Description of the World, covers the area from Constantinople to Japan to Siberia to Africa. Because these locations are told in the third-person, the exact route of Marco Polo is not known. Instead of narrating the journey of the Polos, the book contains historical observations and detailed descriptions of cultures and geography. For this reason Marco Polo's accounts can be used to re-examine the history of China.

Details that the young Polo observed included regional histories, descriptions of cities, architecture, inhabitants, races, languages and governments. Also described are peoples' different lifestyles, diets, styles of dress, marriage customs, rituals, and religions. There are further accounts of the trading practices, crafts, manufactured products, plants, animals, minerals, and **terrain**. Such a diverse and detailed account of the lands that he journeyed earned Polo the name "the father of modern **anthropology.**"

At first, the places that Polo's book tells of were too strange for the Western mind to accept. Crocodiles and coconuts had never been seen before by most Europeans, and were more easily ascribed to the product of one Venetian's overactive imagination than taken as fact. Yet more so than this, that the **ethnocentric** European mind refused to entertain the notion that a civilization larger and more advanced than its own existed seems the most likely reason for the rejection of Polo's story. Europe had come to think of itself as the center of civilization, and this belief was difficult to change. In addition to observations of exotic wildlife, descriptions of the technological advancements of Chinese civilization, such as the use of paper currency, were **staunchly** rejected.

Far from being hailed as a daring adventurer and enlightening explorer, the phrase "It's a Marco Polo" came to **denote** an exaggerated tale. Fearing for his historical reputation, friends of Marco Polo even asked him to **recant** his story on his deathbed in 1323. Polo refused, reportedly saying: "I have not written down the half of those things which I saw." Indeed, several wonders of Chinese civilization, such as the Great Wall, are not mentioned in Polo's book. He either forgot to include things in his book, or knowingly omitted them, thinking that they would not be believed.

Polo's book offered many geographic contributions concerning the layout of the land of Asia. However, it took more than one hundred years for Marco Polo's book to be accepted not as a work of fiction, but as fact. It was not until the nineteenth century that his itineraries were **corroborated** in detail. This eventual verification was made possible by further explorations into Asia. Marco Polo's story also came to encourage further exploration of the world: a well-read edition of Marco Polo's book was taken by Christopher Columbus on his first voyage to the New World.

Marco Polo lived in an interesting period in world history. Europe was awakening from the Dark Ages in a time of religious **crusades** and was quickly expanding trade areas. In contrast, Chinese civilization had very deep roots, but at the time was under Mongol rule. The empire of Kublai Khan was one of the largest kingdoms to ever exist. Marco Polo was one of the very few people to observe this period in traditional China through the eyes of a European. His book, a rare perspective on Asian cultures, is an important work on this era in China's history.

By the 1250s, Venice had conquered its Greek rival trading capitol of Constantinople (present day Istanbul) with the help of the **momentum** of the crusades. Venice, a trading city on the Mediterranean, profited from many ship building contracts for the crusades. Europe had by now come out of the Dark Ages, a time in which trade and development **languished**. Venice at the time was a **bustling** town, thriving with trade.

Up until this time, only fables existed about the far away land of China. Most information had been passed down from the time of Ancient Greek civilization during the time of Alexander the Great. Ever since, the civilization in the Middle East presented itself as an unfriendly barrier between the two realms. It was possible for an exchange of goods through a chain of traveling merchants, but this did not **entail** an exchange of culture and ideas. For example, silk, made from the silkworm, was thought to be a vegetable product or made from bark.

The silk trade had in fact been so heavy since the times of the Roman Empire that a route between Europe and Eastern Asia had been known as the ' Silk Road '. As with the ignorance of Asian civilization in Europe, little was known of Europe in China. Advanced **cartography** did exist, however, within the Middle Kingdom. After its isolated development into a highly organized society, China came to be constantly threatened by tribes of so-called "barbarians" to the North. Although the clans of nomadic horsemen had military superiority over the farmers of China, conquests by these northerners usually led to their absorption into the firmly established Chinese culture.

When Marco Polo arrived in China, Mongols had recently completed a conquest of the entire country. The Sung Dynasty of China had collapsed and had been run over by the descendants of Ghengis Khan. Kublai Khan, born 1215, the grandson of Ghengis Khan, completed the defeat of the stubborn Southern Sung Dynasty in Southern China. The Mongolian invasion of Southern China took longer than most victories of the Mongolian army, which swept across virtually all of Asia, from Hungary to Siberia to Vietnam.

The vast size of the domain of Kublai Khan, which covered most of East Asia, greatly impressed Marco Polo. His book boasts that: "If you put together all the Christians in the world, with their Emperors and their Kings, the whole of these Christians, — aye, and throw in the Saracens to boot, — would not have such power, or be able to do so much as this Kublai, who is Lord of all the Tartars [Mongols] in the world. "

Unlike the Chinese farmers, Mongols lived a nomadic lifestyle out of portable tents. Rather than agricultural products, their diet consisted of mostly meat. Mongols were expert and highly organized horsemen and warriors. Their religion was based on **shamanism**. Due to scarcity of water in the Mongolian Steppe, they did not believe in bathing.

Mongol rule of China established four social classes: the Mongols who ruled the country, non-Chinese aides to the Mongols, Northern Chinese, and lastly, the Southern Chinese. Southern Chinese were viewed as the lowest in the social system because of their stubborn resistance to the Mongol invasion. Because of the high status of foreigners, the Polos were able to find themselves posts as trusted advisors to Kublai Khan.

During the time of Mongol rule in China, most of Chinese culture still survived, although control of the government was temporarily handed over to foreigners. For example, Kublai Khan maintained the practice of Confucianism, but made efforts to halt the use of the Chinese civil service examination system. Even though China was under a foreign rule, it maintained its cultural integrity by remaining true to its deep cultural roots. In fact the years of Mongol rule had a surprisingly small impact on Chinese culture: "Despite this century of contact, things foreign remained superficial in China, as did the Mongol conquerors themselves. " For this reason, Marco Polo's observation of a China under Mongol rule will still provide much information into Chinese civilization.

The history of the Mongolian rise to power that Marco Polo gives is a version that **exalts** the Mongolian culture above all others. In general, the events that Polo describes are somewhat accurate. Having spent so many years in the service of the great Khan, Marco developed a rather one-sided perspective on Asian cultures. He must have come to think of many things in the same way that the Khan did. Polo's agreement with Kublai Khan's claims concerning his rights of conquest can also be ascribed to the fact that the Mongols' position was similar to Venice's stronghold on the Mediterranean at the time. Throughout his book, Marco Polo makes it clear how highly regarded he holds Kublai Khan. A scholar states that: "the book does at times seem to have been intended to celebrate his power and glory."

As he was writing his story in a prison, he must have felt some longing for the civilized methods of Chinese society. As a scholar describes: "His keen eyes must have made mental comparisons every turn, and here, as in many other instances in his book, he appears by his comments to have reached the conclusion that his Venetian townsfolk had much to learn of gentility, **breeding**, and ethical attitudes from the people of the Middle Kingdom."

Many of the aspects of the culture that Marco Polo lived in are not mentioned in his book. Most of these cultural institutions, such as teahouses, acupuncture, and footbinding, represent distinctively Chinese, not Mongol, customs. Furthermore, the tradition of **filial piety** is only hinted at with the misunderstood phrase: "the laws of their ancient kings **ordained** that each citizen should exercise the profession of his father."

Marco did not learn the Chinese language and therefore was not exposed to the Chinese classics. These traditional works had a key role in shaping the core of Chinese culture. For these and other reasons Marco learned to share the Mongols' contempt for their subject populations. Marco Polo's work was mainly written to show glory of the Mongol Empire. Omissions concerning Chinese practices can be taken as Marco's judgment that they are not as important as information such as the vast size of the Mongol Army. Because Marco Polo's work is really a discussion of the Mongol glory, his writings are vital to the examination of Chinese culture under the Mongol Empire.

Marco Polo had learned four languages during his voyages in Asia. His systematic observations of nature, anthropology, and geography were ahead of his time. He was very broad minded, although somewhat **gullible** in relating fables. His book is a mix of accurate descriptions of things that he saw himself, such as the observations that water boils more slowly in the High Pamir and the North Star cannot be seen in the south, and the passing along of fables about far away lands, such as the Mountain of the Ark.

It is remarkable to consider the luck that the Polos had in returning home. Had not the opportunity of returning to Europe by ship had presented itself, they would have likely been stuck in China permanently. Marco closes his book with his explanation of these events: "I believe that it was God's pleasure that we should get back in order that people might learn about the things that the world contains. Thanks to God! Amen! Amen!" After resting in Tabriz, the Polos journeyed back to Italy. In 1295, after an absence of twenty-four years, Maffeo, Nicolo, and Marco Polo returned to Venice.

It is clear from Marco Polo's writings that he was thoroughly impressed with the nature of Chinese civilization. Many of the organized and efficient systems that he saw working in China had yet to be developed in Europe. The history, geography, and anthropology in Marco Polo's book make it an important historical document concerning the era in Traditional

China under Mongol rule.

Retrieved from *Marco Polo's Asia* www. tk421. net/essay/polo. shtml.

New Words and Phrases

unique	adj.	unparalleled 独特的, 罕见的
perspective	n.	the state of one's ideas 观点、看法
bizarre	adj.	unusual 稀奇古怪, 异乎寻常
terrain	n.	a tract of land 地形、地带
anthropology	n.	人类学
ethnocentric	n.	种族中心主义, 种族优越感
staunchly	adv.	firmly and steadfastly 坚定地, 忠诚地
denote	v.	indicate 指示, 表示, 意味着
recant	vt.	to withdraw or disavow, 放弃（信仰、主张）, 撤回声明
crusade	n.	讨伐, 宗教战争
corroborate	v.	证实
momentum	n.	impetus 势头, 力量
languish	vi.	to become weaker 变得衰落, 失去活力
bustling	adj.	thriving or energetic 忙忙碌碌的, 活跃的
entail	v.	牵涉, 使必要
cartography	n.	制图学, 制图法
shamanism	n.	the animistic religion of northern Asia 萨满教
exalt	vt.	使提升
breeding	n.	good manners 教养
filial	adj.	子女的, 后代的
piety	n.	dutiful respect for parents 孝顺, 孝敬
ordain	vt.	to enact by law, to order or command 制定, 规定, 命令
gullible	adj.	easily deceived or cheated 易上当的, 轻信的

Notes to the text

Marco Polo 马可·波罗是出生于意大利威尼斯的旅行家, 曾在 13 世纪中国元朝忽必烈统治时期来到中国, 回国后撰述了著名的《马可·波罗游记》。A Venetian trader and explorer who gained fame for his worldwide travels, recorded in the book *Il Milione* ("The Million" or *The Travels of Marco Polo*). Polo, together with his father Niccolò and his uncle Maffeo, was one of the first Westerners to travel the Silk Road to China (which he called *Cathay*, after the Khitan) and visit the Great Khan of the Mongol Empire, Kublai Khan (grandson of Genghis Khan).

1. **Mongol rule**：公元 1279 年,蒙古统治者忽必烈在北京建立了元朝,开始对中国进行长达近百年的统治。By the mid-thirteenth century, the Mongols had subjugated north China, Korea, and the Muslim kingdoms of Central Asia and had twice penetrated Europe. In 1279, Genghis Khan's grandson Kublai Khan established the first alien dynasty to rule all China — the Yuan (1279—1368).

2. **Venice**：威尼斯是位于意大利北部的著名"水上城市", 13 世纪已是贸易和商业中心。A city in northern Italy, it has been known as the "City of Water", "City of Bridges", and "The City of Light". The Venetian Republic was a major maritime power during the Middle Ages and Renaissance, and a staging area for the Crusades and the Battle of Lepanto, as well as a very important center of commerce (especially silk, grain and spice trade) and art in the 13th century up to the end of the 17th century.

3. **Genoa**：热那亚,a city and a seaport in northern Italy

4. **Constantinople**：君士坦丁堡,拜占庭帝国首都,今土耳其的首都伊斯坦布尔。the capital of the Roman Empire (330—395), the Byzantine / East Roman Empire (395—1204 and 1261—1453), the Latin Empire (1204—1261), and the Ottoman Empire (1453—1922). In 1930, the Turkish government declared its name to be Istanbul.

5. **Dark Ages**：指公元 476 年至公元 1000 年间的欧洲中世纪早期 Refers to the Early Middle Ages, the period encompassing (roughly) 476 to 1000 AD. This concept of a Dark Age was created by the Italian scholar Petrarch (Francesco Petrarca) in the 1330s and was originally intended as a sweeping criticism of the character of Late Latin literature. Later historians expanded the term to refer to the transitional period between Classical Roman Antiquity and the High Middle Ages, including not only the lack of Latin literature, but also a lack of contemporary written history, general demographic decline, limited building activity and material cultural achievements in general.

6. **Kublai khan**：(1215—1294),忽必烈是成吉思汗之孙,中国元朝的创立者,也是蒙古帝国的最后一位皇帝。A grandson of Genghis Khan (1167? —1227), he was the fifth and last Khagan (1260—1294) of the Mongol Empire. In 1271, he founded the Yuan Dynasty, and became the first Yuan emperor. He was the second son of Tolui and Sorghaghtani Beki and a grandson of Genghis Khan. The civil war between him and his younger brother Ariq Böke over the succession of their older brother Möngke (died in 1259) essentially marked the end of a unified Mongol empire.

7. **Ghengis khan**：成吉思汗是蒙古帝国的创立者。He was the founder of the Mongol Empire, the largest empire in history. He came to power by uniting many of the nomadic tribes of northeast Asia. After founding the Mongol Empire and being proclaimed "Genghis Khan", he pursued an aggressive foreign policy by starting the Mongol invasions of East and Central Asia. During his life, the Mongol Empire eventually occupied most of Asia.

8. **Saracen**：古代居住在叙利亚和阿拉伯沙漠一带的游牧民族撒拉逊人，后指所有信仰伊斯兰教的人。It was a term used in the Middle Ages for Fatimids at first, then later all those who professed the religion of Islam.

9. **Shamanism**：撒满教，一种原始宗教，该教具有较冥杂的灵魂观念，认为世界上各种物类都有灵魂，自然界的变化给人们带来的祸福，都是各种精灵、鬼魂和神灵意志的表现。It refers to a range of traditional beliefs and practices concerned with communication with the spiritual world. There are many variations of Shamanism throughout the world.

10. **Tabriz**：塔布里茨，伊朗西北部最大城市。It is the largest city in northwestern Iran.

Exercises

I. Answer the following questions based on Text. The words and expressions listed below are for your reference.

1. **What information does the book provide us about Marco Polo's journeys?**
   perspective / civilization / Mongol rule

2. **What did Marco Polo see during his journey in the Orient?**
   lands / lifestyles / Asia

3. **Why do so many different books about Marco Polo's journey exist today?**
   dictate / written / prisoner / copied / transcript

4. **Why was Marco Polo named "the father of Modern anthropology"?**
   observation / descriptions / cultures / geography / language / races / customs

5. **Why was Marco Polo's story rejected by Europeans in his time?**
   imagination / advanced / belief / center of civilization

6. **What did the phrase "It's a Marco Polo" mean?**
   exaggerated / story / unreal

7. **Describe the comercial and cultural exchange between the West and China before and during the time of Marco Polo.**
   civilization / trade / merchant / advanced / isolated / highly organized / silk / culture / ideas

8. **Say something about the social life and political system in China under Mongol rule.**
   social class / culture / survive / maintain / practice of Confucianism / civil service examination system / cultural integrity / cultural roots

II. Further questions for discussion.

1. Some scholars suspect that Marco Polo had not actually been to China, because he did not mention the famous Great Wall, Chinese love of tea, women's bound feet and the use of chopsticks for eating. Do you think Marco Polo could have made up his stories about his journey to China?

2. Retrace Marco Polo's route and mark the cities he visited. Can you name some modern-day cities Marco Polo might have passed through? Select a city and prepare an outline or brief summary about how its culture, government and borders have changed since Marco Polo's time. Try to find a picture or map of Marco Polo's route to China.

3. Discuss the significance of Marco Polo's journey in the culural exchange between the West and the East.

III. Vocabulary study.

1. Word in Use.

1) **due to**: because of sb. / sth., caused by sb. / sth. 由于,因为

The fail of the plan was due to his lack of experience.

The delay of the air flight was due to the storm.

Due to poor management, the company was forced out of business.

2) **Bizarre**: very strange and unusual 稀奇古怪的,

When he talked about his bizarre experience in the small island, everyone was shocked.

All the audiences were crazy for the pop star's bizarre costume.

The bizarre scene in the huge cave was designed by the creative genius.

3) **take down**: to write or record 记录

I will tell you how to get to the railway station, you'd better take it down.

The traveler took down what he had seen on his journey to Tibet.

The fantastic event was taken down by a famous historian 200 years ago, that is why we know it has really happened.

4) **ascribe to**: to consider that sth. is caused by a particular thing of person 把……归因于,认为是…… 写的,认为……具有

He ascribed his success to the support of his family.

This novel is ascribed to the writer who lived in 13th century.

We ascribed great importance to the new proposal.

5) **corroborate** (**often passive**): to provide evidence or information that supports a statement, etc. 证实,确证

The theory was corroborated by a lot of experience.

His statement was corroborated by three independent witnesses.

The accounts provided by the stranger could not be corroborated by evidence.

6) **languish** (**in sth.**): to become weaker or fail to make progress 变得衰弱,无法取得进展

Though the government tried great effort to enhance the economy, the domestic consumption languished.

The price of oil has languished for three months.

7) **thriving**：*adj.* prosperous, successful 繁荣的,旺盛的

This small town has been thriving with trade for many years.

The economy of the coastal area depends on its thriving real estate.

This is a city thriving with tourism.

8) **pass down**：to give or teach sth. to someone younger than you 世代相传,流传

This blue pottery vase is passed down from his grandfather, it is a treasure of the family.

We should maintain the integration of our culture passed down from our ancestors.

He was not able to manage the enterprise passed down by his father, and decided to sell it.

9) **entail**：to involve sth. that can not be avoided 使······成为必要,牵涉

The task entails working days and nights.

Writing a book entails great patience and rich experience.

Only the athlete himself knows what is entailed in winning an Olympic medal.

10) **exalt**：to make sb. rise to a higher rank or position,提拔,提升

In the past political campaign, people exalted the leader to the position of God.

He was exalted to a post not suitable for him.

The superstitious villagers exalted the witch to a superman who could communicate with God.

2. **Word Distinctions.**

1) **perspective, in perspective**

课文中 '...an outsider's perspective on Chinese civilization would yield further information.' 此处 perspective 的含义是 '观点','视角';

但 He tries to handle this issue in perspective. in perspective 意为客观或正确地。

选择以上适当的词填空：

His rich experience provides a wide _____ on this issue.

Being a team leader, he needs to solve all these problems _____.

Nowadays, managers should maintain a global _____.

How to reward and punish the employees is not an easy task for managers, it requires them to judge _____.

2) **thrive, thrive on**

课文中 Venice at the time was a bustling town, thriving with trade. 此处 thrive 意为繁荣,旺盛,充满活力；

但 He thrives on laboring in the field. 此处 thrive on 意为以某事为乐,因某事而有成。

选择以上适当的词填空：

The African country was once _____ with diamond export business, now it has languished.

He was regarded as an eccentric person, because he closed himself in the small room everyday and _____ those meaningless experiments.

To some people, this is a boring job. But to him, it must be quite interesting, for he _____ it day and night without any complaint.

For only one decade, this small coastal village develops into a _____ city.

3. **Decide the meanings of the following words by matching each word in Column A with the word or expression in Column B that is similar in meaning.**

A	B
1) ordain	a. religious war
2) gullible	b. to claim to give up
3) momentum	c. strong and loyal in one's opinions and attitude
4) nomadic	d. to order or command
5) staunch	e. becoming part of a culture or country
6) recant	f. moving with their animals from place to place
7) crusade	g. being whole and not divided
8) breeding	h. easy to be cheated
9) integrity	i. to raise animals and livestock
10) absorption	j. the ability to increase or develop

4. **Try to write a brief story with the following words and phrases.**

schedule, itinerary, essential, supplies, map, country, culture, customs, view, restaurant, motel, scenery

IV. Translation.

1. **Put the following Chinese expressions into English.**

   1) 用作　　2) 除了之外　　3) 从……牟利　　4) 从……走出

   5) 优于　　6) 融合　　7) 横扫　　8) 由……组成

2. **Translate the following sentences into English, using the words and expressions in the bracket.**

   1. 由于路上遇到车祸,她很迟才来参加会议。她的老板很不高兴。(due to)

   2. 那位歌星穿着奇装异服出现在舞台上,使歌迷们非常疯狂。(bizarre)

   3. 那位学者记录了许多历史事件,为我们的研究提供了依据。(take down)

   4. 他把公司的经营的失败归因于资金不足。(ascribe to)

   5. 他被判谋杀,因为没有证人证实他的陈述。(corroborate)

   6. 股市疲软,股民天真地希望政府能出台干预政策。(languish)

   7. 许多收入不高的年轻人喜欢逛跳蚤市场,所以它很繁荣。(thrive)

   8. 这把丝绸扇子是她祖母传下来的,她很珍惜它,所以不会借给你的。(pass down)

9. 翻译一本书要花很长的时间和辛苦。(entail)

10. 我们没有理由把西方文化提升到我们传统文化之上。(exalt)

3. Translate the following Chinese into English.

维多利亚时代的女性不能外出旅行,除非她们非常富有,或想要与众不同,挑战社会准则。即便富有的女性想要旅行,也极少单独出门。她们只能与自己的丈夫或家人同行。和一群朋友一起出行也不可以,因为这样做闻所未闻,也不被人们接受。维多利亚时代女性的服饰是阻碍她们旅行的一个重要因素。那时的女性穿着紧身胸衣,高跟鞋,长至脚踝的长裙和外披短上衣的长袖衬衫。男人们也认为女性应该呆在家里,并希望此传统保持不变。他们觉得女性根本不必要旅行,因而对任何外出旅行的女性持极端不良的印象。为了避免被沾上污点,大多数维多利亚时代的女性除了自己居住的城镇外,从没接触过外面的世界。

4. Put the following quotes into Chinese.

History consists of a series of accumulated imaginative invention.　　—— Voltaire

Who does not know that the first law of historical writing is the truth.　—— Cicero

We learn from history that we never learn from history.　　　　　—— Hegel

Happy people have no history.　　　　　　　　　　　　　—— Leo Tolstoy

Man's history is waiting in patience for the triumph of the insulted man.

　　　　　　　　　　　　　　　　　　　　　　　　　—— Tagore

5. Translate the following passage into Chinese.

While there are almost as many definitions of history as there are historians, modern practice most closely conforms to one that sees history as the attempt to recreate and explain the significant events of the past. Caught in the web of its own time and place, each generation of historians determines anew what is significant for it in the past. In this search the evidence found is always incomplete and scattered; it is also frequently partial or partisan. The irony of the historians craft is that its practitioners always know that their efforts are but contributions to an unending process.

V. Comment on the structure of the text.

The text is a book review on *The Travels of Marco Polo*. A book review often begins with a very brief introduction to the book and then it may focus on aspects of the form and the matter, the form, such as the writing style, structure, or the use of language, etc. and the matter, that is, the theme. This is a review that devotes its attention to the historical significance of the book *The Travels of Marco Polo* in helping Europeans then and later to know and understand China and its civilization.

A book review is like any other essays often composed of three parts: introduction, body and conclusion. In this book review, the introductory paragraph starts with a clear statement that grabs the reader's attention: 'This book serves as an important work on Chinese civilization during Mongol rule.'

The body of the essay contains several paragraphs which develop the thesis. They are all similarly constructed, and provide supporting facts. In these paragraphs, the writer may discuss them, give examples and analyze them. All these paragraphs work together to prove the thesis.

One good way to conclude an essay is to end the last paragraph with a statement that echoes what has been stated and proved, as is illustrated in this review: 'The history, geography, and anthropology in Marco Polo's book make it an important historical document concerning the era in Traditional China under Mongol rule.', which re-enforces the impression made on the reader and provokes further thought.

Extended Exercises

1. **In the following article, some paragraphs have been removed. Choose the most suitable paragraph from the list A-E to fit into each of the numbered gaps. There is ONE paragraph which does not fit in any of the gaps.**

Glory is as ephemeral as smoke and clouds

As this millennium dawns, New York is the most important city in the world, the unofficial capital of planet Earth. But before New Yorkers become too full of themselves, it might be worthwhile to glance at dilapidated Kaifeng in central China.

1) _____

As the world's only superpower, America may look today as if global domination is an entitlement. But if you look back at the sweep of history, it's striking how fleeting supremacy is, particularly for individual cities.

2) _____

Today, Kaifeng is grimy and poor, not even the provincial capital and so minor it lacks even an airport. Its sad state only underscores how fortunes change. In the 11th century, when it was the capital of Song Dynasty China, its population was more than one million. In contrast, London's population then was about 15,000.

3) _____

Kaifeng's stature attracted people from all over the world, including hundreds of Jews. Even today, there are some people in Kaifeng who look like other Chinese but who consider themselves Jewish and do not eat pork.

4) _____

"China is booming now," said Wang Ruina, a young peasant woman on the outskirts of town. "Give us a few decades, and we'll catch up with the United States, even pass it." She's right. The United States has had the biggest economy in the world for more than a century, but most projections show that China will surpass it in about 15 years, as measured by purchasing power parity.

So what can New York learn from a city like Kaifeng?

One lesson is the importance of sustaining a technological edge and sound economic policies. Ancient China flourished partly because of pro-growth, pro-trade policies and technological innovations like curved iron plows, printing and paper money. But then China came to scorn trade and commerce, and per capita income stagnated for 600 years. A second lesson is the danger of hubris, for China concluded it had nothing to learn from the rest of the world — and that was the beginning of the end.

5) _____ .

Beside the Yellow River, I met a 70-year-old peasant named Hao Wang, who had never gone to a day of school. He couldn't even write his name — and yet his progeny were different.

"Two of my grandsons are now in university," he boasted, and then he started talking about the computer in his home.

Thinking of Kaifeng should stimulate Americans to struggle to improve their high-tech edge, educational strengths and pro-growth policies. For if they rest on our laurels, even a city as great as New York may end up as Kaifeng-on-the-Hudson.

(Nicholas D. Kristof The New York Times)

A: My vote for most important city in the world in the period leading up to 2000 B. C. would be Ur, Iraq. In 1500 B. C. , perhaps Thebes, Egypt. There was no dominant player in 1000 B. C. , though one could make a case for Sidon, Lebanon. In 500 B. C. , it would be Persepolis, Persia; in the year 1, Rome; around A. D. 500, maybe Chang An, China; in 1000, Kaifeng, China; in 1500, probably Florence, Italy; in 2000, New York; and in 2500, probably none of the above.

B: I worry about the United States in both regards. America's economic management is so lax that it can't confront farm subsidies or long-term budget deficits. American technology is strong, but public schools are second-rate in math and science. And Americans' lack of interest in the world contrasts with the restlessness, drive and determination that are again pushing China to the forefront.

C: Kaifeng, an ancient city along the mud-clogged Yellow River, was by far the most important place in the world in A. D. 1000. And if you've never heard of it, that's a useful warning for Americans. As expressed in this column's headline — translated from Chinese, a language of the future that more Americans should start learning — "glory is as ephemeral as smoke and clouds. "

D: An ancient painted scroll, now in the Palace Museum in Beijing, shows the bustle and prosperity of ancient Kaifeng. Hundreds of pedestrians jostle each other on the streets, camels carry merchandise in from the Silk Road, and teahouses and restaurants do a thriving business.

E: As I roamed the Kaifeng area, asking local people why such an international center had sunk so low, I encountered plenty of envy of New York. One man said he was arranging to be smuggled into the United States illegally, by paying a gang $25,000, but many local people insisted that China is on course to bounce back and recover its historic role as world leader.

F: China's move for Unocal neatly sums up the two forces driving the country's ongoing bid to acquire foreign assets: the thirst for raw materials to feed and maintain its booming economy, and the desire to obtain western brands to help market Chinese exports.

2. Matching subheadings to paragraphs.

Choose the most suitable subheading from the list 1 – 6 for paragraph D, E, G, H and I. There is one subheading which does not fit in any of the paragraphs.

Lessons from the Titanic

A From the comfort of our modern lives we tend to look back at the turn of the twentieth century as a dangerous time for sea travelers. With limited communication facilities, and shipping technology still in its infancy in the early nineteen hundreds, we consider ocean travel to have been a risky business. But to the people of the time it was one of the safest forms of transport. At the time of the Titanic's maiden voyage in 1912, there had only been four lives lost in the previous forty years on passenger ships on the North Atlantic crossing. And the Titanic was confidently proclaimed to be unsinkable. She represented the pinnacle of technological advance at the time. Her builders, crew and passengers had no doubt that she was the finest ship ever built. But still she did sink on April 14, 1912, taking 1,517 of her passengers and crew with her.

B The RMS Titanic left Southampton for New York on April 10, 1912. On board were some of the richest and most famous people of the time who had paid large sums of money to sail on the first voyage of the most luxurious ship in the world. Imagine her placed on her end: she was larger at 269 metres than many of the tallest buildings of the day. And with nine decks, she was as high as an eleven-storey building. The Titanic carried 329 first class, 285 second class and 710 third class passengers with 899 crew members, under the care of the very experienced Captain Edward J. Smith. She also carried enough food to feed a small town, including 40,000 fresh eggs, 36,000 apples, 111,000 lbs of fresh meat and 2,200 lbs of coffee for the five-day journey.

C RMS Titanic was believed to be unsinkable because the hull was divided into sixteen watertight compartments. Even if two of these compartments flooded, the ship could still float. The ship's owners could not imagine that, in the case of an accident, the Titanic would not be able to float until she was rescued. It was largely as a result of this confidence in the ship and in the safety of ocean travel that the disaster could claim such a great loss of life.

D   In the ten hours prior to the Titanic's fatal collision with an iceberg at 11:40pm, six warnings of icebergs in her path were received by the Titanic's wireless operators. Only one of these messages was formally posted on the bridge; the others were in various locations across the ship. If the combined information in these messages of iceberg positions had been plotted, the ice field which lay across the Titanic's path would have been apparent. Instead, the lack of formal procedures for dealing with information from a relatively new piece of technology, the wireless, meant that the danger was not known until too late. This was not the fault of the Titanic crew. Procedures for dealing with warnings received through the wireless had not been formalised across the shipping industry at the time. The fact that the wireless operators were not even Titanic crew, but rather contracted workers from a wireless company, made their role in the ship's operation quite unclear.

E   Captain Smith's seemingly casual attitude in increasing the speed on this day to a dangerous 22 knots or 41 kilometres per hour, can then be partly explained by his ignorance of what lay ahead. But this only partly accounts for his actions, since the spring weather in Greenland was known to cause huge chunks of ice to break off from the glaciers. Captain Smith knew that these icebergs would float southward and had already acknowledged this danger by taking a more southerly route than at other times of the year. So why was the Titanic travelling at high speed when he knew, if not of the specific risk, at least of the general risk of icebergs in her path? As with the lack of coordination of the wireless messages, it was simply standard operating procedure at the time. Captain Smith was following the practices accepted on the North Atlantic, practices which had coincided with forty years of safe travel. He believed, wrongly as we now know, that the ship could turn or stop in time if an iceberg was sighted by the lookouts.

F   There were around two and a half hours between the time the Titanic rammed into the iceberg and its final submersion. In this time 705 people were loaded into the twenty lifeboats. There were 473 empty seats available on lifeboats while over 1,500 people drowned. These figures raise two important issues. Firstly, why there were not enough lifeboats to seat every passenger and crew member on board. And secondly, why the lifeboats were not full.

G   The Titanic had sixteen lifeboats and four collapsible boats which could carry just over half the number of people on board her maiden voyage and only a third of the Titanic's total capacity. Regulations for the number of lifeboats required were based on outdated British Board of Trade regulations written in 1894 for ships a quarter of the Titanic's size, and had never been revised. Under these requirements, the Titanic was only obliged to carry enough lifeboats to seat 962 people. At design meetings in 1910, the shipyard's managing director, Alexander Carlisle, had proposed that forty eight lifeboats be installed on the Titanic, but the idea had been quickly rejected as too expensive. Discussion then turned to the ship's décor, and as Carlisle later described the incident. . . "we spent two hours discussing carpet for the first class cabins and fifteen minutes discussing lifeboats".

H　The belief that the Titanic was unsinkable was so strong that passengers and crew alike clung to the belief even as she was actually sinking. This attitude was not helped by Captain Smith, who had not acquainted his senior officers with the full situation. For the first hour after the collision, the majority of people aboard the Titanic, including senior crew, were not aware that she would sink, that there were insufficient lifeboats or that the nearest ship responding to the Titanic's distress calls would arrive two hours after she was on the bottom of the ocean. As a result, the officers in charge of loading the boats received a very half-hearted response to their early calls for women and children to board the lifeboats. People felt that they would be safer, and certainly warmer, aboard the Titanic than perched in a little boat in the North Atlantic Ocean. Not realising the magnitude of the impending disaster themselves, the officers allowed several boats to be lowered only half full.

I　Procedures again were at fault, as an additional reason for the officers' reluctance to lower the lifeboats at full capacity was that they feared the lifeboats would buckle under the weight of 65 people. They had not been informed that the lifeboats had been fully tested prior to departure. Such procedures as assigning passengers and crew to lifeboats and lifeboat loading drills were simply not part of the standard operation of ships nor were they included in crew training at this time.

J　As the Titanic sank, another ship, believed to have been the Californian, was seen motionless less than twenty miles away. The ship failed to respond to the Titanic's eight distress rockets. Although the officers of the Californian tried to signal the Titanic with their flashing Morse lamp, they did not wake up their radio operator to listen for a distress call. At this time, communication at sea through wireless was new and the benefits not well appreciated, so the wireless on ships was often not operated around the clock. In the case of the Californian, the wireless operator slept unaware while 1,500 Titanic passengers and crew drowned only a few miles away.

K　After the Titanic sank, investigations were held in both Washington and London. In the end, both inquiries decided that no one could be blamed for the sinking. However, they did address the fundamental safety issues which had contributed to the enormous loss of life. As a result, international agreements were drawn up to improve safety procedures at sea. The new regulations covered 24 hour wireless operation, crew training, proper lifeboat drills, lifeboat capacity for all on board and the creation of an international ice patrol.

(Sample Reading Text from Holmesglen Institute of TAFE)

List of subheadings:

1. Low priority placed on safety
2. Ignorance of the impending disaster
3. Iceberg locations not plotted
4. Inadequate training
5. Captain's over-confidence
6. Ice warning ignored

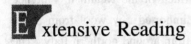xtensive Reading

Passage One

Italy — The Cradle of the Renaissance

14 世纪,随着贸易和纺织业的繁荣,意大利北部城市佛罗伦萨逐渐发展成欧洲的一个商业中心。在这过程中,以美第奇家族为代表的商人和银行家凭借经济力量获得政治权力。他们热爱古典艺术,为艺术家提供丰厚的经济赞助,吸引他们来到佛罗伦萨进行艺术创作,使该城市成为欧洲文艺复兴的发源地。

The Renaissance marks the end of medieval Europe and the beginning of a time of learning, questioning and development. Although the medieval mindset was still present, it was starting to give way to a completely new Europe. The Renaissance, a European phenomenon by all standards, that affected most of the continent, was born and focused in, to a large extent, in Italy. From its epicentre in Italy, the Renaissance spread to all corners of Europe. Florence in particular was the home for many of the greatest thinkers and artists of the time, if not of all time.

In the thirteenth century urban growth in Italy was on the increase once more, and the once rural and sparsely populated peninsula became dotted with great cities. These cities in turn grew into centres of trade and banking. The trade they conducted was mostly directed towards the east, the Byzantine Empire and the Islamic world, but there was also a lot of coming and going to and from Western Europe. During this time Italy was as disunited as ever, far from a united nation. The larger cities then became city-states, autonomous regions that were formed from great cities and the surrounding area. These regions or city-states were governed from the main city within the region. The governing city of the region usually gave its name to the whole city-state. These city-states included The Papal States, Florence, Venice, the Duchy of Milan and the Kingdom of Naples. In these centres of wealth and commerce, a new social class was born among the merchants and bankers, alongside the nobility and peasants. The wealth in these city-states changed owners as the nobility lent money from bankers and used it to unproductive ends, and were then unable to pay back their loans. Because of this they were obliged to hand over some of their property to the bankers as payment. As wealth changed hands, the wealthy middle class, a very commercially orientated one, was born from these merchants and bankers. They invested their wealth to generate more income and so they quickly became the wealthiest class and, ultimately, ruled the city-states.

One of these wealthy merchant families was the Medici family of Florence. Florence was at the very heart of the Renaissance, largely thanks to the funding and opportunities the Medici family (美第奇家族) provided for young talents. Much of the wealth in Florence was acquired through its booming textile industry. Florence imported raw wool from Spain and England, the dyes from the east and the work force was from around northern Italy. The Medici family took pride in their city-state and wanted it to be the most beautiful and awe-inspiring urban centre in all of Italy. They also sought to legitimize their rule of Florence, which they had gained in secret from the republic. They hired numerous patrons and gave them tasks to design and build palaces, sculpt statues, paint murals (壁画), and more. Around a hundred palaces were built in Florence in the 15th century alone. The artists and architects, painters and sculptors, were all rewarded handsomely for their work, but only the best individuals would suffice. These individuals included geniuses like Leonardo da Vinci (达芬奇), Michelangelo (米开朗基罗) and Brunelleschi (布涅莱斯奇). The Renaissance was going on all over Italy, of course, but the wealth and the will to use it on art and learning displayed by the Medici family made Florence the centre of gravity in the Italian Renaissance. The opportunities presented to artists, architects, poets, philosophers and sculptors by the Medici family attracted learning and skill from outside of Florence as well.

The Renaissance was really only for the wealthier classes of society to take part in, and in Italy there was a large, wealthy class of merchants that took part in the Renaissance and encouraged it. The Medici family also paid a hefty pay-check to those who created great works of art, learning and architecture, and this must have acted as a major motivating force as well, as probably for the first time in history, artists were able to make a very comfortable living with their art. Both the artistic and the philosophical side of the Renaissance were influenced by Classical Greek and Roman thinkers, architects, artists and the Classical Greek way of thinking in general. Especially architecture and philosophy were influenced, and this was aided by the influx of Classical Greek and Roman literature from Constantinople, triggered by the fall of Constantinople in the hands of the Muslim Turks. Constantinople, perhaps the greatest city in the christened world was a store of Classical Greek and Roman literature and many who escaped the Turkish occupation brought with them many of the documents that had been kept in Constantinople. The fall of Constantinople and the Byzantine Empire also meant that a rivaling trade centre was "out of order" for a while, which further increased the flow of trade and wealth through the Italian city-states. The Popes in Rome also funded many works of art in the Vatican. They summoned artists from other parts in Italy to create art to the glory of God (and themselves).

Italy had all that was needed for a phenomenon such as the Renaissance: wealthy urban centres (which were also large centres of trade) in which the flow of ideas was great and the sources of ideas were diverse, a wealthy merchant class accumulating more wealth, rulers willing to spend on such things as art, thinking and learning in general and give opportunities to young talents. The revival of the same spirit that reigned in Athens during its Golden Age, was also an important factor. Many of the Italian artists and thinkers thought of themselves as the ones who would continue from where the Greeks and Romans left off. The Renaissance has its roots deep in the soil of Northern Italy, and Florence was its seed. The city's economy and its writers, painters, architects, and philosophers all made Florence a model of Renaissance culture.

Several of the greatest artists of the age studied or worked in Florence, including Michelangelo and Botticelli. Michelangelo began to study painting in Florence with Ghirlandaio and later learned sculpture under the patronage of Lorenzo the Magnificent. It was for the Florence cathedral that Michelangelo created his famous sculpture of David. The Renaissance aesthetic is apparent in the careful and accurate depiction of the human body and its representation as a nude.

The painter Botticelli (波提切利) was a friend of both Michelangelo and Leonardo da Vinci, and the principal painter of the Medici family. His works represent Renaissance style in his use of classical subject matter and in the effect of motion that he achieves. It was for the home of a Medici that he created his two most famous works: *Primavera* (春) and *The Birth of Venus*. In both works Botticelli uses figures from antiquity, such as the goddess Venus and the three Graces (三仙女). He balances his figures in nearly symmetrical groupings, yet never loses a feeling of motion and lightness.

Renaissance style in art, exemplified in works from Florentine artists, flourished largely because of the patronage, or financial support, of wealthy citizens and the church. By purchasing numerous works of art, Renaissance men and women provided a livelihood for many painters, sculptors, and architects. It was also the Renaissance humanist desire to imitate and revive the beauty of ancient Greece, and to have that beauty surround them in their daily lives, that produced the wealth of superb art that is one of the hallmarks of Renaissance culture.

Retrieved from *www. allempires. com / article/*

I. Reading comprehension.

1. In 13th century, the rulers of city-states in Italy were _____

    A. wealthy nobility and bankers.

    B. born of the merchants and bankers' families.

    C. in those autonomous regions.

    D. in the main cities within the region.

2. Medici family of Florence was famous for _____

    A. owning textile industry.

    B. their rule of Florence.

    C. their patron of the talented artists.

    D. building about a hundred palaces in Florence.

3. The source of Renaissance's artistic style and philosophy was from _____

    A. documents kept in Constantinople.

    B. wealthy class of society in Italy.

    C. classical Greek and Roman literature.

    D. a rivaling trade centre of Byzantine Empire.

4. Italy became the cradle of Renaissance, because it had _____

    A. wealthy merchant class.

    B. diverse sources of ideas.

    C. generous rulers who were keen on art, and willing to be patrons the talented artists.

    D. all the above.

5. The artists studied or worked in Florence included _____

    A. Botticelli, Michelangelo and Da Vinci.

    B. David and Michelangelo.

    C. Da Vinci and Lorenzo.

    D. Medici and Botticelli.

II. Topics for further discussion.

    1. How did the merchants and bankers rise to power in Italy during the 13th century?

    2. Discuss the relation between Medici family and Renaissance.

    3. Why is the period from 13th to 15th century called Renaissance?

Passage Two

The Breakdown of Medieval Civilization
(中世纪文明的解体)

Bill Gilbert

    When a new historical epoch (纪元,时代) comes to birth, the travail (分娩) is likely to be painful and prolonged. Our own century appears to be such a time; our discomforts arise partly from our position in an age that we know is dying while we are in the dark about what will emerge. This should give us some understanding and fellow feeling for the people of fourteenth-and fifteenth-century Europe, who also lived in an age of crisis and upheaval, as the old yielded to the new. The distresses of the time resulted largely from the desperate resistance of entrenched ideas and institutions to the thrust of the different and unfamiliar. The changes that run through these years were hastened by a purely accidental occurrence, the Black Death（黑死病）that struck in the middle of the fourteenth century. Plagues or epidemics were not uncommon; what distinguished the Black Death was its severity. The disease was apparently the bubonic plague, carried by rats. It may have come from outside Europe, on ships landing in European harbors. It started in 1348 and swept through western Europe. Some areas were little affected by it, but where it did strike it carried off tremendous numbers of people. Statistics are not available for this period, but there were places where as much as a third of the population died. The incidence of the disease varied with social position; the poor city workers, crowded together in unsanitary conditions from which they could not hope to escape, suffered the greatest number of casualties. The well-to-do, living in much more healthful surroundings and able to get out of the crowded cities like the company of young men and women who told each other stories in Boccaccio's Decameron had a much better prospect of survival.

After the initial impact of the plague, which had exhausted itself by 1350, the disease remained endemic, recurring in some places until the seventeenth century. Until its first appearance, Europe had been experiencing a consistent growth in population. This growth was now checked, and it was not until the sixteenth century that population reached its former levels and continued. The plague was not the only factor that depressed the growth of European population. From about 1350, western Europe generally expcrienced depressed business conditions, and this economic decline also lasted until the sixteenth century. The economic slump was partly result, partly cause, of the other disturbed conditions of the time.

The church passed through a period of severe strain. One of its problems was the prevalence of abuses, of which people were becoming increasingly conscious. Those reached all the way to the top; hence the cry for a reformation "in head and in members". Many of these abuses were intimately connected with the wealth of the church. The fiscal system of the church was highly developed, more so than those of contemporary secular governments. Christendom（基督教世界）was divided into collectorates（收税员的职位及管区）, each with a papal collector backed by formidable authority from the pope. Numerous payments had to be made to Rome, mostly by the clergy, who then got it back in one way or another from the laity（俗人,以别于教士或僧侣）. One of the worst abuses was simony, the buying and selling of church offices. (For the origin of this word, see the Biblical story of Simon Magus, who tried to buy the gift of the Holy Ghost, Acts 8.) As the financial needs of the papacy grew, simony came to be increasingly resorted to as a revenue-raising device. Since these offices were purchased for money, they were expected to produce a financial return for their holders. As economic conditions worsened and the misery of the poor increased, social protest reinforced complaints against the clergy. It was unbearable that the sheep should be shorn for the benefit of their unworthy shepherds. The wealth and luxurious living of bishops and other prelates were a constant offense, and in the violent uprisings of the period this was a familiar grievance. Because of growing frustration and dissatisfaction with formal religion, movements sprang up in the late Middle Ages to provide a richer and more satisfying spiritual life. These movements, which provide part of the background of the Protestant Reformation.

While these conditions were weakening the church from within, there were also external forces which threatened it. Among these the most dangerous were powerful monarchs in developing nations who were determined not to submit to external authority and were supported by the patriotic feeling of their people. The problems that popes, with their claims to supranational authority, would be meeting from this source are well illustrated by the famous quarrel between the French king Philip IV, known as Philip the Fair, and Pope Boniface VIII, around the beginning of the fourteenth century.

The question of the powers of the church and of earthly authority and their relation to one another had been fought out for hundreds of years in the realm of theoretical writings and in concrete cases. Popes had claimed superiority over secular rulers, sometimes using the figure of the two great lights mentioned in the first chapter of Genesis ("圣经"中的"创世纪"). The "greater light" was the church, and the "lesser light" the civil power or state. The conflict of Philip the Fair and Boniface VIII was a practical one with theoretical implications.

The Hundred Years' War (英法百年战争)

The late Middle Ages was an age of turmoil and conflict in secular and ecclesiastical (基督教会的) affairs. International and civil wars characterized the fourteenth and fifteenth centuries, and the most serious was the Hundred Years' War. England and France were the chief antagonists (对手) in this struggle, which lasted from 1337 to 1453. The precipitating occasion for the war was the refusal of Edward III, king of England, to swear homage to Philip VI, king of France, for England's Continental possessions. The underlying cause was the existence of these English possessions on French territory. The war exemplified the incipient (早期的) growth of nation-states and the accompanying spirit of nationalism or patriotism. It was also a stimulus to the further development of these nations and of the national spirit.

This period of civil strife in England is known as the Wars of the Roses (玫瑰战争). The contending factions were the houses of Lancaster, symbolized by the red rose, and of York, represented by the white rose. As Henry VI grew to manhood, it became apparent that he had inherited from his maternal grandfather, Charles VI of France, a tendency toward insanity, along with a mild and devout character. Under these conditions, it is not surprising that he proved unable to maintain order. Eventually the Yorkists gained the throne in the person of Edward IV (1461—1470; 1471—1483) and his brother Richard III (1483—1485). At the battle of Bosworth in 1485, Richard was killed, and the crown passed to Henry Tudor, who as Henry VII opened a new era in English history.

Both countries emerged from their long struggle with a heightened self-consciousness and a stronger sense of national and patriotic pride, brought about by the presence of a dangerous and easily identified enemy. War is one of the sources of nationalism.

Social Upheaval and Revolutionary Movements

Another indication that the fourteenth and fifteenth centuries were witnessing the breakdown of an existing society and the birth of a new one is the prevalence of social protest and class struggle, often assuming the character of revolutionary movements. In England the question was asked, "When Adam delved and Eve spanned, Who was then the gentleman?" A spirit of Christian egalitarianism （平均主义） began to spread, challenging the great discrepancies between rich and poor on the grounds of men's common status as children of one God. The wealth of the clergy was a particularly sore grievance.

After the Black Death the size of the laboring population was seriously diminished, and wages went up. The government attempted to hold down wages, and this generated discontent. Radical leaders like John Ball, Jack Straw, and Wat Tyler influenced the masses.

The climax was the Peasants' Revolt of 1381, which involved a broader section of English society than the name implies, since many of the London poor became part of it. The rebels gathered in many of the counties and marched on London, where their movement was joined by numerous apprentices, workers, and unemployed. Before they were pacified, they had sacked several noble houses and Lambeth Palace, the London home of the archbishop of Canterbury, and murdered the archbishop. To quiet them, King Richard II met them at Blackheath. Since they consistently claimed to be protesting, not against the king but against his evil advisers, they allowed themselves to be satisfied with royal promises and they disbanded. After this, little if anything was done to meet their grievances, and the causes of their discontent remained.

In France the Hundred Years' War brought great suffering to the countryside, and waves of peasant discontent swept the country, particularly in the year 1358. This peasant unrest was called the Jacquerie from the nickname applied to the French peasant, Jacques Bonhomme. Another significant social development in France during the war was the rising importance of the city of Paris. In the years 1356 – 1358, one of the leading figures in French political life was tienne Marcel, who held the important office of provost （教长） of the merchants in Paris and for a while was master of the city, until he was assassinated in 1358. Under his leadership the interests and needs of the bourgeoisie, or town dwellers, made themselves heard at the highest levels of government.

The Atmosphere of the Middle Ages

It is clear that in the fourteenth and fifteenth centuries western Europe was in the throes of a more or less continuing crisis. Tension and conflict within church and society, as well as between states, brought about constant unrest and disorder. The strong attachment of contemporary observers to the ideals of order and stability caused them to look on their times with gloomy foreboding.

The emotional atmosphere of the late Middle Ages has been brilliantly defined in the book, *The Waning of the Middle Ages*, by the great Dutch historian Johan Huizinga. In this book he is particularly concerned with Flanders and France. It was a time, he says, when "a sombre melancholy weighs on people's souls". There was an intense preoccupation with death. Depictions of the Dance of Death were common in woodcuts, drawings, and paintings. Over and over the theme was repeated that Death comes to all: Popes, kings, emperors are subject to it along with the humblest peasant.

There was a factual basis for the concern with death. Life expectancy was shorter, and infant mortality was high. Unsanitary living conditions, plague, poor or insufficient food, to say nothing of war and crime, all made the risks of life and the chances of death greater than they are now.

Religion was powerful in this age, but in a society breaking away from familiar moorings and obsessed with death it took some extreme forms. An apocalyptic（启示）mood was common: Men had visions and dreamed dreams. Many thought that they were living in the last days of the world. A common theme of art in this period was the Passion, the most tragic of religious subjects; the suffering Jesus was emphasized rather than the glorified Christ. Religious devotion sometimes assumed abnormal forms, among them hysterical repentance and extreme ascetic practices, such as flagellation. But these acts of almost excessive piety might alternate, in the same persons, with orgies of sensual indulgence.

The ideals of knighthood, of chivalry, continued to receive lip service, but they were becoming increasingly anachronistic（时代的错误，与时代不合的）in the age of rising towns. The historian Froissart, writing about the events in France and Flanders during the Hundred Years' War, concentrates on the deeds of nobles and princes, regarding the movements among the city populations as a rather irritating distraction from the main events. There were no doubt many of his contemporaries who, like Froissart, failed to grasp the fact that what to them seemed of paramount interest belonged to a dying society, while the future was being shaped largely by forces that they either ignored or affected to disdain.

Retrieved from *http*://vlib. iue. it/carrie/texts/carrie_books/gilbert/

Decide whether the following statements are True or False.

1. During 14th and 15th century, plague or epidemics seldom happened except the Black Death. (　　)

2. The Black Death cut down the growth of European population and slowed down the economic development in Western Europe. (　　)

3. Those who bought offices from church tried to get financial return when they took them. (　　)

4. During 15th century, the kings were equal to Popes in power. (　　)

5. Henry VI was unable to maintain order in England under his rule because he was mad. (　　)

6. Many urban citizens participated in the Peasants' Revolt of 1381. (　　)

7. In the late Middle Ages, people of all social classes were obsessed with death. (　　)

Unit 6

Same Sex Marriage in the United States

本单元课文综述

Text 精读　在欧美国家,同性恋已是司空见惯的现象了。可是,对同性恋者争取同性婚姻权利却一直争议颇多,至今在美国这样的自由国家仍难以合法化。本文从宪法角度探讨美国同性婚姻的合法性问题。

Passage One 泛读　关于假设同性婚姻可行,同性恋者是否有资格当父母的争论。

Passage Two 泛读　联合国所颁布的《世界人权宣言》。同性婚姻是否有违人权精神?

ext　　**Same Sex Marriage in the United States**

Matthew Brigham

The proposed legalization of same-sex marriage is one of the most significant issues in contemporary American family law. Presently, it is one of the most vigorously advocated reforms discussed in law reviews, one of the most explosive political questions facing lawmakers, and one of the most **provocative** issues emerging before American courts. If same-sex marriage is legalized, it could be one of the most revolutionary policy decisions in the history of American family law. The potential consequences, positive or negative, for children, parents, same-sex couples, families, social structure, public health, and the status of women are enormous. Given the importance of the issue, the value of comprehensive debate of the reasons for and against legalizing same-sex marriage should be obvious. Marriage is much more than merely a commitment to love one another. Aside from **societal** and religious conventions, marriage **entails** legally imposed financial responsibility and legally authorized financial benefits. Marriage provides automatic legal protections for the spouse, including medical **visitation**, **succession** of a **deceased** spouse's property, as well as pension and other rights. When two adults desire to "**contract**" in the eyes of the law, as well as perhaps promise in the eyes of the Lord and their friends and family, to be responsible for the **obligations** of marriage as well as to enjoy its benefits, should the law prohibit their request merely because they are of the same **gender**? I intend to prove that because of Article IV of the United States Constitution, there is no reason why the federal government nor any state government should restrict marriage to a **predefined heterosexual** relationship.

Marriage has changed throughout the years. In Western law, wives are now equal rather than **subordinate** partners; interracial marriage is now widely accepted, both in **statute** and in society; and **marital** failure itself, rather than the fault of one partner, may be **grounds for** a divorce. Societal changes have been felt in marriages over the past 25 years as divorce rates have increased and have been **integrated into** even upper class families. Proposals to legalize same-sex marriage or to **enact** broad domestic partnership laws are currently being promoted by gay and **lesbian** activists, especially in Europe and North America. The trend in western European nations during the past decade has been to increase legal aid to homosexual relations and has included marriage benefits to some same-sex couples. For example, within the past six years, three **Scandinavian** countries have enacted domestic partnership laws allowing same-sex couples in which at least one partner is a citizen of the specified country therefore allowing many benefits that heterosexual marriages are given. In the Netherlands, the Parliament is considering domestic partnership status for same-sex couples, all major political parties favor recognizing same-sex relations, and more than a dozen towns have already done so. Finland provides governmental social benefits to same-sex partners. Belgium allows gay prisoners the right to have **conjugal** visits from same-sex partners. An overwhelming majority of European nations have granted partial legal status to homosexual relationships. The European Parliament also has passed a **resolution** calling for equal rights for gays and lesbians.

In the United States, efforts to legalize same-sex domestic partnership have had some limited success. The Lambda Legal Defense and Education Fund, Inc. reported that by mid-1995, thirty-six **municipalities**, eight counties, three states, five state agencies, and two federal agencies **extended some benefits to,** or registered for some official purposes, same-sex domestic partnerships. In 1994, the California legislature passed a domestic partnership bill that provided official state registration of same-sex couples and provided limited marital rights and privileges relating to hospital visitation, wills and estates, and powers of **attorney**. While California's Governor Wilson eventually **vetoed** the bill, its passage by the legislature represented a notable political achievement for advocates of same-sex marriage.

The most significant prospects for legalizing same-sex marriage in the near future are in Hawaii, where advocates of same-sex marriage have won a major judicial victory that could lead to the judicial legalization of same-sex marriage or to legislation authorizing same-sex domestic partnership in that state. In 1993, the Hawaii Supreme Court, in Baehr v. Lewin,

vacated a state **circuit court** judgment dismissing same-sex marriage claims and **ruled** that Hawaii's marriage law allowing heterosexual, but not homosexual, couples to obtain marriage licenses constitutes sex discrimination under the state constitution's Equal Protection Clause and Equal Rights Amendment. The case began in 1991 when three same-sex couples who had been denied marriage licenses by the Hawaii Department of Health **brought suit** in state court against the director of the department. Hawaii law required couples wishing to marry to obtain a marriage license. While the marriage license law did not **explicitly** prohibit same-sex marriage at that time, it used terms of gender that clearly indicated that only heterosexual couples could marry. The couple sought a judicial decision that the Hawaii marriage license law is unconstitutional, as it prohibits same-sex marriage and allows state officials to deny marriage licenses to same-sex couples **on account of** the heterosexuality requirement. Baehr and her attorney sought their objectives entirely through state law, not only by filing in state rather than federal court, but also by **alleging** exclusively violations of state law — the Hawaii Constitution. The state **moved for** judgment on the pleadings and for dismissal of the complaint for failure to state a claim, and the state's motion was granted in October, 1991. Thus, the circuit court **upheld** the heterosexuality marriage requirement as a matter of law and dismissed the **plaintiffs'** challenges to it.

Yet recently the Circuit Court of Hawaii decided that Hawaii had violated Baehr and her partner's constitutional rights by the fourteenth amendment and that they could be recognized as a marriage. The court found that the state of Hawaii's constitution **expressly** discriminated against homosexuals and that because of Hawaii's anti-discrimination law they must reevaluate the situation. After the ruling the state immediately asked for a stay of judgment, until the appeal had been **convened**, therefore putting off any marriage between Baehr and her partner for at least a year.

By far Baehr is the most positive step toward actual marriage rights for gay and lesbian people. Currently there is a high tolerance for homosexuals throughout the United States and currently in Hawaii. Judges do not need the popularity of the people on the Federal or circuit court level to make new **precedent**. There is no clear majority that homosexuals should have marriage rights in the general public, and yet the courts voted for Baehr. The **judiciary has its own mind on** how to interpret the constitution which is obviously very different than most of American popular belief. This is the principal reason that these judges are not elected by the people, so they do not have to **bow to people's pressure**.

The constitutional rights argument for same-sex marriage **affirms** that there is a fundamental constitutional right to marry, or a broader right of privacy or of **intimate association**. The essence of this right is the private, intimate association of consenting adults who want to share their lives and commitment with each other and that same-sex couples have just as much intimacy and need for marital privacy as heterosexual couples; and that laws allowing heterosexual, but not same-sex, couples to marry **infringe upon** and discriminate against this fundamental right. Just as the Supreme Court compelled states to allow interracial marriage by recognizing the claimed right as part of the fundamental constitutional right to marry, of privacy and of intimate association so should states be compelled now to recognize the fundamental right of homosexuals to do the same.

If Baehr ultimately leads to the legalization of same-sex marriage or broad marriage like domestic partnership in Hawaii, the impact of that legalization will be felt widely. Marriage recognition principles derived from choice-of-law and full-faith-and-credit rules probably would be **invoked** to recognize same-sex Hawaiian marriages as valid in other states. The impact of Hawaii's decision will immediately impact marriage laws in all of the United States. The full faith and credit clause of the U. S. Constitution provides that full faith and credit shall be given to the "public acts, records, and judicial proceedings of every other state."

It would seem evident that if heterosexual couples use Article IV as a safety net and guarantee for their **wedlock** then that same right should be given to homosexual couples. This Article has often been cited as **a reference point** for interracial marriages in the south when those states do not want to recognize the legitimacy of that union by another state. As this is used for that lifestyle, there is no logical reason it should be denied to perhaps millions of homosexuals that want the opportunity to get married. The obstacles being out in front of homosexual couples is in the name of the "normal" people that actively seek to define their definition to all. It is these "normal" people that are the definition of surplus **repression** and social domination. Yet as they cling to the Constitution for their freedoms they deny those same freedoms to not "normal" people because they would lose their social domination and could be changed. Therefore it would seem they are afraid to change, and have not accepted that the world does change.

Unfortunately the full faith and credit clause has rarely been used as anything more than an excuse to get a quick divorce. A man wants a divorce yet his wife does not or will not **void** their marriage. He then goes to Reno, Nevada, buys a house and gets a job for six weeks. After that six weeks when he can declare himself a legal resident he applies for a singular marriage void and because Nevada law allows one side to void their marriage as they are a resident of Nevada their marriage is now void. The man now moves back to his home state, and upon doing so this state must now recognize the legitimacy that Nevada has voided out the marriage. Even if the wife does not consent, the new state cannot do anything about it. That is what usually full faith and credit is used under.

Leaving aside, as government should, objections that may be held by particular religions, the case against same-gender marriage is simply that people are unaccustomed to it. **Bigotry** and prejudice still exist in our evolving society, and traditionally people fear what is strange and unfamiliar to them. One may argue that change should not be pushed along hastily. At the same time, it is an argument for legalizing homosexual marriage through **consensual politics** as in Denmark, rather than by court order, as may happen in

Hawaii.

Retrieved from *http://www.antiessays.com/free-essays/1908.html*

New Words and Phrases

provocative	*adj.*	causing argument, anger, interest(often of a sexual kind) etc.　发人深思的,引起讨论的,挑逗的
societal	*adj.*	social, concerning society　社会的
entail	*v.*	make(an event, or action) necessary　使成为必要,需要
visitation	*n.*	a very formal visit paid by someone　探视
succession	*n.*	the right to be the next heir after　继承权
deceased	*adj.*	(fml. & law) (of people) no longer living, esp. recently dead　已死的,死去的
contract	*v.*	to settle or arrange by formal agreement　订合同,立契约
obligation	*n.*	a duty　(法律或道义上的) 义务,责任 be/place under an ~
gender	*n.*	(infml.) sex　(生理上的) 性,性别
predefine	*v.*	预先限定,预先明确
heterosexual	*adj.*	异性的,不同性别的
subordinate	*adj.*	to be considered of less importance　隶属的,顺从的
statute	*n.*	(fml.) a law　成文法,法令,法规
marital	*adj.*	of or concerning (the duties of) marriage　婚姻的
grounds for	*n. + prep.*	(常作 ~s) 理由,根据
integrate into	*v. + prep.*	to join to sth. else so as to form a whole　使成一体,使结合
enact	*v.*	(often pass.) to make or pass (a law)　制订, 通过(法律)
lesbian		同性恋女子(源出居于莱斯博斯岛的古希腊女诗人 Sappho 同性恋的传说)
Scandinavian		斯堪的纳维亚(北欧地区,包括挪威、瑞典和丹麦,有时也包括冰岛,芬兰和法罗群岛)
conjugal	*adj.*	(fml.) concerning the relationship between husband and wife　婚姻的,夫妻之间的
resolution	*n.*	a formal decision made by a group vote　正式决定,决议
municipality	*n.*	自治市
extend some benefits to		给予……一些好处
attorney	*n.*	(esp. AmE.) lawyer　(美) 律师 (英国称 solicitor)

		powers of attorney　授权书,委托书
veto	*v.*	prevent or forbid（some action）; refuse to allow（sth.）否决,反对
vacate	*v.*	（in law）to give up（sth.）（律）撤销,使无效
circuit court		（美）巡回法院
rule	*v.*	（esp. in law）to decide officially　裁决,裁定
bring suit（against）		起诉
explicitly	*adv.*	（of statements etc.）clearly and fully expressed　详尽地,明确地
on account of		为了……的缘故,因为
allege	*v.*	（fml.）to state or declare without proof　断言;宣称,声称
move for		（in Parliament）to make a formal request for　申请,提出请求
uphold	*v.*	to support; confirm　支持,维护
plaintiff	*n.*	（law）a person who brings a charge against sb. in court（律）起诉人,原告
expressly	*adv.*	clearly 明显地,明确地
convene	*v.*	to summon to appear, as before a tribunal. 传唤……到场
precedent	*n.*	a former action or case that may be used as an example or rule for present or future action　先例,前例
judiciary	*n.*	（GC）the judges（in law）considered as one group　（总称）法官
has one's mind on:		对……有自己的看法（见解）
bow to people's pressure		屈从于人们的压力, 对人们的压力让步
affirm	*v.*	to declare（in answer to a question）断言,声明,坚持声称
intimate association		亲密关系
infringe upon	*v.* + *prep.*	go against or take over（the right of another）　侵犯,侵害
invoke	*v.*	call into use　求助于（法律等）,援引
wedlock	*n.*	the state of being（lawfully）married　婚姻,已婚状态 in（out of）wedlock　婚内（外）
a reference point		（空）（海）基准点（指测量距离时用作基准的一点）
repression	*n.*	the act of holding back（feelings, actions etc.）抑制,压制
void	*v.*	（law）to cause to be without effect　（律）使无效,取消
bigotry	*n.*	（derog.）prejudice　偏见;偏执的行为（或态度）
consensual	*adj.*	（律）经双方同意而产生的,两厢情愿的 consensual politics　共识政治

About the author:
Mr. Brigham received his law degree from the University of California, Davis. Prior to attending law school, he received his Bachelor of Science degree in Mechanical Engineering from the University of California, San Diegon. He is admitted to practice before the U. S. Patent and Trademark Office, and is a member of the State Bar of California(加州律师公会会员).

Notes to the text

1. **Article IV of the United States Constitution:** Article Four of the United States Constitution relates to the states. It provides for the responsibilities states have to each other, and the responsibilities the federal government has to the states. Furthermore, it provides for the admission of new states and the changing of state boundaries.
   美国宪法第四条,共四款,主要规定各州与联邦的关系,其中第一款即是完全信任条款(见 Note 2)。

2. **choice-of-law and full-faith-and-credit rules:**
   choice of law clause: In Anglo-American law, the term "choice of law principle[法律适用原则]" is sometimes referred to as "conflicts of law principle [法律冲突原则], commonly incorporated in English contracts." whereby the court determines what law governs the dispute when the laws of two or more jurisdictions are in conflict with each other. In international private law, the choice is between the laws of two or more nations, and is in the area of international private law (国际私法). In United States, the choice is mostly between the laws of different states, and can be translated into 法律适用.
   full faith and credit: shall be given in each state to the public acts, records, and judicial proceedings of every other State. And the Congress may by general laws prescribe the manner in which such acts, records and proceedings shall be proved, and the effect thereof.
   州与州之间的完全信任条款,要求每个州政府承认另一个州政府的法令、纪录与判决。例如承认在另一个州登记的婚姻与核发的驾照等。不过如果一个州对另一个州的一项法令强烈反感时,可以不采纳,例如同性恋婚姻,有的州合法有的不合法。

3. **Equal Protection Clause and Equal Rights Amendment**
   Equal Protection Clause: nor shall any state deny to any person within its jurisdiction the equal protection of the laws (平等保护条款).
   Equal Rights Amendment (ERA): is a failed proposed amendment to the United States Constitution intended to guarantee equal rights under the law for Americans regardless of sex, which failed to gain ratification before the end of the deadline. Although the ERA has been reintroduced in every Congress since 1982, public attention to the ERA has greatly diminished(平等权利修正案).

4. **the Defense of Marriage Act（DOMA）**：In 1996, Congress passed the Defense of Marriage Act（DOMA）. It defines marriage as a legal union between one man and one woman for purposes of all federal laws, prohibits federal recognition of same-sex marriages and also allows a state to ignore gay marriages performed outside its borders（维护婚姻法或保障一夫一妻婚姻制度）.

5. **the Fourteenth Amendment**：The Fourteenth Amendment of the Constitution was passed by both houses on 8th June and the 13th June, 1866. The amendment was designed to grant citizenship to and protect the civil liberties of recently freed slaves. It did this by prohibiting states from denying or abridging the privileges or immunities of citizens of the United States, depriving any person of his life, liberty, or property without due process of law, or denying to any person within their jurisdiction the equal protection of the laws. 第十四条修正案条款被理解成是法律公平、正义的基本保障。

6. **the Uniform Marriage and Divorce Act**：It's a so-called "model law" promulgated（颁布）by a national lawyers' group. This "model law", which included the blueprint for "no-fault" divorce, was promoted as a way to eliminate the rancor（积怨，敌意）of the civil divorce process, whereby one party needed to "accuse" the other party of serious transgression（过失）. 美国 the 1974 Uniform Marriage and Divorce Act 201 款规定，"Marriage is a personal relationship between a man and a woman arising out of a civil contract to which the consent of the parties is essential". 美国 1970 年通过《统一结婚离婚法》。

7. **The state moved for judgment on the pleadings and for dismissal of the complaint for failure to state a claim**：The state applied to the court for judgment on the charge and for the refusal to deal with the plaintiffs' complaint because they failed to present sufficient facts in the court：州政府向法院申请对原告的上诉做出判决并申请驳回原告，因为他们未能提出充足的证据。

for failure to state a claim：原告未能提出充足的证据。

Exercises

I. **Answer the following questions based on Text and the words and expressions listed below are for your reference.**

1. **What is the author's attitude towards the legalization of same-sex marriage in the U. S.?**

   （for/in favor of/support or against/oppose）

2. **How does the author define marriage?**

   （commitment/responsibility/benefit）

3. **What changes has the society undergone in marriage in the past 25 years?**

   （divorce rate）

4. **Give some examples to show the efforts made by some European countries in the legalization of same-sex marriage.**

5. **What progress has been made in the U. S. in the legalization of same-sex marriage?**
   (limited success)

6. **Why will the most significant prospects be in Hawaii for legalizing same-sex marriage in the near future according to the author?**
   (major judicial victory)

7. **Give a brief account of Baehr's case in fighting for her same-sex marriage license.**

8. **What leads to the changes of attitude of judges in this case?**
   (high tolerance/the popularity of people not needed)

9. **What's the essence of the 'fundamental constitutional right to marry'?**
   (private/intimate association)

10. **What will be the significance of Baehr's possible success in legalization of same-sex marriage or broad marriage like domestic partnership?**
    (change of marriage recognition principle)

11. **Why, according to the author, do "normal" people object to same-sex marriage?**
    (afraid to change) **And why does the author use quotation mark for the word "normal"?**

12. **According to the author, how do people exploit the full-faith-and-credit clause in their divorce case?**
    (an excuse)

13. **How does the author conclude the article?**

II. Further questions for discussion.

1. In most of Chinese people's eyes, what would marriage possibly mean?

2. How do you understand sexual discrimination? Do you think the objection to the same-sex marriage is a kind of sexual discrimination?

3. In your opinion, is same-sex marriage abnormal in our present society?

4. Have you watched the movie The Backbroke Mountain? What's your view about the affection between two gays or lesbians?

III. Vocabulary study.

1. Word in Use.

1) **entail**: *vt.* to make (an event or action) necessary 使成为必要,需要

   To get the ship back into full working order would entail spending huge amounts of money.

   Changing the computer system would entail substantial periods of retraining.

   The position entails frequent domestic business travel.

2) **integrate into**：to bring together different people, things, ideas etc, which were formerly kept separate 使结合,使合并

integration *n.*

The group's function is to integrate the refugees into the local community.

Many young people successfully integrated themselves into the new surroundings.

3) **extend ... to ...**：(fml.) to give or offer (help, friendship, etc.) to someone 提供,给予,发出(邀请,欢迎等)

The bank extended credit to customers who enjoyed a reputation of credibility.

They extended a warm welcome to the newcomers to their class.

His friends came to extend their congratulations on his promotion.

4) **uphold**：*vt.* to declare to be right; confirm 赞成,认可,维护,确认

It is the duty of the court to uphold the law and punish law-breakers.

The principal upheld the teacher's decision.

The Supreme Court is expected to uphold the death sentence.

5) **bow to**：to bend forward the upper part of the body to show respect or to yield to 鞠躬,欠身;让步,屈服

Industry has to bow to consumer tastes and people want environment-friendly products.

Ideals bow to practicality.

I bow to your opinion and take your advice.

6) **infringe upon**：go against or take away (the right of another) 侵犯,侵害,侵入

infringement *n.*

The new arrangements infringed upon the widows' right of equal pay and treatment.

The government infringed upon a nation's fishing rights at sea.

This act infringed upon the rights of the citizens.

7) **invoke**：*vt.* to put into effect; to call into use 求助于(法律等),实施;援引

We have to invoke the powers of the law to prevent a crime.

The president invoked an emergency act as a reason for barring a sale.

After the outbreak of the war, the government had invoked economic sanctions on this area.

8) **void**：*vt.* (law) to cause to be without effect 使无效,把……作废,取消

void *n.* (C usu. sing.) & *adj.*

The lack of signature of the other party voided the contract.

Their failure to have a talk with the company voided the contract.

The agreement was voided because it was signed by a child.

2. Word Distinctions.

1) **allege; charge** 两个词均有'指控'的意思：

allege：在没有证据或得到证据之前指控(To assert without or before proof)：课文中 Baehr and her attorney sought their objectives … by **alleging** exclusively violations of state law，所以州政府以 failure to state a claim(未能提出充足的证据)申请州法院将其起诉驳回。

charge：掌握证据后正式起诉(make a formal accusation)。

选择以上适当的词填空：

The former mayor will appear before the local court today _____ with taking bribes.

His classmates _____ that he was cheating in the exam, but they failed to produce any solid proof.

She's been arrested after being _____ with murdering her husband.

The _____ murderer was proved innocent.

2) **affirms；confirm** 两个词均指'确认'

affirm：to state something as true；

confirm：to make an arrangement or meeting certain, often by telephone or writing

选择以上适当的词填空：

Six people have _____ that they will be attending and ten haven't replied yet.

The suspect _____ that he had been at home all evening.

I've accepted the job over the phone, but I haven't _____ in writing yet.

She _____ her intention to apply for the post.

Flights should be _____ 48 hours before departure.

3. **Decide the meanings of the following words from the context by matching each word in Column A with the word or expression in Column B that is similar in meaning.**

A	B
1) vacate	a. to meet or gather
2) conjugal	b. a person who brings a charge against sb. in court
3) enact	c. (of statements etc.)clearly and fully expressed
4) repression	d. (of the Government)to make or pass (a law)
5) convene	e. cease to use or live in
6) wedlock	f. a woman who is sexually attracted to other women rather than to men
7) explicit	g. giving permission
8) consensual	h. the act of controlling (a feeling or desire)
9) plaintiff	i. the state of marriage
10) lesbian	j. concerning the relationship between husband and wife

4. **Try to write a brief account with the following words or phrases.**

a dominant issue, controversial, civil right, moral standard, traditional ideas, allege, uphold enact, bring suit

IV. Translation.

1. Put the following Chinese expressions into English.

1）有争议的问题　　2）社会和宗教传统　　3）异族通婚　　4）法律援助

5）家庭伴侣关系法　6）异性婚姻　　　　7）违反法律　　8）单方婚姻无效

2. Put the following Chinesse sentences into English with the words or phrases in the bracket.

1）所有的战士都知道他们的秘密任务需要冒一定的风险。(entail)

2）移民们努力地融入到新的文化中。(integrate . . . into)

3）他终于获得这个大奖,同事们都向他表示祝贺。(extend)

4）最高法院驳回上诉,维持原判。(uphold)

5）政府最终屈从于民意,撤销了那项不受欢迎的税。(bow to . . .)

6）参议院认为联邦管理这一原则侵犯了州的权利。(infringe upon . . .)

7）他在演讲中援引了莎士比亚的作品。(invoke)

8）她在任何方面都顺从丈夫。(subordinate)

9）没有董事长的背书,这张支票只能作废。(void)

10）他在位期间,继续实施强硬的镇压政策。(repression)

3. Put the following Chinese paragraph into English.

研究成果发现那些相信自己的伴侣会永远对自己好,永远爱着自己,同意自己每一句话的人会对婚姻的前景保持积极乐观的态度,因为他们能够宽恕并仁慈的解释伴侣的消极行为。然而,那些对婚姻期望太高却又不具备处理婚姻关系技巧的人,一旦他们心中的白马王子或白雪公主从神圣的光环中跌落,他们可能很快就被迫回到现实中。

4. Put the following quotes into Chinese.

1）Marriage may be compared to a cage: the birds outside despair to get in and those within despair to get out. —— Michel de Montaigne, French thinker and essayist

2）Where there is marriage without love, there will be love without marriage.

—— Benjamin Franklin

3）If you fight for yourself, only you can win; when you fight for your marriage, you both win. —— Pearsall Paul

4）To make a lasting marriage we have to overcome self-centeredness.

—— Grorge Goreon Byron, British poet

5）All happy families are like one another; each unhappy family is unhappy in its own way. —— Leo Tolstoy, Russian writer

5. Translate the following passage into Chinese.

Love is the highest value in life: It should not be reduced to stupid rituals. And love and freedom go together — you cannot choose one and leave the other. A man who knows freedom is full of love, and a man who knows love is always willing to give freedom.

If you cannot give freedom to the person you love, to whom can you give freedom? Giving freedom is nothing but trusting. Freedom is an expression of love.

So whether you are married or not, remember, all marriages are fake — just social conveniences. Their purpose is not to imprison you and bind you to each other; their purpose is to help you to grow with each other. But growth needs freedom; and in the past, all the cultures have forgotten that without freedom, love dies.

V. Comment on the structure of the text.

This text is an argumentative essay (论述文), which is a type of discourse in speech or writing that develops or debates a topic in a logical or persuasive way. Most argumentative writings begin with a statement of an idea or opinion, which is then supported with logical evidence. Another technique of argumentation is the anticipation and rebuttal of opposing views.

In the text, the author sets out to prove his argument that it is possible to legalize same-sex marriage in the U. S. by quoting examples of progress that European countries have made in this aspect and by analyzing the American Constitution at large, especially taking Baehr's case as a typical example. Finally he comes to his conclusion that it will just take time for the general public to accept the new family pattern and its constitutionality will be only a matter of time as well.

Extended Exercises

1. **Identify the procedures of rescuing birds that have been exposed to oil pollution by grouping the following numbered paragraphs into effective sections and choose the most suitable subheading from the list A-E for each section.**

Rescuing Birds

1) Many government agencies, universities and private organizations help rescue animals and birds that have been exposed to oil pollution. While the government is responsible for animal rescue efforts, many private organizations assist in rescuing injured wildlife. Before any person or organization can handle or confine birds or mammals for rescue, however, they must get special permits that are issued by state and federal officials.

2) It is unlawful for any person or organization to capture and handle oiled wildlife without training or permits. The training that they need prepares them to capture, handle, and treat injured wildlife without causing pain and suffering to the animals or causing injury to themselves as they treat wildlife.

3) Rescue parties usually contact rehabilitation workers before they arrive to make sure that they are prepared to care for the captured birds immediately. This ensures that the birds are treated as quickly as possible. Birds that are most likely to be affected by oil spills are those that remain in, dive in, or feed in the water, such as ducks, gulls, herons, pelicans, bald eagles, and ospreys.

4) Once a bird has been brought to a rehabilitation center, certain basic procedures are followed. First, birds are given complete physical exams, including checking body temperature, breathing rates, and heart rates. Birds are examined for broken bones, skin burns and cuts. Oil is flushed from birds eyes and ears. Heavily oiled birds are wiped with absorbent cloths to remove patches of oil.

5) Certain medicine is administered orally to prevent additional absorption of oil inside the bird's stomach and to help remove internal oil from the bird. The bird is then warmed and placed in a quiet area. Curtains, towels, and sheets are often hung to limit visual contact with people.

6) Nutrition is essential for the recovery of oiled birds. Birds are fed and given water using a special solution and mix of fish, vitamins, minerals until they are washed. Birds need up to five days to get normal levels of water back into their system and strengthen themselves before being washed.

7) After a bird is alert, responsive, and stable, it can be washed. Dishwashing detergent thinned with water has been found to be the most effective washing means for oiled birds. Beads of water will roll freely from the feathers, and down will begin to fluff up and appear dry when a bird has been acceptably rinsed. Failure to properly rinse birds is one of the most common causes of unsuccessful treatment.

8) After its feathers are completely rinsed, the bird is placed in a clean holding pen lined with meshed nets and a ceiling made of sheets or towels. The pen is warmed with pet dryers, and, again, minimizing human contact is important.

9) If behavior appears normal and a bird's condition remains stable, it is placed in a recovery pool and allowed to swim. The bird then begins to groom itself and straighten out its feathers to restore them to their original structure, helping the bird to become waterproof again.

10) Before a bird is released, it must pass the waterproofing test; it must demonstrate buoyancy (the ability to float) and water-repellency (the ability to keep water away from its body).

11) Once a bird passes this test, it is slowly exposed to temperatures comparable to outside weather. Its weight should be close to the average for the species, and it should show no signs of abnormal behavior.

12) Rehabilitated birds are banded and released early in the day into appropriate habitat. Release location is a very important element in rehabilitation. Birds must not be

allowed to return to oiled areas nor should they be released into an unsuitable habitat.

A：Waterproof test

B：Physical examinations and initial treatments.

C：Release of birds.

D：Prevention from human contact

E. Careful cleanup.

2. **Read the following text and choose the best word for each numbered blank.**

In general, ill health becomes more common with advancing age. More than three ____1)____ of those over sixty-five suffer from some ____2)____ health condition. But ill health need not have only physiological causes; it can have social and psychological causes ____3)____ . People tend to follow social ____4)____ to fill the roles that are offered to them. In a ____5)____ , all we offer the aged is a sick role — the role of the infirm person who has ____6)____ his or her usefulness to society. An urbanized, industrialized society such as the United States is ____7)____ towards youth, mobility, and activity. It does little to ____8)____ the old into the social structure. ____9)____ the elders in a traditional society, the American aged can no longer lay automatic ____10)____ on their relatives for support and social participation; on the contrary, they are more ____11)____ to have to try not to be a "nuisance" to their now ____12)____ adult offspring. Nor are they regarded as the wisest members of the community ____13)____ the elders in a traditional society would be; ____14)____ , any advice they give is likely to be considered ____15)____ in a changing world about which their descendants consider themselves much better informed. ____16)____ retirement and the loss of an economic role can have a disastrous effect. ____17)____ all the decent words about "senior citizens" and their "golden age", the fact is that retirement often ____18)____ little more than a swift shift from a meaningful ____19)____ to a meaningless one. The change is not simply from work to leisure. It can also be a ____20)____ form relative affluence to economic hardship; and if the old person is still living with mature children, he or she becomes, overnight, a dependent in the household.

1) A. numbers   B. quantities   C. quarters   D. fractions

2) A. fatal   B. chronic   C. mortal   D. acute

3) A. as well   B. at all   C. as yet   D. at stake

4) A. preferences   B. reputation   C. choices   D. expectations

5) A. sense   B. extent   C. result   D. consequence

6) A. surpassed   B. overtook   C. exceeded   D. outlived

7) A. advanced   B. oriented   C. tended   D. prompted

8) A. encourage   B. inspire   C. integrate   D. involve

9) A. As   B. Like   C. Alike   D. Unlike

10) A. claim   B. demand   C. request   D. assertion

11) A. possible   B. able   C. likely   D. capable
12) A. single   B. independent   C. individual   D. credible
13) A. as   B. though   C. since   D. if
14) A. moreover   B. however   C. otherwise   D. instead
15) A. irrelevant   B. impartial   C. irregular   D. unsettled
16) A. Indispensable B. Compulsory   C. Volunteer   D. Optional
17) A. For   B. After   C. Above   D. In
18) A. resembles   B. signifies   C. designates   D. verifies
19) A. occupation   B. career   C. circumstance   D. role
20) A. transmission   B. transaction   C. transition   D. transformation

3. **The passage contains TEN errors. Each indicated line contains a maximum of ONE error. In each case, only ONE word is involved. You should proofread the passage and correct it.**

For a wrong word, underline it and write the correct one in the blank provided at the end of the line.

For a missing word, mark its position with a "^" sign and write the word you believe to be missing in the blank provided at the end of the line.

For an unnecessary word, cross use a slash"/" and put the word in the blank provided at the end of the line.

The law is a great mass of rules shows when and how far a man is	1) _____
liable to be punished, or to be made to hand over money or property	2) _____
for his neighbors, and so forth. A lawyer learns them mainly by	
reading books. He begins by doing little else than reading and after he	
had prepared himself by, say, three years' study to practice, still, all	3) _____
his life long and almost every day, he will be looking into books to	
read little more than he already knows about some new questions to	4) _____
which he has to answer.	5) _____
The power to use books, then, is a talent about which a good	6) _____
lawyer ought to possess. He ought to have enough flexibility to make it	
easy for him to collect ideas from printing words. He ought to have	
some readiness in finding what a book contains, and something of an	7) _____
instinct to where to look for what he wants. But although this is the	8) _____
power of that he will first feel the need, it is not the most important. A	9) _____
lawyer does not study law to recite it; he studies it and acts for the	
rules which he has learned in real life. His business is to try cases in	10) _____
court and to advise men what to do in order to keep or get out of the	
trouble. He studies his books in order to advise and to try his cases in	
the right manners.	

Extensive Reading

Passage One

Gay Parenting
如果同性婚姻可行,同性恋者是否有资格当父母

The conception that lesbians and gay men may be parents is frequently perceived in today's society as impossible or immoral. Gay men and lesbians are often viewed as excluded from having children because sexual reproduction is related to men and women only. My approach to this uniquely controversial topic of gay parenting will be that of attempting to analyze the Pro side first. Gays and lesbians are human too and who is to say that they don't deserve equal rights in society. Society has to realize that the modern family has developed into many different forms in recent years in that the "nuclear family" is not necessarily the most common form anymore.

Then I will attempt to analyze the Con side which expresses the fact that two people of the same sex should not be raising and rearing children together. Many believe that if the couple is unable to produce children together, then they shouldn't be raising them as parents. Children need a balance in their lives and different sexed parents can provide that balance efficiently. Each parent (mom or dad) socializes the child differently and the child needs to be introduced to both worlds.

I will then *proceed to*(开始做) critique both sides on strengths and weaknesses, based on facts, studies, and my own opinion, and then draw some of my own conclusions on this controversial topic of Gay Parenting.

Pro Position

There is no valid reason for refusing to call lesbian and gay headed household families. They fall under every conceivable *criterion*(标准) for identifying families and the concept of a Family. "They are groups of *co-resident kin*(同居关系) providing jointly through *income-pooling*(共同收入) for each other's need of food and shelter. They socialize children, engage in emotional and physical support, and make up part of a larger kin network". (O. Brien and Weir, 128).

There are also many *homophobic*(对同性恋者憎恶的)(the irrational fear or hatred of homosexuality or gay people, Biery 88) individuals in today's society who are the main cause of negative *stereotypes*(陈规,偏见) against lesbians and gay parents. These negative stereotypes all prove to be untrue and irrational, revealing that gay and lesbian parents could be equally as fit to *straight parents*(异性父母).

The accusation that majority of gay men are *child molesters* (猥亵儿童者) has been rejected in that the overwhelming majority of child *sexual abusers* (性虐待) are heterosexual men, who abuse both boys and girls. The fear that children of lesbian and gay parents will become lesbian or gay is irrational in that studies show that the *sexual orientation* (性取向) of the parents has no effect whatsoever on sexual orientation of youths. The concern that the children of *gay and lesbian headed families* (同性恋者为父母的家庭) will not develop so called appropriate *gender identity* (性别特性) or gender behavior has been introduced. This was proved incorrect in that when comparing children of gay parents to children of straight parents, there was no significant difference in these two areas. The last stereotype involving the fear that emotional damage will effect the child due to coping with the issue of having lesbian or gay parents. Once again this was proved to be false and the general psychological well being of children in gay and lesbian households matches that of children of heterosexual parent households. (O. Brien and Weir, 129).

These common stereotypes heard frequently in today's society have all been proved incorrect and ignorant. Therefore they illustrate that gay and lesbian parents are continually stereotyped against unfairly and unjustly. Lesbians and gay men are popularly and commonly thought of by society to have a negative influence on children. This *places an enormous strain* (施加巨大压力) and great pressure on lesbian and gay headed families, which is totally unnecessary.

"When we assume male-headed nuclear families to be central units of kinship, and all alternative patterns to be extensions or exceptions, we accept as aspect of *cultural hegemony* (文化霸权) instead of studying it. In the process, we miss the *contested domain* (竞争领域) in which symbolic innovation may occur. Even *continuity* (持续性) may be the result of innovation". (Weston, 145). This is a very powerful statement in that it reinforces the argument that lesbian and gay families are overlooked in society as even being a family unit.

Society must come to realize that every family, not just gay headed families, experience problems in their homes. An article which *depicts* (描述) some of the major problems that some single mothers experience is: Manhunts (侠盗猎魔,一种电脑单机游戏) and Bingo (一种赌博游戏) Blabs? Single mothers speak out-M. Little, p. 164 - 181. This article will assist one in realizing that some individuals will face some *dilemmas* (两难境地) and issues in life, but it is those issues and how a family deals with them effectively that will make them stronger as a family unit. Everyone deals with pressures of everyday life and it is those who learn by them that are prosperous.

With specific reference to *child rearing* (抚养孩子), parents were told that problems arise in all homes, with all children, and at all ages, the interesting fact being that the problems do or do not arise but what method should be employed in dealing with them when they arise (Dickinson, 392). Problems in the home are inevitable, in all forms of families, and those who believe that one form of family will have more problems and issues than others will need to reassess their outlook to a more rational *perception* (认识).

Society has to realize that it is not one's *sexual preference* (性偏好) that allows a family to grow and flourish but the efforts of the people who make up that family unit. A family is based on trust and love, and if that is what these gays' and lesbians' parents are providing for their children, then why not let them live as they want.

Con Position

Many will argue that children of lesbian and gay parents do not grow up the "same" as children of heterosexual parents. Concern usually *revolves around* (围绕) the issue that the children will also grow up to become lesbian or gay themselves (Baker, 105).

In most cultures, children are raised to take on specific roles associated with their biological sex very early in life. Therefore, in most cases people maintain an identity of themselves in terms of gender (Blumenfeld and Raymond, 45). (This statement is expanded on in the Chapter of Socialization and gender roles in Looking at Gay and Lesbian Life).

Many also believe that children need parents of the opposite sex to find balance in their lives. Each heterosexual parent socializes their children differently and children need to view this difference for themselves.

An *elaborate* (详尽的) description of *masculinity* (男子气概) and fatherhood takes place in, "Fatherhood, Masculinity, and the Good life during Canada's baby boom", 1945 – 1965, Robert Rutherdale. This article depicts how the dad of the nuclear family "had secured his family place in the consumer markets and recreational opportunities of a profoundly acquisitive period" (369). It depicts some activities which fathers endured with the son to ensure masculinity and *machoness* (男子气概) as the son matured into a man himself.

Children need to realize and witness how men and women deal with certain situations differently. They need to be informed of different situations that will occur to them throughout their lives (depending on their sex), and they need each of their parents at different times of their lives (example — a girl needs her mom at *menarche* (月经初期) and her dad to help her with her car). Some feel that if there is an imbalance then the child will never learn to identify with the one sex that is absent from their life. This issue of balance has never been proved to be true yet still remains an issue to some.

Another major issue facing gay parents is AIDS. "The fact that the *epidemic* (流行病) was first identified in the early 1980 in the gay male communities of North America." (Weeks, chapter 1 p. 15 – 45). AIDS is known as the gay disease. It has been studied and many feel that homosexuals are more *prone and susceptible to* (易于……,易受影响的) *contracting the disease* (得病) than heterosexuals. Many feel that the children of gay parents are in increased danger due to the fact that AIDS is increasingly spreading and if their parent has it then they are at high risk to contracting it.

The Chapter, "HIV and the State of the Family" in the text *"Transgressing Borders"*

（越界）（p. 19 – 33）, clearly depicts the issues facing families, of all forms, in direct relation to AIDS. This may help some to realize the seriousness of this incurable disease. AIDS *phobia*（恐惧症）is another issue discussed in this chapter. This is "strongly related to heterosexism and homophobia prejudicial attitudes and practices against lesbians and gay men. Individuals with antigay attitudes are far more likely than others to have irrational fears about HIV transmission (Sears and Adam, 27). AIDS is a growing epidemic with no cure that affects millions. The seriousness of this disease is illustrated in" From Reproduction to HIV: Blurring Categories, Shifting Positions, Martin-256-269, in which individuals narrate stories of people living with AIDS and these individuals, while extremely sick and almost dying, experience abandonment, by family and friends, and discrimination.

A great portion of today's society feel that children should not be exposed to this disease if it may be prevented. Therefore they attack these gay parents seeing that AIDS is the "gay" disease. Society has to realize that anyone may contract it and there is no one in the world that is *immune*（免疫）to it. It is up to gay parents as well as straight parents to assure in preventing the contraction of this disease to any child. Also to protect themselves from contracting it, the loss of a parent is *traumatizing*（使受心理创伤）to a child.

Another main issue against gay parenting is the concern of safety for their children. There is a concern that children of homosexuals will be *harassed*（骚扰）by their peers (Brooks, 362). Many people in today's society have a negative stereotypical attitude towards homosexuals. This influence passed onto their children in turn is then *taken out*（发泄）on peers. This especially affects those who have gay parents. That child may be harassed at school, both mentally and physically, and *teased*（戏弄）constantly. This may then affect the child psychologically, emotionally, and physically, either then or later in life. Children have increasingly become more cruel with peers and this certainly does *take its toll*（造成危害）on the child being harassed, whether the effects are visible or not.

The child living with homosexual parents may not only be harassed for having gay parents, but also for being gay themselves. Many have the idea that children who grow up in a gay home become gay themselves. They believe this to be true in that the child learns the parents' ways and wants to be just like their role model, their parent. People have to realize that in today's society children tease one another for the oddest reasons, if there is not a reason to tease or *gang up on someone*（联合起来对付某人）, someone is sure to find or make up something just to have something to do.

In conclusion, in analyzing all of the facts, both supporting and refuting the controversial topic of gay parenting, I felt that the stronger side proved to be that of supporting gay parenting. The information gathered on negative stereotypes against gay parenting proved to be incorrect and inconclusive. Much of the information *refuting*（反驳）gay parenting was not based on concrete facts or studies. The issue of AIDS, safety, and gender identity are all issues that affect heterosexual headed families as often as homosexual headed families. It is how the family overcomes these issues that is important. If these families are successful this will create a closer and stronger family tie.

In evaluating the issue of gay parenting, one would find it difficult to gather information refuting the issue, majority of the information that I came across was supporting. One will notice that literature and attitudes have changed and are progressing when dealing with homosexuality. More and more individuals are beginning to accept or *come to terms with* (妥协,屈服) this controversial topic. Gay and lesbian parenting should be treated as any other parenting style would be treated. If they are willing and able to love and provide adequately for these children, then society should allow them to do just that. Evidence proves that there is no difference between a child from a gay parent family to a heterosexual parent family, and therefore there is no reason why these family units should be treated so differently.

"I am against gay marriage because I believe that marriage is for men and women. I don't support gay *adoption* (收养) either because I believe that society ought to aim for the ideal, and the ideal is for a man and a woman to adopt children." — *George W. Bush*, *Meet the Press*, 11/21/99

Retrieved from *http*://www. antiessays. com/free-essays/1012. html

I. Reading comprehension.

1. According to the passage, the author suggests that _____
   A) gay-parenting is so abnormal that people should act to oppose it.
   B) he has to remain neutral about gay-parenting for its controversy.
   C) the majority of the society are still hesitant in accepting gay-parenting.
   D) more and more evidence indicates that great progress has been made in the acceptance of gay-parenting as a new family style.

2. Why does the author quote President Bush's statement?
   A) To show Bush's attitude toward gay-parenting.
   B) To show the difficulty for gay-parenting to be legally recognized in the U. S. .
   C) To support the arguments against gay-parenting.
   D) To strengthen his own attitude toward gay-parenting.

3. According to the passage, those who approve of gay-parenting argue that _____
   A) it's reasonable for gay-parenting family to be refused in terms of its children because children's gender identity will be affected by their lesbian or gay parents.
   B) gay-parenting families do not meet the social norms of a family.
   C) Children growing up in a gay-parenting family tend to develop emotional and psychological problems.
   D) what makes up a family unit and leads to its prosperity is determined by the efforts both parters make rather than by their sexual preference.

4. According to the passage, which of the following is not mentioned as a view held by those who are opposed to gay-parenting?

A) Homosexual parents are unable to take good care of their children and bring them up to be normal kids

B) Children living in gay-parenting households will face greater danger of being exposed to AIDS.

C) Children of lesbian and gay parents will not develop appropriate gender identity or behavior.

D) Children need a balanced knowledge from both normal parents in dealing with different situations at different stages of their life.

5. In Pro Position part, what does Weston's statement imply?

A) Innovation is the most important element in promoting the development of society.

B) Cultural hegemony is inevitable in our society.

C) Gay-parenting families should be accepted as a result of social development like other social innovations.

D) Whether gay-parenting families should be given government support is controversial

II. Topics for further discussion.

1. What do you think are the qualities that parents should possess for a healthy growth of children?

2. Do you think a healthy growth of a child is largely determined by parents?

3. How do you think people differ in their attitude towards a single-parent family and a gay-parent family?

III. Decide whether the following statements are True or False based on the text.

1. According to the author, gay and lesbian headed families are acceptable as a new family form. (   )

2. According to those in pro position, people have every reason to believe that gay parenting families will have more problems than other forms of family. (   )

3. According to those in favor of gay parenting, gays and lesbians will perform as well as other heterosexual parents do in supporting the emotional and physical needs of their children. (   )

4. According to those in con position, in almost every culture of the world, people have to depend on 'gender' to maintain a personal identity. (   )

5. According to the author, there will be an increasing number of people accepting gay parenting. (   )

Passage Two

Universal Declaration of Human Rights
联合国颁布的《世界人权宣言》

On December 10, 1948 the General Assembly of the United Nations adopted and proclaimed the Universal Declaration of Human Rights as a common standard of achievement for all peoples and all nations and that every individual and every organ of society, keeping this Declaration constantly in mind, shall strive by teaching and education to promote respect for these rights and freedoms and by progressive measures, national and international, to secure their universal and effective recognition and observance, both among the peoples of Member States themselves and among the peoples of territories under their jurisdiction (管辖范围).

Article 1.

All human beings are born free and equal in dignity and rights. They are *endowed with reason and conscience* (赋有理性和良心) and should act towards one another in a spirit of brotherhood.

Article 2.

Everyone is *entitled to* (有资格) all the rights and freedoms set forth in this Declaration, without distinction of any kind, such as race, color, sex, language, religion, political or other opinion, national or social origin, property, birth or other status. Furthermore, no distinction shall be made on the basis of the political, *jurisdictional or international status* (行政的或者国际的地位) of the country or territory to which a person belongs, whether it be independent, trust, non-self-governing or under any other limitation of sovereignty.

Article 3.

Everyone has the right to life, liberty and security of person.

Article 4.

No one shall be held in slavery or *servitude* (奴役); slavery and the slave trade shall be prohibited in all their forms.

Article 5.

No one shall be subjected to torture or to cruel, inhuman or *degrading treatment* (侮辱性的待遇) or punishment.

Article 6.

Everyone has the right to recognition everywhere as a person before the law.

Article 7.

All are equal before the law and are entitled without any discrimination to equal protection of the law. All are entitled to equal protection against any discrimination in violation of this Declaration and against any incitement to such discrimination.

Article 8.

Everyone has the right to *an effective remedy* (有效的补救) by the competent *national tribunals* (国家法庭) for acts violating the fundamental rights granted him by the constitution or by law.

Article 9.

No one shall be subjected to arbitrary arrest, detention or exile.

Article 10.

Everyone is entitled in full equality to a fair and public hearing by an independent and impartial tribunal, in the determination of his rights and obligations and of any criminal charge against him.

Article 11.

(1) Everyone charged with *a penal offence* (刑事控告) has the right to be presumed innocent until proved guilty according to law in a public trial at which he has had all the guarantees necessary for his defense.

(2) No one shall be held guilty of any penal offence on account of any act or omission which did not constitute a penal offence, under national or international law, at the time when it was committed. Nor shall a heavier penalty be imposed than the one that was applicable at the time the penal offence was committed.

Article 12.

No one shall be subjected to arbitrary interference with his privacy, family, home or correspondence, nor to attacks upon his honor and reputation. Everyone has the right to the protection of the law against such interference or attacks.

Article 13.

(1) Everyone has the right to freedom of movement and residence within the borders of each state.

(2) Everyone has the right to leave any country, including his own, and to return to his country.

Article 14.

(1) Everyone has the right to seek and to enjoy in other countries *asylum*（庇护）from persecution.

(2) This right may not be *invoked*（援用）in the case of prosecutions genuinely arising from non-political crimes or from acts contrary to the purposes and principles of the United Nations.

Article 15.

(1) Everyone has the right to a nationality.

(2) No one shall be arbitrarily deprived of his nationality nor denied the right to change his nationality.

Article 16.

(1) Men and women of full age, without any limitation due to race, nationality or religion, have the right to marry and to found a family. They are entitled to equal rights as to marriage, during marriage and *at its dissolution*（在解除婚约时）.

(2) Marriage shall be entered into only with the free and full consent of the intending spouses.

(3) The family is the natural and fundamental group unit of society and is entitled to protection by society and the State.

Article 17.

(1) Everyone has the right to own property alone as well as in association with others.

(2) No one shall be arbitrarily deprived of his property.

Article 18.

Everyone has the right to *freedom of thought*, *conscience and religion*（思想、良心和宗教自由）; this right includes freedom to change his religion or belief, and freedom, either alone or in community with others and in public or private, to manifest his religion or belief in teaching, practice, worship and observance.

Article 19.

Everyone has the right to freedom of opinion and expression; this right includes freedom to hold opinions without interference and to seek, receive and impart information and ideas through any media and regardless of frontiers.

Article 20.

(1) Everyone has the right to freedom of peaceful assembly and association.

(2) No one may be compelled to belong to an association.

Article 21.

(1) Everyone has the right to take part in the government of his country, directly or through freely chosen representatives.

(2) Everyone has the right of equal access to public service in his country.

(3) The will of the people shall be the basis of the authority of government; this will shall be expressed in periodic and genuine elections which shall be by universal and *equal suffrage* (平等的投票权) and shall be held by secret vote or by equivalent free voting procedures.

Article 22.

Everyone, as a member of society, has the right to social security and is entitled to realization, through national effort and international co-operation and in accordance with the organization and resources of each State, of the economic, social and cultural rights indispensable for his dignity and the free development of his personality.

Article 23.

(1) Everyone has the right to work, to free choice of employment, to just and favourable conditions of work and to protection against unemployment.

(2) Everyone, without any discrimination, has the right to equal pay for equal work.

(3) Everyone who works has the right to just and favourable *remuneration* (报酬) ensuring for himself and his family an existence worthy of human dignity, and supplemented, if necessary, by other means of social protection.

(4) Everyone has the right to form and to join trade unions for the protection of his interests.

Article 24.

Everyone has the right to rest and leisure, including reasonable limitation of working hours and periodic holidays with pay.

Article 25.

(1) Everyone has the right to a standard of living adequate for the health and well-being of himself and of his family, including food, clothing, housing and medical care and necessary social services, and the right to security in the event of unemployment, sickness, disability, widowhood, old age or other lack of livelihood in circumstances beyond his control.

(2) Motherhood and childhood are entitled to special care and assistance. All children, whether born in or out of wedlock, shall enjoy the same social protection.

Article 26.

(1) Everyone has the right to education. Education shall be free, at least in the elementary and fundamental stages. Elementary education shall be compulsory. Technical and professional education shall be made generally available and higher education shall be equally accessible to all on the basis of merit.

(2) Education shall be directed to the full development of the human personality and to the strengthening of respect for human rights and fundamental freedoms. It shall promote understanding, tolerance and friendship among all nations, racial or religious groups, and shall further the activities of the United Nations for the maintenance of peace.

(3) Parents have a prior right to choose the kind of education that shall be given to their children.

Article 27.

(1) Everyone has the right freely to participate in the cultural life of the community, to enjoy the arts and to share in scientific advancement and its benefits.

(2) Everyone has the right to the protection of the moral and material interests resulting from any scientific, literary or artistic production of which he is the author.

Article 28.

Everyone is entitled to a social and international order in which the rights and freedoms set forth in this Declaration can be fully realized.

Article 29.

(1) Everyone has duties to the community in which alone the free and full development of his personality is possible.

(2) In the exercise of his rights and freedoms, everyone shall be subject only to such limitations as are determined by law solely for the purpose of securing due recognition and respect for the rights and freedoms of others and of meeting the just requirements of morality, public order and the general welfare in a democratic society.

(3) These rights and freedoms may in no case be exercised contrary to the purposes and principles of the United Nations.

Article 30.

Nothing in this Declaration may be interpreted as implying for any State, group or person any right to engage in any activity or to perform any act aimed at the destruction of any of the rights and freedoms set forth herein.

Retrieved from *http*://www. un. org/Overview/rights. html

Decide whether the following statements are True or False.

1. Individuals should have free access to any other country even when they commit crimes in their own country. (   )
2. The society and the State have the obligation to protect every family from family violence. (   )
3. Men and women, because of different division of labor, should be offered different job opportunities. (   )
4. Governments should provide social protection to individuals and their families. (   )
5. The society should offer and choose the kind of education for children. (   )

Answer the following question based on the text.

Can you find any supports in the Declaration for the constitutionality of the same-sex marriage?

Unit 7

Winston Smith

本单元课文综述

Text 精读 课文"Winston Smith"节选自英国著名小说家奥威尔的《1984》。该书堪称世界文坛最著名的反乌托邦、反极权的政治讽喻小说。他在小说中创造的"老大哥"、"双重思想"、"新话"等词汇都已收入权威的英语词典,影响深远。在《1984》中我们看到一个科学的专制可以是如何牢固,人性的脆弱又是多么的令人绝望。

Passage One 泛读 从 *Brave New World*《美丽新世界》中,我们可看到人类在科技所提供的自由之前迷失自我,甚至繁育后代也依靠试管在流水线上完成。这两部巨著同属于"反乌托邦三部曲"(Dystopia Fiction)系列。

Passage Two 泛读 *Animal Farm*《动物庄园》和《1984》并称为乔治·奥威尔最重要的代表作。《动物庄园》用动物对人类抗争后自建家园来再现前苏联的整个历史情形。《1984》着重于内心,入木三分地刻划主人公被洗脑,最后变成奴隶的一个心理改变过程。而《动物庄园》则从全局的角度勾画了整个洗脑的操作流程。

ext   **Winston Smith**

George Orwell

It was a bright cold day in April, and the clocks were striking thirteen. Winston Smith, his chin **nuzzled** into his breast in an effort to escape the vile wind, slipped quickly through the glass doors of Victory Mansions, though not quickly enough to prevent a swirl of **gritty** dust from entering along with him.

The hallway smelt of boiled cabbage and old **rag mats**. At one end of it a coloured poster, too large for indoor display, had been **tacked** to the wall. It depicted simply an enormous face, more than a metre wide: the face of a man of about forty-five, with a heavy black moustache and **ruggedly** handsome features. Winston made for the stairs. It was no use trying the lift. Even at the best of times it was seldom working, and at present the electric current was cut off during daylight hours. It was part of the economy drive in preparation for Hate Week. The flat was seven flights up, and Winston, who was thirty-nine and had **a varicose ulcer** above his right ankle, went slowly, resting several times on the way. On each landing, opposite the **lift-shaft,** the poster with the enormous face gazed from the wall. It was one of those pictures which are so **contrived** that the eyes follow you about when you move. BIG BROTHER IS WATCHING YOU, the caption beneath it ran.

Inside the flat a fruity voice was reading out a list of figures which had something to do with the production of pig-iron. The voice came from an **oblong** metal **plaque** like a dulled mirror which formed part of the surface of the right-hand wall. Winston turned a switch and the voice sank somewhat, though the words were still distinguishable. The instrument (the telescreen, it was called) could be dimmed, but there was no way of shutting it off completely. He moved over to the window: a smallish, frail figure, the **meagreness** of his body merely emphasized by the blue overalls which were the uniform of the party. His hair was very fair, his face naturally **sanguine,** his skin roughened by coarse soap and blunt razor blades and the cold of the winter that had just ended.

Outside, even through the shut window-pane, the world looked cold. Down in the street little eddies of wind were whirling dust and torn paper into **spirals,** and though the sun was shining and the sky a harsh blue, there seemed to be no colour in anything, except the posters that were plastered everywhere. The black-mustachios' face gazed down from every commanding corner. There was one on the house-front immediately opposite. BIG BROTHER IS WATCHING YOU, the caption said, while the dark eyes looked deep into Winston's own. Down at street level another poster, torn at one corner, flapped fitfully in the wind, alternately covering and uncovering the single word INGSOC. In the far distance a helicopter skimmed down between the roofs, hovered for an instant like a bluebottle, and **darted away** again with a curving flight. It was the police patrol, **snooping into** people's windows. The patrols did not matter, however. Only the Thought Police mattered.

Behind Winston's back the voice from the telescreen was still babbling away about pig-iron and the overfulfilment of the Ninth Three-Year Plan. The telescreen received and transmitted simultaneously. Any sound that Winston made, above the level of a very low whisper, would be picked up by it, moreover, so long as he remained within the field of vision which the metal plaque commanded, he could be seen as well as heard. There was of course no way of knowing whether you were being watched at any given moment. How often, or on what system, the Thought Police plugged in on any individual wire was guesswork. It was even **conceivable** that they watched everybody all the time. But at any rate they could plug in your wire whenever they wanted to. You had to live — did live, from habit that became instinct — in the assumption that every sound you made was overheard, and, except in darkness, every movement **scrutinized.**

Winston kept his back turned to the telescreen. It was safer, though, as he well knew, even a back can be revealing. A kilometer away the Ministry of Truth, his place of work, towered vast and white above the grimy landscape. This, he thought with a sort of vague **distaste** — this was London, chief city of Airstrip One, itself the third most populous of the provinces of Oceania. He tried to squeeze out some childhood memory that should tell him whether London had always been quite like this. Were there always these **vistas** of rotting nineteenth-century houses, their sides **shored up** with baulks of timber, their windows patched with cardboard and their roofs with corrugated iron, their crazy garden walls sagging in all directions? And the bombed sites where the plaster dust **swirled** in the air and the willow-herb straggled over the heaps of rubble; and the places where the bombs had cleared a larger patch and there had **sprung up sordid** colonies of wooden dwellings like chicken-houses? But it was no use, he could not remember: nothing remained of his childhood except a series of bright-lit **tableaux** occurring against no background and mostly unintelligible.

The Ministry of Truth — Minitrue, in Newspeak — was startlingly different from any other object in sight. It was an enormous **pyramidal** structure of glittering white concrete, **soaring up**, **terrace** after terrace, 300 metres into the air. From where Winston stood it was just possible to read, picked out on its white face in elegant lettering, the three slogans of the Party:

WAR IS PEACE
FREEDOM IS SLAVERY
IGNORANCE IS STRENGTH

The Ministry of Truth contained, it was said, three thousand rooms above ground level, and corresponding **ramifications** below. Scattered about London there were just three other buildings of similar appearance and size. So completely did they **dwarf** the surrounding architecture that from the roof of Victory Mansions you could see all four of them simultaneously. They were the homes of the four Ministries between which the entire **apparatus** of government was divided. The Ministry of Truth, which concerned itself with news, entertainment, education, and the fine arts. The Ministry of Peace, which concerned itself with war. The Ministry of Love, which maintained law and order. And the Ministry of Plenty, which was responsible for economic affairs. Their names, in Newspeak: Minitrue, Minipax, Miniluv, and Miniplenty.

The Ministry of Love was the really frightening one. There were no windows in it at all. Winston had never been inside the Ministry of Love, nor within half a kilometre of it. It was a place impossible to enter except on official business, and then only by penetrating through a maze of barbed-wire entanglements, steel doors, and hidden machine-gun nests. Even the streets leading up to its outer barriers were roamed by gorilla-faced guards in black uniforms, armed with jointed **truncheons**.

Winston turned round abruptly. He had set his features into the expression of quiet optimism which it was advisable to wear when facing the telescreen. He crossed the room into the tiny kitchen. By leaving the Ministry at this time of day he had sacrificed his lunch in the canteen, and he was aware that there was no food in the kitchen except a hunk of dark-coloured bread which had got to be saved for tomorrow's breakfast. He took down from the shelf a bottle of colourless liquid with a plain white label marked VICTORY GIN. It gave off a sickly, oily smell, as of **Chinese rice-spirit.** Winston poured out nearly a teacupful, nerved himself for a shock, and gulped it down like a dose of medicine.

Instantly his face turned scarlet and the water ran out of his eyes. The stuff was like **nitric acid,** and moreover, in swallowing it one had the sensation of being hit on the back of the head with a rubber club. The next moment, however, the burning in his belly died down and the world began to look more cheerful. He took a cigarette from a crumpled packet marked VICTORY CIGARETTES and incautiously held it upright, whereupon the tobacco fell out on to the floor. With the next he was more successful. He went back to the living-room and sat down at a small table that stood to the left of the telescreen. From the table drawer he took out a penholder, a bottle of ink, and a thick, quarto-sized blank book with a red back and a marbled cover.

From《1984》，中国致公出版社 2001

New Words and Phrases

nuzzle	vt.	press close to sb./sth.　紧挨，紧贴
gritty	adj.	full of grit　含砂的，砂粒般的
rag mats		油污的破垫
tack	v.	nail sth with a tack　用平头钉钉住
ruggedly	adv.	roughly, robustly, not gently　粗糙地；粗鲁地
a varicose ulcer		静脉曲张性溃疡
lift shaft		电梯井
contrive	v.	plan cleverly or deceitfully; invent　发明，设计；谋划，策划（坏事，恶事）
oblong	n. & adj.	长方形（的）；长椭圆形（的）
plaque	n.	（建筑物，家具等上的）饰板，匾
meagerness	n.	small in quantity and poor in quality; thin　质量差，瘦，不足
sanguine		ruddy　红润的健康的红颜色的
spiral	n.	螺旋状物体
dart away		move suddenly and quickly in the specified direction　快速离去
conceivable	adj.	that can be conceived or believed　可想象的，可理解的

scrutinize	*v.*	look at or examine (sth.) carefully or thoroughly 详细检查, 仔细观察
distaste	*n.*	dislike; aversion 不喜欢, 厌恶
vistas	*n.*	(从特定角度或从两排树木或房屋间的林荫道看出去的)长条形景色;远景
shore up		to support sth. with a wooden beam 用撑柱支撑;使稳住
corrugated	*adj.*	波纹的
plaster	*n.*	灰浆;石膏
spring up		to appear, develop, grow, etc. quickly or suddenly. 突然出现
swirl	*v.*	move or flow with twists 盘旋;回绕
sordid	*adj.*	dirty and unpleasant; squalid 肮脏的,破破烂烂的
tableaux	*n.*	tableau 的复数,(动人的)画面,场景
pyramidal	*adj.*	金字塔的
soar up		to be very high or tall 高耸,屹立
terrace	*n.*	阶地;梯田;排屋
ramification	*n.*	(通常做复数)某复杂系统的部分, 分支
dwarf	*v.*	to cause to appear small in size, extent 使(某人或某物)相比之下显得小
apparatus	*n.*	complex structure of an organization 机构,组织
truncheon	*n.*	警棍
Chinese rice-spirit		中国米酒
Nitric acid		硝酸

About the author：George Orwell (pseudonym of Eric Arthur Blair) (1903 – 1950), journalist, political author and novelist, wrote *Animal Farm* (1945) and *1984* (1949); throughout his writing life. Orwell worked to achieve a balance between public and private values, between creative work and necessary labour. His major concerns were public and political, yet he was equally aware of the importance of the individual's private life and the matters of everyday existence.

乔治·奥威尔(George Orwell, 1903 — 1950),英国伟大的人道主义作家、新闻记者和社会评论家,著名的英语文体家。他为后人留下了大量的作品。《动物农庄》和《1984》销售达 4,000 万册,近 60 种语言版本,任何一部战后的严肃的或通俗的作品都难以与之相比。现代英语中有一个词叫"奥威尔现象(Orwellian)",指代某些奥威尔所描述过的社会现象。奥威尔作品主要反映两个主题:贫困和政治,而激发他写作的重要动力是良知和真诚。1950 年 1 月,奥威尔病逝,享年 46 岁。

Notes to the text

1. *1984*: is a dystopian satire of totalitarian regimes, nationalism, the class system, bureaucracy and world leader's power struggles. It is also nihilistic prophesy on the downfall of humankind. The book has proven to be a profoundly meaningful work and continues to be one of the world's most widely read and quoted novels into the twenty-first century, with its title and many phrases — such as 'Big Brother is watching you', 'newspeak' and 'doublethink' — entering popular use.

   The story starts, as the title tells us, in the year of 1984, and it takes place in England or as it is called at that time, Airstrip One. Airstrip One itself is the mainland of a huge country, called Oceania, which consists of North America, South Africa, and Australia. The country is ruled by the Party, which is led by a figure called Big Brother. The population of Oceania is divided into three parts:

   The Inner Party (app. 1% of the population)

   The Outer Party (app. 18% of the population)

   The Proles(app. 80% of the population)

   1984 is a political novel written with the purpose of warning readers in the West of the dangers of totalitarian government. Having witnessed firsthand the horrific lengths to which totalitarian governments in Spain and Russia would go in order to sustain and increase their power, Orwell designed 1984 to sound the alarm in Western nations still unsure about how to approach the rise of communism.

   本文节选自政治讽刺小说《1984》,那时德国法西斯在欧洲大陆的肆虐刚刚结束,斯大林的大清洗也已经接近尾声。这是乔治·奥威尔虚拟的一个故事,在这个虚拟的故事里有一个虚拟的人温斯顿生活在一个虚拟的"大洋国"里。故事发生在1984 年(即奥威尔创作此书时的 30 多年后)的"大洋国"。"大洋国"由老大哥实行寡头政治,由核心党员、外围党员、无产阶级三个层面组成一个几乎全封闭的国家。

   这个发生在 1984 年的英国的虚幻故事,却处处可找到现实事件的影子,对全人类的整个历史都是一场反思。《1984》写的虽然是一个近似科幻的小说:世界被分割成三个大格局(大洋国、东亚国、欧亚国),持续的争夺边界的战争,国内狂热的个人崇拜、思想奴役、篡改历史、大清洗、封闭、禁欲。这些现象在人类历史的现实中不断再现。奥威尔的绝妙之处在于把我们都知道的这层意思给形象地传达了出来,那样地生动,扣人心弦,不仅是对历史的总结,也是对未来的警示。

2. **Winston Smith** 主人公温斯顿 Winston Smith is a fictional character and the protagonist of George Orwell's 1949 novel *1984*. His name has become a metaphor for the man in the street, the unwitting and innocent victim of political machination. In the book, Winston is a clerk for the Ministry of Truth, where his job is to rewrite historical documents so that

they match the current party line, which changes on a daily basis.

　　小说主人公温斯顿是个四十岁左右的外围党员,在真理部工作,而真理部的职责就是负责造谣,不断地篡改历史,使历史完全接近于真实,与现实毫无差别。温斯顿干的就是这项工作。"全部历史都象一张不断刮干净重写的羊皮纸。这一工作完成以后,无论如何都无法证明曾经发生过伪造历史的事。最后连他也不知道到底何为真实"。温斯顿的家与所有私人居室一样,有一个无孔不入的现代化设备,叫做"电子屏幕"。每个房间右首墙上都装有这样一面长方形的金属镜子,可以视听两用,也可以发号施令,室内一言一语,一举一动,无时无刻不受这面照妖镜的监视和支配。平时无事,电子屏幕就没完没了地播送大军进行曲、政治运动的口号、"第九个三年计划"超额胜利完成的消息。这些噪音由中央枢纽控制,个人无法关掉。

3. **"Hate Week"** 仇恨周：Hate Week is an event in George Orwell's novel *1984*, designed to increase the hatred for the current enemy of the Party, whichever of the two opposing superstates that maybe. Hate Week is officially celebrated from April 4th to April 10th. The events during that time include waxwork displays, military parades, speeches and lectures. New slogans are also coined and new songs are written. The theme of the Hate Week is called the Hate Song.

4. **"Big Brother"** "老大哥"：not a real person. All-present as he is, all-powerful and forever watching, he is only seen on TV. Although his picture glares out from huge posters that shout, BIG BROTHER IS WATCHING YOU, nobody sees Big Brother in person.

　　小说中党和国家的最高领导人不叫总统,也不叫国王,而叫"老大哥",听起来就像公仆、人民的儿子一样亲近,但人们所受的并不是一种慈祥的统治。社会的根本信念是:老大哥全能,党一贯正确。"老大哥"从不露面,他的大幅照片户内户外却到处张贴。炯炯有神的眼睛,紧盯着臣民。

5. **INGSOC** 新社：Ingsoc is the ideology of the totalitarian government of Oceania. Ingsoc is Newspeak（新话）for **"English Socialism"**.

6. **Thought Police** 思想警察：Thought police is the secret police. It is the job of the Thought Police to uncover and punish thoughtcrime and thought criminals, using psychology and omnipresent surveillance from telescreens to find and eliminate members

of society who were capable of the mere thought of challenging ruling authority.

思想警察身着便衣,日以继夜地监视着人们的一举一动,面部表情的改变都有可能引起怀疑。在街上、在屋内,甚至在卧室,到处都安装了窃听器和监视器。思想警察可以随时使独立思考的思想犯"失踪"。

7. **Newspeak**(新话): artificial language of official communication in George Orwell's novel '1984', from new + speak. Frequently applied to propagandistic warped English

在《1984》里,政府利用不断更新出版的"新话辞典"规定人们只能说什么话。"新话"是世界上"唯一词汇量"在逐年减少的语言。其全部目的就是要缩小思想的范围。

8. **WAR IS PEACE**　战争即和平
FREEDOM IS SLAVERY　自由即奴役
IGNORANCE IS STRENGTH　无知即力量

These words are the official slogans of the Party. Because it is introduced so early in the novel, this creed serves as the reader's first introduction to the idea of doublethink. By weakening the independence and strength of individuals' minds and forcing them to live in a constant state of propaganda-induced fear, the Party is able to force its subjects to accept anything it decrees, even if it is entirely illogical — for instance, the Ministry of Peace (和平部) is in charge of waging war, the Ministry of Love (仁爱部) is in charge of political torture, and the Ministry of Truth (真理部) is in charge of doctoring history books to reflect the Party's ideology.

小说中主人公温斯顿服务的机关是"真理部"。政府除了"真理部"以外还有三大部:"和平部"、"仁爱部"、"富裕部"。和平部负责战争,真理部负责造谣,仁爱部负责拷打,富裕部负责挨饿。四大机构各占据一座300米高的金字塔式建筑。建筑外边大书特书党的三大原则:"战争即和平"、"自由即奴役"、"愚昧即力量"。

9. **Totalitarian** (极权主义): a modern autocratic government in which the state involves itself in all facets of society, including the daily life of its citizens. A totalitarian government seeks to control not only all economic and political matters but the attitudes, values, and beliefs of its population, erasing the distinction between state and society. The citizen's duty to the state becomes the primary concern of the community, and the goal of the state is the replacement of existing society with a perfect society.

Various totalitarian systems, however, have different ideological goals. For example, of the states most commonly described as totalitarian — the Soviet Union under Stalin and Nazi Germany sought the universal fulfillment of humankind through the establishment of a classless society; German National Socialism, on the other hand, attempted to establish the superiority of the so-called Aryan race.

Exercises

I. Answer these questions based on Text and the words and expressions listed below are for your reference.

1. **In "1984" what kind of picture of that time did Orwell draw for us?**

   a totalitarian future/a negative Utopia/no personality nor identity/follow governments without contest/big brother is all knowing and always correct

2. **Although all the events in "1984" take place in the future, there are a couple of elements and symbols taken from the present and past, can you find out any of them through this chosen excerpt?**

   totalitarian/superstates/socialist/cold war/Oceania/USA/Eurasia/Russia/Eastasia/China

3. **How does technology affect the Party's ability to control its citizens? In what ways does the Party employ technology throughout the book?**

   blare constant propaganda and observe citizens/

   Telescreen: security camera-like devices constant monitoring

4. **Discuss the concept of "Newspeak". Give concrete examples of "Newspeak" from the text.**

   "The only language in the world whose vocabulary gets smaller every year."

   removing /the ideas of freedom, rebellion

5. **How important is "Newspeak" to the Party's control of Oceania?**

   thought and language/rebellion and control

6. **The name of the hero Winston Smith is deliberately-chosen by the author. What does the author intend to imply?**

   World War II/England leader

7. **Try to figure out what Orwell had in mind when he created "Big Brother".**

8. **Give a brief description of the hero, Winston Smith.**

   physical appearance/character

9. **What do you think of the Party's slogans (War is Peace, Freedom is Slavery, Ignorance is Strength) in this novel?**

II. Further questions for discussion.

1. Have you ever read anything about "Utopia"? What do you think of a Utopian society? Could it possibly be a reality in future?

2. What do you think of the "Thought Police"?

3. Comment on "Newspeak".

4. What writing techneques does the author employ to depict the hero?

III. Vocabulary study.

1. Word in Use.

1) **nuzzle**: *v.* press close to sb. /sth. , esp. by pushing gently with head or nose. 紧挨,紧贴（尤指用头或鼻子轻拱）

The horse nuzzled my shoulder.

The dog nuzzled up to his master.

The rabbit is nuzzling into the snow.

2) **contrive**: *v.* plan (sth) cleverly or deceitfully; invent; design 谋划或策划（某事）

He contrived to make matters worse, ie unintentionally made them worse by what he did.

The author contrived a clever plot.

He contrived to gain their votes.

3) **conceivable**: *adj.* that can be conceived or believed; imaginable. 可想到的,可相信可想象的

We tried it in every conceivable combination.

He couldn't conceivably have (ie I don't believe he could have) meant what he said.

It is hardly conceivable that she should do such a thing.

4) **scrutinize**: *v.* to look at or examine (sth) carefully or thoroughly. 仔细检查;详细观察

He scrutinized the coin with a magnifying-glass.

The judge scrutinized all the documents relating to the trial.

The candidates ask for a close scrutiny of the election results.

5) **spring up**: appear, develop, grow, etc. quickly or suddenly 突然出现

A breeze sprang up as we were returning.

Industries sprang up in the suburbs.

Weeds are springing up everywhere.

6) **apparatus**: *n.* equipment, a political organization or an underground political movement. 器械, 设备;机关, 机构, 政党组织

medical apparatus

the state apparatus

the apparatus of government

7) **snoop**: *vi.* to prowl or pry; go about in sneaking 窥探, 窥视

Why were you snooping around (about) in my room?

She is always snooping into other people's businesses.

US information security company Cyber-Ark surveyed 300 senior IT professionals, and found that one-third admitted to secretly snooping, while 47 percent said they had accessed information that was not relevant to their role.

8) **dwarf**: *vt.* to cause to appear or seem small in size, extent, character, etc. , as by being much larger or better：使变小

He dwarfed all his rivals in athletic ability.

The oaks were dwarfed from lack of moisture.

This year's debt dwarfs that of last year.

9) **soar**：be very high or tall. 矗立 **Soar up**: rise rapidly；耸立；崛起

Cliffs soar above the sea.

Our spirits soared.

The stock market soared after the cease — fire was announced.

10) **dart**：*v.* to move swiftly；spring or start suddenly and run swiftly：猛冲,突进

A mouse darted out of the closet and ran across the room.

He darted his eyes around the room.

His forefinger darted in all directions as he spoke.

2. Word Distinctions.

1) **contrive**；**devise**

contrive 表示策划、设计时,常含贬义或不诚实之意（often disproving or dishonest）：

如课文中的' It was one of those pictures which are so contrived...'精心谋划

devise 则为中性词。

选择以上适当的词填空：

In the end, the politician _____ a plot to seize the power.

The economist _____ a new mechanism to improve the system.

He _____ to get into the concert without a ticket.

Can you _____ a better approach to have the problem sorted out?

Because of the timing, I'm sure the salary freeze is deliberately _____ rather than coincident.

2) **scatter**；**spread**

scatter, spread, 均含使分散、使散开之意

scatter：指向不同方向散开；spread：指一直延伸、蔓延,侧重遍及。

选择以上适当的词填空：

The protesters _____ at the sound of gunshots.

The fire _____ very rapidly because of the strong wind.

A few small towns _____ across the vast land that was once covered with primitive forests.

The AIDS virus has _____ through contact with blood and other body fluids.

_____ showers are expected this afternoon off the Florida coast and the launch of the space shuttle is to be postponed.

The financial storm clouds continue to _____ around the world.

3. **Decide the meanings of the following words from the context by matching each word in Column A with the word or expression in Column B that is similar in meaning.**

A	B
1）meager	a. representation of a picture or scene by a silent and motionless group of people, esp. on stage
2）sordid	b. part of a complex structure
3）soar	c. having a red complexion; optimistic
4）ramifications	d. dirty and unpleasant
5）spring up	e. imaginable
6）shore up	f. appear suddenly
7）rugged	g. rough; not refined or gentle
8）conceivable	h. support sth with a wooden beam
9）sanguine	i. very tall or high
10）tableau	j. small in quantity and poor in quality; thin

4. **Try to write a brief story with the following words and phrases.**

dwarf, soar, timber, window-pane, hallway, flat, barbed-wire, barriers, scatter, nests, grounded level,

IV. Translation.

1. **Put the following Chinese expressions into English.**

1）一阵沙土 2）喋喋不休 3）在某一特定时间里 4）硬着头皮(强忍着做某事)

5）在远处   6）因公   7）尘土飞扬   8）杂草丛生

2. **Put the following Chinese sentences into English with the words or phrases in the bracket.**

1）狗在沙发上依偎着我。(nuzzle up to/against)

2）他们设法逃税。(contrive)

3）我突然起了疑心。(spring up)

4）律师必须仔细审阅与案子有关的所有文件。(scrutinize)

5）我们的小船跟大游艇一比显得很小。(dwarf)

6）摩天大楼拔地而起高耸入云。(soar up)

7）他们知道他在附近。他们已经窥察他好几天了。(snoop)

8）他将胶卷交给间谍组织。(apparatus)

3. **Put the following Chinese paragraphs into English.**

大量的非人性化、极权政府、世界末日、网络遗传技术、社会混乱和普遍的城市暴力是诸多反乌托邦电影的共同主题。他们勇敢地揭示着这些未来可能呈现的凶兆。

反乌托邦虚构了一个与乌托邦理想完全相反的社会。在乌托邦构建的理想里,世界臻于完善,政治和科技设施健全。世界摆脱了混乱、战争和饥饿的威胁,人们的个性得以充分发挥,自由被放在第一位。

相反的,反乌托邦的未来充斥着贫困和极权个体对世界的强权统治。这一类型的电影常常构建出一个虚拟的宇宙,以人工技术的进步、人为的灾难或者阶级革命这些特殊的环境作为大背景。

4. **Put the following quotes into Chinese.**

1) Men are freest when they are most unconscious of freedom. The shout is a rattling of chains, always was. —— D. H. Lawrence

2) Freedom is the freedom to say that two plus two make four. If that is granted, all else follows. —— George Orwell

3) Truth is beautiful without doubt, and so are lies. —— Emerson

4) Respect for the liberty of others is not a natural impulse in most men. —— Bertrand Russell

5) Smokers and non-smokers cannot be equally free in the same railway carriage. —— Bernard Shaw

5. **Translate the following passage into Chinese.**

He picked up the children's history book and looked at the portrait of Big Brother which formed its frontispiece. The hypnotic eyes gazed into his own. It was as though some huge force were pressing down upon you — something that penetrated inside your skull, battering against your brain, frightening you out of your beliefs, persuading you, almost, to deny the evidence of your senses. In the end the Party would announce that two and two made five, and you would have to believe it. It was inevitable that they should make that claim sooner or later: the logic of their position demanded it. Not merely the validity of experience, but the very existence of external reality, was tacitly denied by their philosophy. The heresy of heresies was common sense. And what was terrifying was not that they would kill you for thinking otherwise, but that they might be right. For, after all, how do we know that two and two make four? Or that the force of gravity works? Or that the past is unchangeable? If both the past and the external world exist only in the mind, and if the mind itself is controllable what then?

V. Comment on the structure of the text.

The narrator of the book is "Third Person Limited"(有限第三人称). The protagonist is Winston Smith, a member of the Outer Party, working in the Records Department of the Ministry of Truth, rewriting and altering records, such as newspaper-articles, of the past.

The third person limited omniscient (全知) is a narrative mode. In this mode, the reader and writer observe the situation from the outside through the senses and thoughts of a single character, although that focal character may shift throughout the course of any given narrative. Furthermore, there is no implied fictional intermediary between the reader and the story, as there would be in the case of a fictional newspaper article with an implied fictional reporter.

Although first person fictional narratives are popular as well, the third person is seen as the current preferred voice in fiction, with the prominent exception of most detective and some police procedural novels.

While an omniscient point of view can change viewpoint characters (视点人物) instantly, the limited omniscient point of view narrative limits narration to what can be known, seen, thought, or judged from a single character's perspective. Thus, the narration is limited in the same way a first person narrative might be, but the text is in third person.

Extended Exercises

1. **In the following article, some paragraphs have been removed. Choose the most suitable paragraph from the list A-E to fit into each of the numbered gaps. There is ONE paragraph which does not fit in any of the gaps.**

George Orwell

George Orwell was born Eric Arthur Blair at Motihari, Bengal, India. His father, Richard Walmesley Blair, was a minor customs official in the opium department of the Indian Civil Service. When Orwell was 4 years old, his family returned to England, where they settled at Henley, a village near London. His father soon returned to India. When Orwell was 8 years old, he was sent to a private preparatory school in Sussex. He later claimed that his experiences there determined his views on the English class system. From there he went by scholarship to two private secondary schools: Wellington for one term and Eton for 4 1/2 years.

1) _____

In the first 6 months after his decision, Orwell went on what he thought of as an expedition to the East End of London to become acquainted with the poor people of England. As a base, he rented a room in Notting Hill. In the spring he rented a room in a working-class district of Paris. It seems clear that his main objective was to establish himself as a writer, and the choice of Paris was characteristic of the period. Orwell wrote two novels, both lost, during his stay in Paris, and he published a few articles in French and English. After stints as a kitchen porter and dishwasher and a bout with pneumonia, he returned to England toward the end of 1929.

2) _____

Orwell's *Down and Out* was issued in 1933. During the next 3 years he supported himself by teaching, reviewing, and clerking in a bookshop and began spending longer periods away from his parents' Suffolk home. In 1934 he published Burmese Days. The plot of this novel concerns personal intrigue among an isolated group of Europeans in an Eastern station. Two more novels followed: *A Clergyman's Daughter* (1935) and *Keep the Aspidistra Flying* (1936).

3) _____

In July 1936 the Spanish Civil War broke out. By the end of that autumn, Orwell was readying himself to go to Spain to gather material for articles and perhaps to take part in the war. After his arrival in Barcelona, he joined the militia of the POUM (Partido Obrero de Unificacion Marxista) and served with them in action in January 1937. Transferring to the British Independent Labour party contingent serving with the POUM militia, Orwell was promoted first to corporal and then to lieutenant before being wounded in the middle of May. During his convalescence, the POUM was declared illegal, and he fled into France in June. His experiences in Spain had made him into a revolutionary socialist.

After his return to England, Orwell began writing *Homage to Catalonia* (1938), which completed his disengagement from the orthodox left. He then wished to return to India to write a book, but he became ill with tuberculosis. He entered a sanatorium where he remained until late in the summer of 1938. Orwell spent the following winter in Morocco, where he wrote *Coming Up for Air* (1939). After he returned to England, Orwell authored several of his best-known essays. These include the essays on Dickens and on boys' weeklies and "Inside the Whale."

4) _____

The year 1943 was an important one in Orwell's life for several reasons. His mother died in March; he left the BBC to become literary editor of the Tribune; and he began book reviewing on a more regular basis. But the most important event occurred late that year, when he commenced the writing of Animal Farm. Orwell had completed this satire by February 1944, but several publishers rejected it on political grounds. It finally appeared in August 1945. This fantasy relates what happens to animals who free themselves and then are again enslaved through violence and fraud.

Toward the end of World War II, Orwell traveled to France, Germany, and Austria as a reporter. His wife died in March 1945. The next year he settled on Jura off the coast of Scotland, with his youngest sister as his housekeeper.

5) _____

Orwell entered a London hospital in September 1949 and the next month married Sonia Brownell. He died in London on Jan. 21, 1950.

A: Orwell used his parents' home in Suffolk as a base, still attempting to establish himself as a writer. He earned his living by teaching and by writing occasional articles, while he completed several versions of his first book, *Down and Out* in London and Paris.

This novel recorded his experiences in the East End and in Paris, and as he was earning his living as a teacher when it was scheduled for publication, he preferred to publish it under a pseudonym. From a list of four possible names submitted to his publisher, he chose "George Orwell" The Orwell is a Suffolk river.

B: Orwell then joined the Indian Imperial Police, receiving his training in Burma, where he served from 1922 to 1927. While home on leave in England, Orwell made the important decision not to return to Burma. His resignation from the Indian Imperial Police became effective on Jan. 1, 1928. He had wanted to become a writer since his adolescence, and he had come to believe that the Imperial Police was in this respect an unsuitable profession. Later evidence also suggests that he had come to understand the imperialism which he was serving and had rejected it.

C: In the spring of 1936 Orwell moved to Wallington, Hertfordshire, and several months later married Eileen O'Shaughnessy, a teacher and journalist. His reputation up to this time, as writer and journalist, was based mainly on his accounts of poverty and hard times. His next book was a commission in this direction. *The Left Book Club* authorized him to write an inquiry into the life of the poor and unemployed. *The Road to Wigan Pier* (1937) was divided into two parts. The first was typical reporting, but the second part was an essay on class and socialism. It marked Orwell's birth as a political writer, an identity that lasted for the rest of his life.

D: By now, Orwell's health was steadily deteriorating. Renewed tuberculosis early in 1947 did not prevent the composition of the first draft of his masterpiece, *Nineteen Eighty-four*. The second draft was written in 1948 during several attacks of the disease. By the end of 1948 Orwell was seriously ill. *Nineteen Eighty-four* (1949) is an elaborate satire on modern politics, prophesying a world perpetually laid waste by warring dictators.

E: Orwell's singleness of purpose in pursuit of his material and the uncompromising honesty that defined him both as a man and as a writer made him critical of intellectuals whose political viewpoints struck him as dilettante. Thus, though a writer of the left, he wrote the most savage criticism of his generation against left-wing authors, and his strong stand against communism resulted from his experience of its methods gained as a fighter in the Spanish Civil War.

F: After World War II began, Orwell believed that "now we are in this bloody war we have got to win it and I would like to lend a hand." The army, however, rejected him as physically unfit, but later he served for a period in the home guard and as a fire watcher. The Orwells moved to London in May 1940. In early 1941 he commenced writing "*London Letters*" for Partisan Review, and in August he joined the British Broadcasting Corporation (BBC) as a producer in the Indian section. He remained in this position until 1943.

2. Identify the six ways of keeping fit between summer and autumn by grouping the following numbered paragraphs into effective sections and choose the most suitable subheading from the list A-F for each section.

Six Ways to Keep Fit Between Summer and Autumn

1) It is easy to become ill during the transition from summer to autumn. There are six pieces of advice on how to stay healthy during the changing of the seasons.

2) By making subtle changes in your daily life, you may be able to improve your health. For instance, if you eat vegetables that are rich in vitamins, you will improve your immune system. Hou Yurui, vice-secretary-general of the China Cuisine Association (CCA), and Liu Yinghua, physician-in-charge of the Nutrition Department of the General Hospital of the People's Liberation Army, or Hospital 301, have provided the following suggestions on how to keep fit between summer and autumn.

3) As the weather changes, you should take steps to improve your immune system. To prevent colds, you should eat vegetables that contain vitamin C.

4) Doctors who practice traditional Chinese medicine (TCM) refer to cauliflower as "white treasure," as its vitamin C content is three or four times higher than that of Chinese cabbage and soybean sprouts, and two times greater than that of oranges and tangerines. Cauliflower will help you prevent colds and some other respiratory diseases, and it will help clean your blood vessels.

5) Lettuce, which is rich in iodine, improves metabolism. There is greater nutrition in lettuce leaves compared with the stems. If you have a cough, you should eat more lettuce leaves.

6) As the weather turns cool, you might feel like eating fish and meat. However, your stomach might have a difficult time digesting too many rich foods within a short period, especially if your stomach adjusted to light foods during the summer. Therefore, you should eat some vegetables to improve digestion.

7) Fragrant-flowered garlic, which contains carotene, protein and coarse fiber, is the best option, as it helps prevent indigestion, improve the functions of the spleen, and sharpen the appetite.

8) Coriander, known for its unique flavor, helps stimulate the appetite and promote digestion. According to TCM theories, the vegetable can warm your stomach and bile, and it can invigorate the functions of the stomach, For instance, if you suffer from a stomachache, you can eat some coriander to ease the pain.

9) As it is dry during the early autumn, you should drink enough water and eat enough vegetables and fruit; otherwise, you might suffer from excessive internal heat, with such symptoms as oral ulcer and inflammation. Spinaches, which is rich in riboflavin, may prevent and cure canker sores, cheilitis, glossitis and dermatitis. Tomatoes help relieve

internal heat and fever, promote the secretion of saliva and quench thirst. They can also cure some illnesses, such as poor appetite, mouth ulcers and bleeding gums.

10) As summer changes to autumn, the temperature will fluctuate throughout the day, as it is usually hot at noon and cool in the morning and evening. This might affect the endocrines and nervous systems of some people, especially some elderly people who have a difficult time adjusting to such changes. As a result, they might suffer from insomnia.

11) If you want to improve the quality of your sleep, you should eat celery. Vegetables that contain vitamins B and C and various trace elements, such as carotene and zinc(Zn), can help reduce blood pressure and cholesterol, and can help you relax before bed. Onions help stimulate the cerebral cortex, which, in turn, will help you relax. In addition, onions are rich in vitamins and minerals, such as calcium(Ca) and phosphorus (P), which benefit your central nervous system.

12) As it becomes cooler with each passing day, some people, who enjoy excessively cold drinks and dishes during the summer, might suffer from gastric diseases. Li Jianhua, deputy director of internal medicine at the People's Hospital in Cangzhou, in North China's Hebei Province, stresses the importance of a regular diet and proper exercise, such as walking and jogging, to strengthen the stomach.

13) Exercises improve the functions of your digestive system, as they promote peristalses of your stomach and intestines, stimulate the secretion of digestive juices, and improve blood circulation in your stomach and intestines. In particular, exercises help cure a peptic ulcer.

A: Digestion
B: Curing an Oral Ulcer
C: Proper Exercise
D: Vegetables
E: Avoiding Colds
F: Sound Sleep

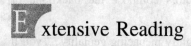xtensive Reading

Passage One

Brave New World（美丽新世界）

Aldous Huxley

赫胥黎（Aldous Huxley, 1884—1963），英国生物学家及作家。作者通过一个由基因改造所制造的一个乌托邦世界（Utopia）的故事，描绘了以"科学方式"组织的理想社会的恐怖情景，辛辣地讽刺了科技奴役人类、使人类沦为机器、使文化艺术趋于毁灭结果。

A squat grey building of only thirty-four stories. Over the main entrance the words, Central London Hatchery（孵化场）and Conditioning Centre, and, in a shield, the World State's motto, Community, Identity, Stability.

The enormous room on the ground floor faced towards the north. Cold for all the summer beyond the panes, for all the tropical heat of the room itself, a harsh thin light glared through the windows, hungrily seeking some draped lay figure, some pallid shape of academic goose-flesh, but finding only the glass and nickel and bleakly shining porcelain（瓷器）of a laboratory. Wintriness responded to wintriness. The overalls of the workers were white, their hands gloved with a pale corpse-coloured rubber. The light was frozen, dead, a ghost. Only from the yellow barrels of the microscopes did it borrow a certain rich and living substance, lying along the polished tubes like butter, streak after luscious streak in long recession down the work tables.

"And this," said the Director opening the door, "is the Fertilizing Room."

Bent over their instruments, three hundred Fertilizers were plunged, as the Director of Hatcheries and Conditioning entered the room, in the scarcely breathing silence, the absentminded, soliloquizing（自言自语）hum or whistle, of absorbed concentration. A troop of newly arrived students, very young, pink and callow, followed nervously, rather abjectly, at the Director's heels. Each of them carried a note-book, in which, whenever the great man spoke, he desperately scribbled（匆匆写下）. Straight from the horse's mouth. It was a rare privilege. The D. H. C. for Central London always made a point of personally conducting his new students round the various departments.

"Just to give you a general idea," he would explain to them. For of course some sort of general idea they must have, if they were to do their work intelligently — though as little of one, if they were to be good and happy members of society, as possible. For particulars, as every one knows, make for virtue and happiness; generalities are intellectually necessary evils. Not philosophers, but fret-sawyers and stamp collectors compose the backbone of society.

"To-morrow," he would add, smiling at them with a slightly menacing geniality, "you'll be settling down to serious work. You won't have time for generalities. Meanwhile..."

Meanwhile, it was a privilege. Straight from the horse's mouth into the note-book. The boys scribbled like mad.

Tall and rather thin but upright, the Director advanced into the room. He had a long chin and big, rather prominent teeth, just covered, when he was not talking, by his full, floridly（红润）curved lips. Old, young? Thirty? fifty? fifty-five? It was hard to say. And anyhow the question didn't arise; in this year of stability, a. f. 632, it didn't occur to you to ask it.

"I shall begin at the beginning," said the D. H. C. and the more zealous students recorded his intention in their note-books: *Begin at the beginning*. "These," he waved his hand, "are the incubators." And opening an insulated (绝缘) door he showed them racks upon racks of numbered test-tubes. "The week's supply of ova (卵子). Kept," he explained, 'at blood heat; whereas the male gametes(配子)," and here he opened another door, "They have to be kept at thirty-five instead of thirty-seven. Full blood heat sterilizes. (消毒)" Rams wrapped in thermogene (热基因) beget (产生) no lambs.

Still leaning against the incubators (孵化器) he gave them, while the pencils scurried illegibly across the pages, a brief description of the modern fertilizing process; spoke first, of course, of its surgical introduction — "the operation undergone voluntarily for the good of Society, not to mention the fact that it carries a bonus amounting to six months' salary"; continued with some account of the technique for preserving the excised ovary alive and actively developing; passed on to a consideration of optimum temperature, salinity, viscosity (粘稠度); referred to the liquor in which the detached and ripened eggs were kept; and, leading his charges to the work tables, actually showed them how this liquor was drawn off from the test-tubes; how it was let out drop by drop on to the specially warmed slides of the microscopes; how the eggs which it contained were inspected for abnormalities, counted and transferred to a porous receptacle; how (and he now took them to watch the operation) this receptacle was immersed in a warm bouillon (肉汤) containing free-swimming spermatozoa (精子) — at a minimum concentration of one hundred thousand per cubic centimetre, he insisted; and how, after ten minutes, the container was lifted out of the liquor and its contents re-examined; how, if any of the eggs remained unfertilized, it was again immersed, and, if necessary, yet again; how the fertilized ova went back to the incubators; where the Alphas and Betas remained until definitely bottled; while the Gammas, Deltas and Epsilons were brought out again, after only thirty-six hours, to undergo Bokanovsky's Process.

"Bokanovsky's Process," repeated the Director, and the students underlined the words in their little note-books.

One egg, one embryo (胚胎), one adult — normality. But a bokanovskified egg will bud, will proliferate, will divide. From eight to ninety-six buds, and every bud will grow into a perfectly formed embryo, and every embryo into a full-sized adult. Making ninety-six human beings grow where only one grew before.

"Essentially," the D. H. C. concluded, "bokanovskification consists of a series of arrests of development. We check the normal growth and, paradoxically enough, the egg responds by budding."

Responds by budding. The pencils were busy.

He pointed. On a very slowly moving band a rack-full of test-tubes was entering a large metal box, another rack-full was emerging. Machinery faintly purred. It took eight minutes for the tubes to go through, he told them. Eight minutes of hard X-rays being about as much as an egg can stand. A few died; of the rest, the least susceptible(易受侵害的) divided into two; most put out four buds; some eight; all were returned to the incubators, where the buds began to develop; then, after two days, were suddenly chilled, chilled and checked. Two, four, eight, the buds in their turn budded; and having budded were dosed almost to death with alcohol; consequently burgeoned (萌芽) again and having budded — bud out of bud out of bud — were thereafter — further arrest being generally fatal-left to develop in peace. By which time the original egg was in a fair way to becoming anything from eight to ninety-six embryos — a prodigious improvement, you will agree, on nature. Identical twins — but not in piddling twos and threes as in the old viviparous (胎生) days, when an egg would sometimes accidentally divide; actually by dozens, by scores at a time.

"Scores," the Director repeated and flung out his arms, as though he were distributing largesse. "Scores."

But one of the students was fool enough to ask where the advantage lay.

"My good boy!" The Director wheeled sharply round on him. "Can't you see? Can't you *see*?" He raised a hand; his expression was solemn. "Bokanovsky's Process is one of the major instruments of social stability!"

Major instruments of social stability.

Standard men and women; in uniform batches. The whole of a small factory staffed with the products of a single bokanovskified egg.

"Ninety-six identical twins working ninety-six identical machines!" The voice was almost tremulous with enthusiasm. "You really know where you are. For the first time in history." He quoted the motto. "Community, Identity, Stability." Grand words. "If we could bokanovskify indefinitely the whole problem would be solved."

Solved by standard Gammas, unvarying Deltas, uniform Epsilons. Millions of identical twins. The principle of mass production at last applied to biology.

"But, alas," the Director shook his head, "we *can't* bokanovskify indefinitely."

Ninety-six seemed to be the limit; seventy-two a good average. From the same ovary and with gametes of the same male to manufacture as many batches of identical twins as possible — that was the best (sadly a second best) that they could do. And even that was difficult.

"For in nature it takes thirty years for two hundred eggs to reach maturity. But our business is to stabilize the population at this moment, here and now. Dribbling (细水长流) out twins over a quarter of a century — what would be the use of that?"

Obviously, no use at all. But Podsnap's Technique had immensely accelerated the process of ripening. They could make sure of at least a hundred and fifty mature eggs within two years. Fertilize and bokanovskify — in other words, multiply by seventy-two — and you get an average of nearly eleven thousand brothers and sisters in a hundred and fifty batches of identical twins, all within two years of the same age.

"And in exceptional cases we can make one ovary yield us over fifteen thousand adult individuals. "

Beckoning (召唤) to a fair-haired, ruddy young man who happened to be passing at the moment, "Mr. Foster," he called. The ruddy young man approached. "Can you tell us the record for a single ovary, Mr. Foster?"

He spoke very quickly, had a vivacious blue eye, and took an evident pleasure in quoting figures. "Sixteen thousand and twelve; in one hundred and eighty-nine batches of identicals. But of course they've done much better," he rattled on, "in some of the tropical Centres. Singapore has often produced over sixteen thousand five hundred; and Mombasa has actually touched the seventeen thousand mark. But then they have unfair advantages. You should see the way a negro ovary responds to pituitary (脑垂体)! It's quite astonishing, when you're used to working with European material. Still," he added, with a laugh (but the light of combat was in his eyes and the lift of his chin was challenging), "still, we mean to beat them if we can. I'm working on a wonderful Delta-Minus ovary at this moment. Only just eighteen months old. Over twelve thousand seven hundred children already, either decanted or in embryo. And still going strong. We'll beat them yet. "

"That's the spirit I like!" cried the Director, and clapped Mr. Foster on the shoulder. "Come along with us and give these boys the benefit of your expert knowledge. "

Mr. Foster smiled modestly, "With pleasure. " They went.

From *Brave New World Harper Perennial Modern Classics*, 1998

I. Reading comprehension.

1. What's the aim of this passage?

A. To introduce a list of stunning scientific achievements.

B. To criticize the overenthusiastic embrace of new scientific discoveries.

C. To record an unusual visit of the young students.

D. To foresee a bright future of human beings.

2. What is the name of the process that allows the Hatchery to produce many clones from a single egg?

A. The Pondansky Technique.

B. The Trotsky Process.

C. The Bokanovsky Process.

D. Centrifugal Bumble-puppy.

3. Which of the followings is not true about "Bokanovsky's Process"?

A. Gammas, Deltas and Epsilons undergo Bokanovsky's Process.

B. Bokanovsky's Process is one of the major instruments of social stability.

C. Bokanovsky's Process consists of a series of arrests of development.

D. We can conduct Bokanovsky Process indefinitely.

4. The higher castes (ie. Gammas, Deltas and Epsilons) _____

A. are more likely to be subject to the forces of anonymity and mechanization.

B. will be decanted one by one without our intervention.

C. retain at least certain level of the individuality and creativity totally denied to the lower castes.

D. are not any different from lower castes as far as the way they were produced.

5. What's the tone of the Text?

A. Praise

B. Positive

C. Satirical

D. Objective

II. Further topics for discussion.

1. How do the castes differ from each other? Do you think they reflect any aspect of contemporary society?

2. Make a comparison between *1984* and *Brave New World*.

Passage Two

Animal Farm

George Orwell

本文节选自《动物农庄》第一章。动物们在夜深人静之时进行了秘密集会,来聆听"长者"分析头天晚上做的一个奇特的梦。"长者"做了一番演说,号召大家一起奋起反抗人类的奴役和掠夺。

Mr. Jones, of the Manor Farm, had locked the hen-houses for the night, but was too drunk to remember to shut the pop-holes. With the ring of light from his lantern(提灯、灯笼) dancing from side to side, he lurched (蹒跚) across the yard, kicked off his boots at the back door, drew himself a last glass of beer from the barrel in the scullery (食品与炊具存放室), and made his way up to bed, where Mrs. Jones was already snoring.

As soon as the light in the bedroom went out there was a stirring and a fluttering (心绪不宁) all through the farm buildings. Word had gone round during the day that old Major, the prize Middle White boar (公猪), had a strange dream on the previous night and wished to communicate it to the other animals. It had been agreed that they should all meet in the big barn (谷仓) as soon as Mr. Jones was safely out of the way. Old Major (so he was always called, though the name under which he had been exhibited was Willingdon Beauty) was so highly regarded on the farm that everyone was quite ready to lose an hour's sleep in order to hear what he had to say.

At one end of the big barn, on a sort of raised platform, Major was already ensconced (安置) on his bed of straw, under a lantern which hung from a beam (横梁). He was twelve years old and had lately grown rather stout, but he was still a majestic-looking pig, with a wise and benevolent (仁慈的) appearance in spite of the fact that his tushes (长牙) had never been cut. Before long the other animals began to arrive and make themselves comfortable after their different fashions. First came the three dogs, Bluebell, Jessie, and Pincher, and then the pigs, who settled down in the straw immediately in front of the platform. The hens perched themselves on the window-sills, the pigeons fluttered up to the rafters, the sheep and cows lay down behind the pigs and began to chew the cud (反刍的食物). The two cart-horses, Boxer and Clover, came in together, walking very slowly and setting down their vast hairy hoofs(马蹄) with great care lest there should be some small animal concealed in the straw.

....

All the animals were now present except Moses, the tame raven (渡鸦), who slept on a perch (禽鸟的栖木) behind the back door. When Major saw that they had all made themselves comfortable and were waiting attentively, he cleared his throat and began:

"Comrades, you have heard already about the strange dream that I had last night. But I will come to the dream later. I have something else to say first. I do not think, comrades, that I shall be with you for many months longer, and before I die, I feel it my duty to pass on to you such wisdom as I have acquired. I have had a long life, I have had much time for thought as I lay alone in my stall, and I think I may say that I understand the nature of life on this earth as well as any animal now living. It is about this that I wish to speak to you. "

"Now, comrades, what is the nature of this life of ours? Let us face it: our lives are miserable, laborious (吃苦耐劳的), and short. We are born, we are given just so much food as will keep the breath in our bodies, and those of us who are capable of it are forced to work to the last atom of our strength; and the very instant that our usefulness has come to an end we are slaughtered (屠杀) with hideous cruelty. No animal in England knows the meaning of happiness or leisure after he is a year old. No animal in England is free. The life of an animal is misery and slavery: that is the plain truth. "

"But is this simply part of the order of nature? Is it because this land of ours is so poor that it cannot afford a decent life to those who dwell upon it? No, comrades, a thousand times no! The soil of England is fertile, its climate is good, it is capable of affording food in abundance (丰富,充裕) to an enormously greater number of animals than now inhabit it. This single farm of ours would support a dozen horses, twenty cows, hundreds of sheep —

and all of them living in a comfort and a dignity that are now almost beyond our imagining. Why then do we continue in this miserable condition? Because nearly the whole of the produce of our labour is stolen from us by human beings. There, comrades, is the answer to all our problems. It is summed up in a single word — Man. Man is the only real enemy we have. Remove Man from the scene, and the root cause of hunger and overwork is abolished for ever. "

"Man is the only creature that consumes without producing. He does not give milk, he does not lay eggs, he is too weak to pull the plough, he cannot run fast enough to catch rabbits. Yet he is lord of all the animals. He sets them to work, he gives back to them the bare minimum that will prevent them from starving, and the rest he keeps for himself. Our labour tills (耕种) the soil, our dung (粪肥) fertilizes it, and yet there is not one of us that owns more than his bare skin. You cows that I see before me, how many thousands of gallons of milk have you given during this last year? And what has happened to that milk which should have been breeding up sturdy calves? Every drop of it has gone down the throats of our enemies. And you hens, how many eggs have you laid in this last year, and how many of those eggs ever hatched into chickens? The rest have all gone to market to bring in money for Jones and his men. And you, Clover, where are those four foals you bore, who should have been the support and pleasure of your old age? Each was sold at a year old — you will never see one of them again. In return for your four confinements (分娩) and all your labour in the fields, what have you ever had except your bare rations (食物的定量) and a stall?"

"And even the miserable lives we lead are not allowed to reach their natural span. For myself I do not grumble (抱怨), for I am one of the lucky ones. I am twelve years old and have had over four hundred children. Such is the natural life of a pig. But no animal escapes the cruel knife in the end. You young porkers who are sitting in front of me, every one of you will scream your lives out at the block (案板) within a year. To that horror we all must come — cows, pigs, hens, sheep, everyone. Even the horses and the dogs have no better fate. You, Boxer, the very day that those great muscles of yours lose their power, Jones will sell you to the knackers (无用的家畜的收买者), who will cut your throat and boil you down for the foxhounds. As for the dogs, when they grow old and toothless, Jones ties a brick round their necks and drowns them in the nearest pond. "

"Is it not crystal clear, then, comrades, that all the evils of this life of ours spring from the tyranny of human beings? Only get rid of Man, and the produce of our labour would be our own. Almost overnight we could become rich and free. What then must we do? Why, work night and day, body and soul, for the overthrow of the human race! That is my message to you, comrades: Rebellion! I do not know when that Rebellion will come, it might be in a week or in a hundred years, but I know, as surely as I see this straw beneath my feet, that sooner or later justice will be done. Fix your eyes on that, comrades, throughout the short remainder of your lives.! And above all, pass on this message of mine to those who come after you, so that future generations shall carry on the struggle until it is victorious. "

"And remember, comrades, your resolution must never falter（犹豫、畏缩）. No argument must lead you astray（迷路）. Never listen when they tell you that Man and the animals have a common interest, that the prosperity of the one is the prosperity of the others. It is all lies. Man serves the interests of no creature except himself. And among us animals let there be perfect unity, perfect comradeship in the struggle. All men are enemies. All animals are comrades. "

. . .

"And now, comrades, I will tell you about my dream of last night. I cannot describe that dream to you. It was a dream of the earth as it will be when Man has vanished. But it reminded me of something that I had long forgotten. Many years ago, when I was a little pig, my mother and the other sows used to sing an old song of which they knew only the tune and the first three words. I had known that tune in my infancy（婴儿期）, but it had long since passed out of my mind. Last night, however, it came back to me in my dream. And what is more, the words of the song also came back — words, I am certain, which were sung by the animals of long ago and have been lost to memory for generations. I will sing you that song now, comrades. I am old and my voice is hoarse（嘶哑的）, but when I have taught you the tune, you can sing it better for yourselves. It is called *Beasts of England*. "

Old Major cleared his throat and began to sing. As he had said, his voice was hoarse, but he sang well enough, and it was a stirring tune, something between *Clementine* and *La Cucaracha*. The words ran:

> *Beasts of England, beasts of Ireland,*
> *Beasts of every land and clime,*（地方,风土）
> *Hearke（倾听）to my joyful tidings（音讯）*
> *Of the golden future time.*
> *Soon or late the day is coming,*
> *Tyrant Man shall be o'erthrown,*
> *And the fruitful fields of England*
> *Shall be trod by beasts alone.*
>
> *Rings shall vanish from our noses,*
> *And the harness from our back,*
> *Bit and spur shall rust forever,*
> *Cruel whips no more shall crack.*

Riches more than mind can picture,
Wheat and barley, oats and hay,
Clover（三叶草）*, beans, and mangel-wurzels*（一种甜菜）
Shall be ours upon that day.

Bright will shine the fields of England,
Purer shall its waters be,
Sweeter yet shall blow its breezes
On the day that sets us free.

For that day we all must labour,
Though we die before it breaks;
Cows and horses, geese and turkeys,
All must toil for freedom's sake.

Beasts of England, beasts of Ireland,
Beasts of every land and clime,
Hearken well and spread my tidings
Of the golden future time.

The singing of this song threw the animals into the wildest excitement. Almost before Major had reached the end, they had begun singing it for themselves. Even the stupidest of them had already picked up the tune and a few of the words, and as for the clever ones, such as the pigs and dogs, they had the entire song by heart within a few minutes. And then, after a few preliminary tries, the whole farm burst out into *Beasts of England* in tremendous unison （齐唱）. The cows lowed it, the dogs whined （发哀鸣声） it, the sheep bleated （咩咩叫） it, the horses whinnied it, the ducks quacked it. They were so delighted with the song that they sang it right through five times in succession, and might have continued singing it all night if they had not been interrupted.

From *Aninal Farm* 中国致公出版社 2000

Decide whether the following statements are True or False.

1. All of the farm animals except Clover, Boxer — the cart-horse whose incredible strength, dedication, and loyalty play a key role in the early prosperity of Animal Farm, convene in the big barn to hear a speech by Old Major. （   ）
2. The dogs, being the most intelligent animals in the group, take control of the planning and government of the farm. （   ）

3. Major blames the animals' suffering solely on their own cowardice. They are irresistible to human being's false notion that humans and animals share the same interest. (   )

4. The song called "Beasts of England" paints a dramatic picture of the utopian — an ideal animal community of Major's dream. (   )

5. Orwell chose to use a fable in his condemnation of Soviet communism and totalitarianism, because historically fables or parables have allowed writers to criticize individuals or institutions without endangering themselves: an author could always claim that he or she had aimed simply to write a fairy tale — a hypothetical, meaningless children's story. (   )

Unit 8

Summerhill Education vs Standard Education

本单元课文综述

Text 精读 节选自英国教育家 A. S. Neill 的文章 *Summerhill*。作者指出传统教育的缺陷在于忽略孩子情感的培养,创造力的开发;过于强调"学"的方面,而忽略了"玩"的方面,因而传统教育是片面的、强制性的教育。

Passage One 泛读 著名哲学家与数学家 Alfred North Whitehead 阐述了大学的功能:既非传授知识,也非为教员提供科研机会,而在于开发学生的想象力。

Passage Two 泛读 幽默作家里柯克(Leacock)阐述他对牛津校舍及教育的看法。

Text　Summerhill Education vs Standard Education

I hold that the aim of life is to find happiness, which means to find interest. Education should be a preparation for life. Our culture has not been very successful. Our education, politics, and economics lead to war. Our medicines have not **done away with** disease. Our religion has not **abolished usury** and robbery. Our **boasted humanitarianism** still allows public opinion to approve of the barbaric sport of hunting. The advances of the age are advances in mechanism — in radio and television, in electronics, in jet planes. New world wars threaten, for the world's social conscience is still primitive.

If we feel like questioning today, we can pose a few awkward questions. Why does man seem to have many more diseases than animals have? Why does man hate and kill in war when animals do not? Why does cancer increase? Why are there so many suicides? So many insane sex crimes? Why the hate that is **anti-Semitism**? Why Negro hating and **lynching**? Why **backbiting** and **spite**? Why is sex **obscene** and a **leering** joke? Why is being a **bastard** a social disgrace? Why the continuance of religions that have long ago lost their love and hope and charity? Why, a thousand whys about our **vaunted** state of civilized eminence!

I ask these questions because I am by profession a teacher, one who deals with the young. I ask these questions because those so often asked by teachers are the unimportant ones, the ones about school subjects. I ask what earthly good can come out of discussions about French or ancient history or what not when these subjects **don't** matter **a jot** compared to the larger question of life's natural fulfillment — of man's inner happiness.

How much of our education is real doing, real self-expression? Handiwork is too often the making of a pin tray under the eye of an expert. Even the Montessori system, well-known as a system of directed play, is an artificial way of making the child learn by doing. It has nothing creative about it.

In the home, the child is always being taught. In almost every home, there is always at least one ungrown-up grownup who rushes to show Tommy how his new engine works. There is always someone to lift the baby up on a chair when the baby wants to examine something on the wall. Every time we show Tommy how his engine works we are stealing from that child the joy of life — the joy of discovery — the joy of overcoming an obstacle. Worse! We make that child come to believe that he is inferior, and must depend on help.

Parents are slow in realizing how unimportant the learning side of school is. Children, like adults, learn what they want to learn. All prize-giving and marks and exams **sidetrack** proper personality development. Only **pedants** claim that learning from books is education.

Books are the least important apparatus in a school. All that any child needs is the **three R's**; the rest should be tools and **clay** and sports and theater and paint and freedom.

Most of the school work that adolescents do is simply a waste of time, of energy, of patience. It robs youth of its right to play and play and play; it puts old heads on young shoulders.

When I lecture to students at teacher training colleges and universities, I am often shocked at the ungrownupness of these lads and lasses stuffed with useless knowledge. They know a lot; they **shine in** dialectics; they can quote the classics — but in their outlook on life many of them are infants. For they have been taught to know, but have not been allowed to feel. These students are friendly, pleasant, eager, but something is lacking — the emotional factor, the power to subordinate thinking to feeling. I talk to these of a world they have missed and go on missing. Their textbooks do not deal with human character, or with love, or with freedom, or with **self-determination**. And so the system goes on, aiming only at standards of book learning — goes on separating the head from the heart.

It is time that we were challenging the school's notion of work. It is taken for granted that every child should learn mathematics, history, geography, some science, a little art, and certainly literature. It is time we realized that the average young child is not much interested in any of these subjects.

I prove this with every new pupil. When told that the school is free, every new pupil cries, "Hurrah! You won't catch me doing dull arithmetic and things!"

I am not **decrying** learning. But learning should come after play. And learning should

not be deliberately **seasoned with** play to make it **palatable**.

Learning is important — but not to everyone. **Nijinsky** could not pass his school exams in St. Petersburg, and he could not enter the State Ballet without passing those exams. He simply could not learn school subjects — his mind was elsewhere. They **faked** an exam for him, giving him the answers with the paper — so a biography says. What a loss to the world if Nijinsky had had to really pass those exams!

Creators learn what they want to learn in order to have the tools that their originality and genius demand. We do not know how much creation is killed in the classroom with its emphasis on learning.

I have seen a girl weep nightly over her geometry. Her mother wanted her **geometry**. Her mother wanted her to go to the university, but the girl's whole soul was artistic. I was delighted when I heard that she had failed her college entrance exams for the seventh time. Possibly, the mother would now allow her to go on the stage as she longed to do.

Some time ago, I met a girl of fourteen in Copenhagen who had spent three years in Summerhill and had spoken perfect English here. "I suppose you are at the top of your class in English," I said.

She **grimaced ruefully**. "No, I'm at the bottom of my class, because I don't know English grammar," she said. I think that disclosure is about the best commentary on what adults consider education.

Indifferent scholars who, under discipline, **scrape through** college or university and become unimaginative teachers, mediocre doctors, and incopetent lawyers would possibly be good mechanics or excellent **bricklayers** or first-rate policemen.

We have found that the boy who cannot or will not learn to read until he is, say, fifteen is always a boy with a mechanical **bent** who later on becomes a good engineer or electrician. I should not dare **dogmatize** about girls who never go to lessons, especially to mathematics and physics. Often such girls spend much time with needlework, and some, later on in life, take up dressmaking and designing. It is an absurd curriculum that makes a **prospective** dressmaker study **quadratic equations** or Boyle's Law.

Caldwell Cook wrote a book called *The Play Way*, in which he told how he taught English by means of play. It was a fascinating book, full of good things, yet I think it was only a new way of bolstering the theory that learning is of the utmost importance. Cook held that learning was so important that the pill should be sugared with play. This notion that unless a child is learning something the child is wasting his time is nothing less than a curse — a curse that **blinds** thousands of teachers and most school inspectors. Fifty years ago the **watchword** was "Learn through doing". Today the watchword is "Learn through playing". Play is thus used only as a means to an end, but to what good end I do not really know.

If a teacher sees children playing with mud, and he thereupon improves the shining moment by holding forth about river-bank erosion, what end has he in view? What child cares about river erosion? Many so-called educators believe that it does not matter what a child learns as long as he is taught something. And, of course, with schools as they are — just massproduction factories — what can a teacher do but teach something and come to believe that teaching, in itself, matters most of all?

When I lecture to a group of teachers, I commence by saying that I am not going to speak about school subjects or discipline or classes. For an hour my audience listens in **rapt** silence; and after the sincere applause, the chairman announces that I am ready to answer questions. At least three-quarters of the questions deal with subjects and teaching.

I do not tell this in any superior way. I tell it sadly to show how the classroom walls and the prisonlike buildings narrow the teacher's outlook, and prevent him from seeing the true essentials of education. His work deals with the part of a child that is above the neck; and **perforce**, the emotional, vital part of the child is foreign territory to him.

I wish I could see a bigger movement of rebellion among our younger teachers. Higher education and university degrees do not make a **scrap** of difference in confronting the evils of society. A learned neurotic is not any different from an unlearned neurotic.

In all countries, capitalist, socialist, or communist, elaborate schools are built to educate the young. But all the wonderful labs and workshops do nothing to help John or Peter or Ivan **surmount** the emotional damage and the social evils bred by the pressure on him from his parents, his schoolteachers, and the pressure of the **coercive** quality of our civilization.

From *Subject and Structure by John Wasson Little Brown and Company Limited* 1981

New Words and Phrases

do away with		to stop having sth/make sth end　废除,结束
abolish	*v.*	to officially end a law,　废除,废止
usury	*n.*	放高利贷
boast	*v.*	自夸,自吹自擂
humanitarianism	*n.*	人道主义
anti-Semitism	*n.*	hatred of Jew　反犹主义
lynch	*v.*	kill someone illegally,　用私刑处死
backbiting	*n.*	背后中伤,诽谤
spite	*n.*	malice　恶意,怨恨
obscene	*a.*	下流的
leering	*a.*	smiling at sb in an unpleasant way　奸笑的
bastard	*n.*	私生子
vaunted	*a.*	praised as being very good,　被吹嘘,夸耀的

not a jot		not at all 丝毫,一点不
sidetrack	*v.*	使转移目标
pedant	*n.*	a person too concerned with small details or rules 书呆子,学究
three R's		reading, writing, and arithmetic
clay	*n.*	heavy, sticky earth for making pots and bricks 陶土
shine in sth		be very good at sth 出类拔萃
self-determination	*n.*	个人自主权力、能力
decry	*v.*	condemn 公开谴责,强烈批评
season sth with sth		add salt, pepper, to food to give it more flavour 给食物调味
palatable	*a.*	pleasant/acceptable 宜人的,可接受的
Nijinsky		尼仁斯基,俄国芭蕾舞演员
fake	*v.*	伪造,冒充
geometry	*n.*	几何学
grimace	*v.*	to make an ugly expression with your face 做鬼脸,怪相
ruefully	*adv.*	sorrowfully 懊悔,沮丧地
scrape through sth		to succeed in doing sth with difficulty 艰难完成,勉强通过
bricklayer	*n.*	a person whose job is to build walls, etc. with bricks 瓦工,砌砖工
bent	*n.*	gift 天赋,爱好
dogmatize	*v.*	武断判断
prospective	*n.*	potential 可能,有望
quadratic equation		二次方程式
blind	*v.*	使思维混乱,使失去判断力
watchword	*n.*	标语,口号
rapt	*a.*	preoccupied 全神贯注,专心致志的
perforce	*adv.*	必定,势必
scrap	*n.*	a small amount of sth 丝毫,一丁点
surmount	*v.*	overcome 克服,解决
coercive	*a.*	using force or the threat of force 用武力强迫的,胁迫的

About the author: Alexander S. Neill (1883 — 1973) was born in Scotland and educated in Edinburgh. A prolific writer, educator, and child psychologist, Neill founded, in Suffolk, England, the famous Summerhill School, an experimental school aimed at freeing the child's creative imagination from the restrictions of conventional education. Besides *Summerhill*, from which this text comes, Neill's books on unregimented education are *The Problem Child*, *The problem Parent*, *The Problem Teacher*, and *The Problem Family*.

Notes to the text

1. 英国教育家 A. S. Neill 因不满传统教育模式,与妻子共同创办了著名的 Summerhill 学校。该学校重在培养学生的创造力,独立自主的精神,个性的发挥。

The Summerhill School in Leiston, Suffolk was started in the 1920's as an experiment by Neill and his wife, ardent believers in the idea of inculcating (灌输) happiness as the main, if not the only purpose of education. It is a radical example of English education without the fear of authority and respectful of children's freedom, independence and creativity. Education in Summerhill School needs to be seen in light of (鉴于) children's overall experience in the boarding school. The principle of life and schooling in Summerhill community is that the children are free to pursue their interests and choose what they want to learn, do, wear, say and become. All lessons are optional (选修的) and the timetable (课程表) exists only for teachers. However, according to Neill (1973) children who come to the school from the beginning do not show the problems for other children who come from other schools, where there is an average three-month period of "recovery from lesson aversion (厌恶)". Examinations exist only as an option, usually pursued by the children who want to go to university. Another striking difference in Summerhill is in the social relations that encourage approval of child's individuality and equality between children and adults. All school rules are voted in a general school meeting where the voice of a six-year old counts (重要) as much as that of the headmaster.

Not surprisingly, the school met with much disapproval and criticism and was seen as a too far liberal experiment which did not provide its pupils with the standard of education that would help them succeed in the real world. It is also clear that the school functioned for a small number of children whose parents were themselves believers in this freedom and the sense of fulfillment from non-material benefits. The ethos (道德观) of Summerhill was that human beings are innately (天生) good and, if provided with an opportunity to develop without repression (压抑), will ordinarily grow into happy, self-satisfied human beings who will not "preach a war" or "lynch a Negro" (Neill, 1973). Judging by the experiences of pupils and their later lives, it seems that Summerhill did mange to bring up self-confident adults that have no fear of authority, are courageous to independently pursue their own dreams and live in harmony with others — very much the kind of people that the progressive education professes to educate.

Yet, these are also the products of the very traditional methods of instruction at Summerhill, an ordinary timetable of forty minute periods on five mornings a week, with old fashioned classrooms and teachers. Indeed, the traditional pedagogy (教学法) does not seem to impinge on (影响) children's attitudes once they choose what they wish to learn, or as Neill expresses it: Whether a school has or has not a special method for teaching long division is of no significance, for long division is of no importance except to those who want to learn it. And the child who wants to learn long division will learn it no matter how it is taught (Neill, 1973: 5). There are countless examples of inspirational teachers who made a decisive impact on the development of positive values in their pupils long before behaviorist (行为主义) psychologists claimed the discovery that learning can be scientifically studied and inspired the subsequent research into most effective educational methods. There are many instances of progressive methods failing to encourage genuine open enquiry and producing citizens who can fearlessly express and inform their individual and social action by liberal ideas. While acknowledging a tremendous advance of teaching and learning practices with the adoption of progressive methods, there seem to be valid (有根据的) grounds for suggesting that it might not be the pedagogy that makes that critical difference between education for obedience and conformity (遵从) vs. a socially critical education for liberal civilization.

2. **Montessori System**: 意大利著名的儿童教育学家蒙台梭利的教育思想,其核心是重视儿童个性的发展和培养,并为保证儿童个性的健康成长提供了一个行之有效的教育模式。In this educational system, each child is a unique being (独特的个体). He is encouraged to develop social and emotional skills, in addition to intellectual ones. The main premises of Montessori education are:

Children are to be respected as different from adults and as individuals who differ from each other.

The child possesses an unusual sensitivity (情感) and intellectual ability, unlike those of the adult, to absorb and learn from his environment, both in quality and quantity.

The first six years of life are the most important years of a child's growth when unconscious (无识的) learning gradually emerges to the conscious level.

3. **The three Rs**: a widely-used abbreviation for the basic elements of a primary school curriculum: *reading*, *'riting* (*writing*), *and 'rithmetic* (*arithmetic*) 读,写,算

Exercises

I. Answer the following questions.

1. **If the aim of life is happiness and the aim of education is preparation for life, does it follow that the goal of education is happiness**?

   interest in life/integrating the head with the heart

2. **Neill asks a number of embarrassing questions in Paragraph 2. Does he demonstrate that his brand of education should eliminate the need for such questions? Does he mean to imply that standard education is the source of these problems or that it ignores them**?

ignoring the fundamental issue of life — pursuit of inner happiness

3. How, according to Neill, does his system of education differ from the Montessori system and from "learning through playing"?

focusing more on fostering students' creativity/independence/confidence

4. Would you agree that creative people will learn what they need without being taught and that non-creative people would be better off without being taught things they will never use? Does emphasis on learning kill creativity? Does a student learn anything from a standard curriculum besides "knowledge"?

Knowledge should be taught in a creative way.

5. Neill asserts, perhaps correctly, that the average child is "not much interested" in the standard subjects taught in school. Does it follow that such subjects should not be taught?

learning coming after play/seasoning learning with play to make it enjoyable/fostering students' creativity in the learning process

6. What do you think might be the chief advantages of attending a school like Summerhill? What might be the disadvantages?

freedom of pursuing one's interests/bring up self-confident adults that have no fear of authority/courage to independently pursue one's own dreams/live in harmony with others.

failure to provide pupils with the standard of education

II. Further questions for discussion.

1. What is the basis of contrast between Summerhill education and standard education?

2. Comment on the Neill's use of specific examples. Do they provide effective support for his position? Do they seem typical rather than "loaded"? (That is, could one find examples of people who "failed" in life because they didn't learn enough in school? Keep in mind that Neill's definition of success is not getting a high-paying job.)

3. Does Neill's complete commitment to his own system interfere with the drawing of a valid contrast with the standard system?

III. Vocabulary study.

1. Word in Use.

1) **do away with**: to stop having sth/make sth end

He thinks it is time we did away with the monarchy.

They did away with uniforms at that school years ago.

These ridiculous rules and regulations should have been done away with years ago.

2) **boast**: to talk with too much pride about sth that you have or can do

He didn't talk about his top exam results in case people thought he was boasting.

Parents enjoy boasting about their children's achievements.

She boasted of how she had written a novel when she was only 15.

3) **vaunted**: proudly talked about or praised as being very good, esp. when this is not deserved

His much vaunted new scheme has been shown to have serious weaknesses.

Their much vaunted reforms did not materialize.

Their much vaunted plan end up in failure.

4) **sidetrack**: to direct one's attention away from an activity or subject to less important ones 使转移目标

Ruth was looking for an envelope in a drawer when she was sidetracked by some old letters.

The students sidetracked their teacher into talking about her hobby.

I was supposed to be writing a letter but I'm afraid I got sidetracked.

5) **shine in sth**: be good at sth

She is hopeless at languages, but she shines in science.

He failed to be excellent academically but he shined in sports.

She has set a good example of shining in loyal service over four decades.

6) **scrape through**: manage to accomplish sth with difficulty

He managed to scrape through his exam with 60%.

I might scrape through the exam if I am lucky.

With its big body, the bear scraped through a narrow opening.

7) **surmount**: overcome

She has had to surmount the difficulty of bringing up six children on her own.

They managed to surmount all the opposition to their plans.

There are still a few technical obstacles to be surmounted before the product can be put on sale to the public.

2. Word Distinctions.

1) **It/that depends** 那得看情况　　**depend on/upon sb./sth.** 依靠,信赖;指望

选择以上适当的词填空:

I don't know if we can help — it all _____.

He was the sort of person you can _____.

I might not go. It _____ how tired I am.

I shouldn't be too late. But it _____ if the traffic is bad.

Can we _____ you coming in on Sunday?

The community _____ the shipping industry for its survival.

2) **feel like (doing) sth**, 想要某物,想做某事　　**feel sth**, 意识到,感觉到;触,深深体会到

选择以上适当的词填空：

I could _____ the warm sun on my back.

We all _____ celebrating.

She could not _____ her legs.

Can you _____ the tension in the room?

I _____ a drink.

Try to tell what this is just by _____ it.

The effects of the recession are being _____ everywhere.

3）**Scrape, scrape through**

Scrape sth：刮掉，削去

Scrape through：艰难完成；勉强通过（考试）

选择以上适当的词填空：

She _____ the mud off her boots.

The kids had _____ their plates clean.

I might _____ the exam if I am lucky.

I _____ the side of my car on the wall.

Sorry, I've _____ some paint off the car.

The wire had _____ the skin from her fingers.

3. **Decide the meanings of the following words by matching each word in Column A with the word or expression in Column B that is similar in meaning.**

A	B
1）ruefully	a. condemn
2）decry	b. make a face
3）spite	c. gift
4）bent	d. overcome
5）prospective	e. malice
6）rapt	f. regretfully
7）surmount	g. attentive
8）grimace	h. potential
9）perforce	i. acceptable
10）platable	j. certainly

4. **Try to write a brief story with the following words and phrases.**

academic   be motivated   curriculum   subject   graduate with
honor   take courses in   extracurricular activity

IV. Translation.

1. **Put the following Chinese expressions into English.**

  1）综合大学   2）主/副修课程   3）知名高等学府   4）脱产培训

5）多元教育　　6）学制　　　　7）校训　　　　　　8）实习生

2. Put the following Chinesse sentences into English.

1）她全神贯注地听演讲者讲话。（rapt）

2）她很清楚必须克服哪些困难。（surmount）

3）他的赤诚忠心使他看不清真相。（blind）

4）他一尝那苦味，做了个苦相。（grimace）

5）他们大肆吹嘘的改革并没有实现。（vaunted）

6）吉姆吹嘘说打扑克牌谁都不是他的对手。（boast）

7）她有数学天赋。（ bent ）

8）这些措施受到指责，说是不起作用。（decry）

3. Put the following Chinese paragraph into English.

挑起一场学术争论最容易的法子莫过于提出这样一个问题：一个受过教育的人应该知道些什么？哈佛大学上次应对这个问题是在 1978 年，在那一年该校确立了它的核心课程。核心课程侧重于学生学会掌握思考的方式而非单纯的知识内容。与哈佛在 1945 年出台的所谓"红皮书"标准类似，核心课程在其他各主要院校引起了广泛共鸣。现在，哈佛正在重新思考应该传授给学生什么以及如何教育学生。翻开新的一页的一个主要目标，便是帮助学生把他们在课堂上所学的东西应用到实践中去。"如果看到所学的知识和以后生活中所遇到的各种各样的难题、问题和需要解决的事情有所联系，学生们学习将会更有动力。"哈佛过渡期的校长如是说。在重新考虑应该传授给学生什么以及如何教育学生这方面，哈佛并非是孤家寡人。耶鲁大学最近也进行了类似的改革。一旦这所全国最负盛名的大学也这样做了，那么其他院校很有可能会步其后尘。

4. Put the following quotes into Chinese.

1）And gladly would learn, and gladly teach.　　　—— Chaucer, British poet

2）Better be unborn than untaught, for ignorance is the root of misfortune.

—— Plato, Ancient Greek philosopher

3）Genius17 without education is like silver in the mine.

—— Benjamin Franklin, American president

4）The roots of education are bitter, but the fruit is sweet.

—— Aristotle, Ancient Greek philosopher

5）Knowledge, in truth, is the great sun in the firmanent. Life and power are scattered with all its beams.　　　—— Daniel Webster

5. Translate the following passage into Chinese.

In the current climate of international test competitions and increased student exchanges, science and science education teaching practices have come under closer scrutiny in the United States. The European style of teaching has been touted by some educators because of the ranking of European students on international tests. Based on comparative statistical data, however, I believe that the U. S. approach to science education is more efficient and appropriate than the European one.

European students conclude their liberal arts education, including the sciences, at the secondary level of schooling with comprehensive examinations. Consequently, European universities are for specialization only and exclude general education components. Students often follow a strict and rigid curriculum in both high school and college that allows for very few electives.

The level of science instruction in Europe is relatively high. For example, 90 percent of Bulgarian students graduate from high school having completed trigonometry and with scientific knowledge equivalent to introductory courses for science majors at an American college.

V. Comment on the structure of the text.

This text is an extract from the book *Summerhill* by the Scottish educator and child psychologist Alexander S. Neill. This extract is a comparison and contrast essay that focuses on the different notions of teaching philosophy between free education (Summerhill education) and forced education (standard education).

In the beginning of the three paragraphs, the writer states his personal view about the aim of education — to achieve "life's natural fulfillment... man's inner happiness". The writer also points out a major problem resulting from the current educational system, that is: modern education is inadequate in cultivating the world's social conscience. Rhetorical questions and parallelism are used to achieve a very strong effect so that the reader's interest is aroused. The remainder of the essay unfolds on the basis of his definition of the aim and success of education.

From paragraphs 4 to 9, the writer lays out the drawbacks of modern school education which, in spite of its systematic teaching curriculum, basically stifles the creativity in the student and deprives the student of emotional development which is essential in understanding the truth of life.

Paragraphs 10 through 12 serve as a transition in which the writer states his view on learning ("Learning is important — but not to everyone.") which is contrasted to the notion of learning in standard education.

From paragraphs 13 to 19, the writer uses specific examples to support his position that forced learning can in no way benefit the personal and emotional development of the student. And this notion clashes with the notion of standard education.

Paragraphs 20 and 21 echo the writer's view on learning stated in paragraphs 10 through 12 and illustrated through examples in paragraphs 13 through 19.

In paragraphs 22 through 25, the writer further traces the cause of the drawbacks of modern education: most school teachers are not aware of the aim and essence of education; and it is exactly this that brings about the failure of the modern educational system and the inability to cultivate the world's social conscience.

Extended Exercises

1. In the following article, some paragraphs have been removed. Choose the most suitable paragraph from the list A-D to fit into each of the numbered gaps.

The First Major Turning Point

I kept close to the top of the class, though. The topmost scholastic standing, I remember, kept shifting between me, a girl named Audrey Slaugh, and a boy named Jimmy Cotton.

1) _____

Somehow, I happened to be alone in the classroom with Mr. Ostrowski, my English teacher. He was a tall, rather reddish white man and he had a thick mustache. I had gotten some of my best marks under him, and he had always made me feel that he liked me. He was, as I have mentioned, a natural-born "advisor", about what you ought to read, to do, or think — about any and everything. We used to make unkind jokes about him: why was he teaching in Mason instead of somewhere else, getting for himself some of the "success in life" that he kept telling us how to get?

2) _____

He told me, "Malcolm, you ought to be thinking about a career. Have you been giving it thought?"

The truth is, I hadn't. I never have figured out why I told him, "Well, yes sir, I've been thinking I'd like to be a lawyer." Lansing certainly had no Negro lawyers — or doctors either — in those days, to hold up an image. I might have aspired to. All I really knew for certain was that a lawyer didn't wash dishes, as I was doing.

Mr. Ostrowski looked surprised, I remember, and leaned back in his chair and clasped his hands behind his head. He kind of half-smiled and said, "Malcolm, one of life's first needs is for us to be realistic. Don't misunderstand me, now. We all here like you, you know that. But you've got to be realistic about being a nigge. A lawyer — that is no realistic goal for a nigger. You need to think about something you can be. You are good with your hands — making things. Everybody admires your carpentry shop work. Why don't you plan on carpentry? People like you as a person — you'd get all kinds of work. "

3)_____

What made it really begin to disturb me was Mr. Ostrowski's advice to others in my class — all of them white. Most of them had told him they were planning to become farmers, like their parents — to one day take over their family farms. But those who wanted to strike out on their own, to try something new, he had encouraged. Some, mostly girls, wanted to be teachers. A few wanted other professions, such as one boy who wanted to be a nurse. They all reported that Mr. Ostrowski had encouraged whatever they had they wanted. Yet nearly none of them had earned marks equal to mine.

4)_____

It was then that I began to change — inside.

A: It was a surprising thing that I had never thought of it that way before, but I realized that whatever I wasn't, I was smarter than nearly all of those white kids. But apparently I was still not intelligent enough, in their eyes, to become whatever I wanted to be.

B: It went on that, as I become increasingly restless and disturbed through the first semester. And then one day, just about when those of us who had passed were about to move up to 8 – A, from which was to become the first major turning point of my life.

C: The more I thought afterwards about what he said, the more uneasy it made me. It just kept treading around in my mind.

D: I know that he probably meant well in what he happened to advise me that day. I doubt that he meant any harm. It was just in his nature as an American white man. I was one of his top students, one of the school's top students — but all he could see for me was the future "in your place" that all white people see for black people.

2. **Identify the four principal ideas of the passage by grouping the following numbered paragraphs into effective sections and choose the most suitable subheading from the list A-D for each part.**

Doctor's Dilemma: Treat or Let Die

1) Medical advances in wonder drugs, daring surgical procedures, radiation therapies, and intensive-care units have brought new life to thousands of people. Yet to many of them, modern medicine has become a double-edged sword. Doctor's power to treat with an array of space-age techniques has outstripped the body's capacity to heal. More medical problems can be treated, but for many patients, there is little hope of recovery. Even the fundamental distinction between life and death has been blurred.

2）Many Americans are caught in medical limbo, as was the South Korean boxer Duk Koo Kim, who was kept alive by artificial means after he had been knocked unconscious in a fight and his brain ceased to function. With the permission of his family, doctors in Las Vegas disconnected the life-support machines and death quickly followed. In the wake of technology's advances in medicine, a heated debate is taking place in hospitals and nursing homes across the country — over whether survival or quality of life is the paramount goal of medicine.

3）"It gets down to what medicine is all about," says Daniel Callahan, director of the Institute of Society, Ethics, and the Life Sciences in Hastings-on-Hudson, New York. "It is really to save a life? Or is the larger goal the welfare of the patient?" Doctors, patients, relatives, and often the courts are forced to make hard choices in medicine. Most often it is at the two extremes of life that these difficult ethical questions arise — at the beginning for the very sick newborn and at the end for the dying patient.

4）The dilemma posed by modern medical technology has created the growing new discipline of bioethics. Many of the country's 127 medical schools now offer courses in medical ethics, a field virtually ignored only a decade ago. Many hospitals have chaplains, philosophers, psychiatrists, and social workers on the staff to help patients make crucial decisions, and one in twenty institutions has a special ethics committee to resolve difficult cases.

5）Of all the patients in intensive-care units who are at risk of dying, some 20 percent present difficult ethical choices — whether to keep trying to save the life or to pull back and let the patient die. In many units, decisions regarding life-sustaining care are made about three times a week. Even the definition of death has been changed. Now that the heart-lung machine can take over the functions of breathing and pumping blood, death no longer always comes with the patient's "last gasp" or when the heart stops beating. Thirty-one states and the District of Columbia have passed brain-death statutes that identify death as when the whole brain ceases to function.

6）More than a dozen states recognize "living wills" in which the patients leave instructions to doctors not to prolong life by feeding them intravenously or by other methods if their illness becomes hopeless. A survey of California doctors showed that 20 to 30 percent were following instructions of such wills. Meanwhile, the hospice movement, with its emphasis on providing comfort — not cure — to the dying patient, has gained momentum in many years.

7）Despite progress in society's understanding of death and dying, thorny issues remain. Example: A woman, 87, afflicted by the nervous-system disorder of Parkinson's disease, has a massive stroke and is found unconscious by her family. Their choices are to put her in a nursing home until she dies or to send her to a medical center for diagnosis and possible treatment. The family opts for a teaching hospital in New York city. Tests show the woman's stroke resulted from a blood clot that is curable with surgery. After the operation, she says to her family, "Why did you bring me back to this agony?" Her health continues to worsen, and two years later she dies.

8) On the other hand, doctors say prognosis is often uncertain and that patients, just because they are old and disabled, should not be denied life-saving therapy. Ethicists also fear that under the guise of medical decisions not to treat certain patients, death may become too easy, pushing the country toward the acceptance of euthanasia. For some people, the agony of watching high-technology dying is too great. Earlier this year, Woodrow Wilson Collums, a retired dairyman from Poteet, was put on probation for the mercy killing of his older brother Jim, who lay helpless in his bed at a nursing home, a victim of severe senility resulting from Alzheimer's disease. After the killing, the victim's widow said, "I thank God, Jim's out of his misery. I hate to think it had to be done the way it was done, but I understand it."

9) At the other end of the life span, technology has so revolutionized newborn care that it is no longer clear when human life is viable outside the womb. Twenty-five years ago, infants weighing less than three and one-half pounds rarely survived. The current survival rate is 70 percent, and doctors are "salvaging" some babies that weigh only one and one-half pounds. Tremendous progress has been made in treating birth deformities such as spina bifida. Just ten years ago, only 5 percent of infants with transposition of the great arteries — the congenital heart defect most commonly found in newborns — survived. Today, 50 percent live.

10) Yet, for many infants who owe their lives to new medical advances, survival has come at a price. A significant number emerge with permanent physical and mental handicaps. "The question of treatment and nontreatment of seriously ill newborns is not a single one," says Thomas Murray of the Hastings Center. "But I feel strongly that retardation or the fact someone is going to be less than perfect is not good grounds for allowing an infant to die."

11) For many parents, however, the experience of having a sick newborn becomes a lingering nightmare. "Two years ago, an Atlanta mother gave birth to a baby suffering from Down's Syndrome, a form of mental retardation; the child also had blocked intestines. The doctors rejected the parents' plea not to operate, and today the child, severely retarded, still suffers intestinal problems. "Every time Melanie has a bowel movement, she cries," explains her mother. "She is not able to take care of herself, and we won't live forever. I wanted to save her from sorrow, pain, and suffering. I don't understand the emphasis on life at all costs, and I am very angry at the doctors and the hospital. We felt doing nothing to sustain her life was best for her. The doctors went against nature. I asked the doctors, who threatened to take us to court if we didn't go along with their procedures: "Who will take care of Melanie after we are gone? Where

will you doctors be then?"

12) The choices posed by modern technology have profoundly changed the practice of medicine. Until now, most doctors have been activists, trained to use all the tools in their medical arsenals to treat disease. The current trend is toward nontreatment as doctors grapple with questions not just of who should get care but when to take therapy away. Always in the background is the threat of legal action. In August, two California doctors were charged with murdering a comatose patient by allegedly disconnecting the respirator and cutting off food and water. In 1981, a Massachusetts nurse was charged with murdering a cancer patient with massive doses of morphine but was subsequently acquitted.

13) Between lawsuits, government regulations, and patients' rights, many doctors feel they are under siege. Modern technology actually has limited their ability to make choices, More recently, these actions are resolved by committees.

14) In recent years, the debate on medical ethics has moved to the level of national policy. "It's just beginning to hit us that we don't have unlimited resources," says Washington Hospital Center's Dr. Lynch. "You can't talk about ethics without talking about money." Since 1972, Americans have enjoyed unlimited access to a taxpayer-supported, kidney-dialysis program that offers life-prolonging therapy to all patients with kidney failure. To a number of policy analysts, the program has grown out of control — to a $1.4 billion operation supporting 61,000 patients. The majority are over 50, and about a quarter have other illnesses, such as cancer or heart disease, conditions that could exclude them from dialysis in other countries.

15) Some hospitals are pulling back from certain lifesaving treatments. Massachusetts General Hospital, for example, has decided not to perform heart tranplants on the ground that the high costs of providing such surgery help too few patients. Burn units — though extremely effective — also provide very expensive therapy for very few patients.

16) As medical scientists push back the frontiers of therapy, the moral dilemma will continue to grow for doctors and patients alike, making the choice of to treat or not to treat the basic question in modern medicine.

A: Death and Dying

B: Crisis in Newborn Care

C: Changing Standards

D: Public Policy

Extensive Reading

Passage One

Universities and Their Function

Alfred North Whitehead

Alfred North Whitehead 是英国数学家与哲学家,曾在剑桥大学和伦敦大学教授数学,后在哈佛大学教授哲学。著有多本哲学著作,其中之一为《科学与现代世界》(1925)。虽然下面这篇文章写于 50 年前,其中所提出的问题仍然值得当今教育者的关注。

The universities are schools of education, and schools of research. But the primary reason for their existence is not to be found either in the mere knowledge conveyed to the students or in the mere opportunities for research afforded to the members of the faculty. The justification for a university is that it preserves the connection between knowledge and the zest(热情) of life, by uniting the young and the old in the imaginative consideration of learning. The university imparts (传授) information, but it imparts it imaginatively. At least, this is the function which it should perform for society. A university which fails in this respect has no reason for existence. This atmosphere of excitement, arising from imaginative consideration, transforms(改变) knowledge. A fact is no longer a bare fact: it is invested with(具备某种性质) all its possibilities. It is no longer a burden on the memory: it is energizing as the poet of our dreams, and as the architect of our purposes. Imagination is not to be divorced from(分离) facts: it is a way of illuminating the facts. It works by eliciting(引发) the general principles which apply to the facts, as they exist, and then by an intellectual survey of alternative possibilities which are consistent with those principles. It enables men to construct an intellectual vision of a new world, and it preserves the zest of life by the suggestion of satisfying purposes.

Youth is imaginative, and if the imagination be strengthened by discipline this energy of imagination can in great measure be preserved through life. The tragedy of the world is that those who are imaginative have but slight experience, and those who are experienced have feeble(贫乏的) imaginations. Fools act on imagination without knowledge; pedants(学究) act on knowledge without imagination. The task of a university is to weld together imagiantion and experience.

These reflections upon the general functions of a university can be at once translated in terms of the particular functions of a business school. We need not flinch from(畏缩不前) the assertion that the main function of such a school is to produce men with a greater zest for business.

In a simpler world, business relations were simpler, being based on the immediate contact of man with man and on immediate confrontation with all relevant material circumstances. Today business organization requires an imaginative grasp(理解)of the psychologies of populations engaged in differing modes of occupation; of populations scattered through cities, through mountains, through plains; of populations on the ocean, and of populations in mines, and of populations in forests. It requires an imaginative grasp of conditions in the tropics, of conditions in temperate zones. It requires an imaginative grasp of the interlocking interests of great organizations, and of the reactions of the whole complex to any change in one of its elements. It requires an imaginative understanding of laws of political economy, not merely in the abstract, but also with the power to construe(解释)them in terms of the particular circumstances of a concrete business. It requires some knowledge of the habits of government, and of the variations of those habits under diverse conditions. It requires an imaginative vision of the binding(有法律约束力的)forces of any human organization, a sympathetic vision of the limits of human nature and of the conditions which evoke loyalty of service. It requires some knowledge of the laws of health, of the laws of fatigue, and of the conditions for sustained reliability. It requires an imaginative understanding of the social effects of the conditions of factories. It requires a sufficient conception of the role of applied science in modern society. It requires that discipline of character which can say "yes" and "no" to other men, not by reason of blind obstinacy(固执), but with firmness derived from a conscious evaluation of relevant alternatives.

The universities have trained the intellectual pioneers of our civilization — the priests, the lawyers, the statesmen, the doctors, the men of science, and the men of letters. The conduct of business now requires intellectual imagination of the same type as that which in former times has mainly passed into those occupations.

There is one great difficulty which hampers(阻碍)all the higher types of human endeavor. In modern times this difficulty has even increased in its possibilities for evil. In any large organization the younger men, who are novices, must be set to jobs which consist in carrying out fixed duties in obedience to orders. No president of a large corporation meets his youngest employee at his office door with the offer of the most responsible job which the work of that corporation includes. The young men are set to work at a fixed routine, and only occasionally even see the president as he passes in and out of the building. Such work is a great discipline. It imparts knowledge, and it produces reliability of character; also it is the work for which they are hired. There can be no criticism of the custom, but there may be an unfortunate effect — prolonged routine work dulls the imagination.

The way in which a university should function in the preparation for an intellectual career, such as modern business or one of the older professions, is by promoting the imaginative consideration of the various general principles underlying that career. Its students thus pass into their period of technical apprenticeship with their imaginations already practised in connecting details with general principles. The routine then receives its meaning, and also illuminates the principles which give it that meaning. Hence, instead of a drudgery（繁重无聊的工作）issuing in a blind rule of thumb, the properly trained man has some hope of obtaining an imagination disciplined by detailed facts and by necessary habits.

Thus the proper function of a university is the imaginative acquisition of knowledge. Apart from this importance of the imagiantion, there is no reason why business men, and other professional men, should not pick up their facts bit by bit as they want them for particular occasions. A university is imaginative or it is nothing — at least nothing useful.

Subject and Structure — An Anthology for Writers Little Brown and Company Limited 1981

I. Reading comprehension.

1. According to the writer, the justified existence of a university is _____.
   A. conveying knowledge to students imaginatively
   B. affording research opportunities to the faculty
   C. preserving the connection between knowledge and the enthusiasm of life
   D. offering imaginative reflection of the society

2. In business areas, young novices are required to complete fixed duties assigned to them. The long-term negative effect of the practice is _____.
   A. blind obedience to their superiors
   B. diminishing their initiative
   C. their being over-disciplined
   D. their imagination being stifled

3. Today a business organization requires _____.
   A. an imaginative grasp of psychologies of customers of different occupations
   B. an imaginative grasp of various circumstances in various places
   C. an insight into human nature, an understanding of the role of science applied in various industries and a reasonable amount of knowledge of how a government functions
   D. all of the above

4. In universities, imagination is to be _____.
   A. welded together with experience
   B. divorced from the facts
   C. strengthened by discipline
   D. disciplined by education

5. The way in which a university should function for students in their preparation for an intellectual career such as modern business or one of the older professions is _____.
   A. by offering students enough opportunities for practices

    B. by sharpening the students' imagination

    C. by provoking students' interest to probe into the principles underlying a career

    D. by instilling the students with knowledge

II. Topics for further discussion.

1. What does the writer see as the chief function of a university?

2. Why does the writer choose business administration as his primary example rather than some more "speculative" study such as philosophy?

Passage Two

Oxford as I See It

Stephen Leacock

    My private station being that of a university professor, I was naturally deeply interested in the system of education in England. I was therefore led to make a special visit to Oxford and to submit the place to a searching scrutiny (仔细检查). Arriving one afternoon at four o'clock, I stayed at the Mitre Hotel and did not leave until eleven o'clock next morning. The whole of this time, except for one hour spent in addressing the undergraduates, was devoted to a close and eager study of the great university. When I add to this that I had already visited Oxford in 1907 and spent a Sunday at All Souls with Colonel L. S. Amery, it will be seen at once that my views on Oxford are based upon observations extending over fourteen years.

    On the strength of (凭借) this basis of experience I am prepared to make the following positive and emphatic (坚决的) statements. Oxford is a noble university. It has a great past. It is at present the greatest university in the world; and it is quite possible that it has a great future. Oxford trains scholars of the real type better than any other place in the world. Its methods are antiquated (过时的,陈旧的). It despises science. Its lectures are rotten. It has professors who never teach and students who never learn. It has no order, no arrangement, no system. Its curriculum is unintelligible (难懂的). It has no president. It has no state legislature to tell it how to teach, and yet, — it gets there. Whether we like it or not, Oxford gives something to its students, a life and a mode of thought, which in America as yet we can emulate (模仿) but not equal.

    I persist in my assertion that I believe that Oxford, in its way, is the greatest university in the world. I am aware that this is an extreme statement and needs explanation. Oxford is much smaller in numbers, for example, than the State University of Minnesota, and is much poorer. It has, or had till yesterday, fewer students than the University of Toronto. To mention Oxford beside the 26,000 students of Columbia University sounds ridiculous (可笑的). In point of money, the 39,000,000 dollar endowment (捐赠,资助) of the University of Chicago, and the $35,000,000 one of Columbia, and the $43,000,000 of Harvard seem to leave Oxford nowhere. Yet the peculiar thing is that it is not nowhere. By some queer process of its own it seems to get there every time. It was therefore of the very greatest interest to me, as a profound scholar, to try to investigate just how this peculiar excellence of Oxford arises.

It can hardly be due to anything in the curriculum or programme of studies. Indeed, to any one accustomed to the best models of a university curriculum as it flourishes in the United States and Canada, the programme of studies is frankly quite laughable. There is less Applied Science in the place than would be found with us in a theological college. Hardly a single professor at Oxford would recognise a dynamo (发电机) if he met it in broad daylight. The Oxford student learns nothing of chemistry, physics, heat, plumbing, electric wiring, gas-fitting or the use of a blow-torch (喷灯). Any American college student can run a motor car, take a gasoline engine to pieces, fix a washer on a kitchen tap, mend a broken electric bell, and give an expert opinion on what has gone wrong with the furnace. It is these things indeed which stamp (表明是) him as a college man, and on occasion a very pardonable pride in the minds of his parents.

But in all these things the Oxford student is the merest amateur.

This is bad enough. But after all one might say this is only the mechanical side of education. True: but one searches in vain in the Oxford curriculum for any adequate recognition of the higher and more cultured studies. Strange though it seems to us on this side of the Atlantic, there are no courses at Oxford in Housekeeping, or in Salesmanship, or in Advertising, or on Comparative Religion, or on the influence of the Press. There are no lectures whatever on Human Behaviour, on Altruism (利他主义), on Egotism (利己主义), or on the Play of Wild Animals. Apparently, the Oxford student does not learn these things. This cuts him off from a great deal of the larger culture of our side of the Atlantic. "What are you studying this year?" I once asked a fourth year student at one of our great colleges. "I am electing Salesmanship and Religion," he answered. Here was a young man whose training was destined (注定) inevitably to turn him into a moral business man: either that or nothing. At Oxford Salesmanship is not taught and Religion takes the feeble form of the New Testament. The more one looks at these things the more amazing it becomes that Oxford can produce any results at all.

The effect of the comparison is heightened by the peculiar position occupied at Oxford by the professors' lectures. In the colleges of Canada and the United States the lectures are supposed to be a really necessary and useful part of the student's training. Again and again I have heard the graduates of my own college assert that they had got as much, or nearly as much, out of the lectures at college as out of athletics or the Greek letter society or the Banjo and Mandolin Club. In short, with us the lectures form a real part of the college life. At Oxford it is not so. The lectures, I understand, are given and may even be taken. But they are quite worthless and are not supposed to have anything much to do with the development of the, student's mind. "The lectures here," said a Canadian student to me, "are punk." I appealed to another student to know if this was so. "I don't know whether I'd call them exactly punk," he answered, "but they're certainly rotten." Other judgments were that the lectures were of no importance: that nobody took them: that they don't matter: that you can take them if you like: that they do you no harm.

It appears further that the professors themselves are not keen on their lectures. If the lectures are called for they give them; if not, the professor's feelings are not hurt. He merely waits and rests his brain until in some later year the students call for his lectures. There are men at Oxford who have rested their brains this way for over thirty years: the accumulated brain power thus dammed up is said to be colossal（巨大的）.

I understand that the key to this mystery is found in the operations of the person called the tutor. It is from him, or rather with him, that the students learn all that they know: one and all are agreed on that. Yet it is a little odd to know just how he does it. "We go over to his rooms," said one student, "and he just lights a pipe and talks to us." "We sit round with him," said another, "and he simply smokes and goes over our exercises with us." From this and other evidence I gather that what an Oxford tutor does is to get a little group of students together and smoke at them. Men who have been systematically（有系统有条理地）smoked at for four years turn into ripe scholars. If anybody doubts this, let him go to Oxford and he can see the thing actually in operation. A well-smoked man speaks, and writes English with a grace that can be acquired in no other way.

In what was said above, I seem to have been directing criticism against the Oxford professors as such: but I have no intention of doing so. For the Oxford professor and his whole manner of being I have nothing but a profound respect. There is indeed the greatest difference between the modern up-to-date American idea of a professor and the English type. But even with us in older days, in the bygone time when such people as Henry Wadsworth Longfellow were professors, one found the English idea; a professor was supposed to be a venerable（值得尊重）kind of person, with snow-white whiskers（络腮胡子）reaching to his stomach. He was expected to moon around（闲逛）the campus oblivious of（未察觉到）the world around him. If you nodded to him he failed to see you. Of money he knew nothing; of business, far less. He was, as his trustees（委托人）were proud to say of him, "a child."

On the other hand he contained within him a reservoir（大量的储藏）of learning of such depth as to be practically bottomless. None of this learning was supposed to be of any material or commercial benefit to anybody. Its use was in saving the soul and enlarging the mind.

At the head of such a group of professors was one whose beard was even whiter and longer, whose absence of mind was even still greater, and whose knowledge of money, business, and practical affairs was below zero. Him they made the president.

Now the principal reason why I am led to admire Oxford is that the place is little touched as yet by the measuring of "results", and by this passion for visible and provable "efficiency". The whole system at Oxford is such as to put a premium on（珍视）genius and to let mediocrity（平庸）and dullness go their way. On the dull student Oxford, after a proper lapse（间隔时间）of time, confers（授予）a degree which means nothing more than that he lived and breathed at Oxford and kept out of jail. This for many students is as much as society can expect. But for the gifted students Oxford offers great opportunities. There is no question of his hanging back（继续留在原处）till the last sheep has jumped over the fence. He need wait for no one. He may move forward as fast as he likes, following the bent of his genius. If he has in him any ability beyond that of the common herd, his tutor, interested in his studies, will smoke at him until he kindles（点燃）him into a flame. For the tutor's soul is not harassed（困扰）by herding dull students, with dismissal hanging by a thread over his head in the class room. The American professor has no time to be interested in a clever student. He has time to be interested in his "deportment", his letter-writing, his executive work, and his organising ability and his hope of promotion to a soap factory. But with that his mind is exhausted. The student of genius merely means to him a student who gives no trouble, who passes all his "tests", and is present at all his "recitations". Such a student also, if he can be trained to be a hustler（耍诡计骗钱的人）and an advertiser, will undoubtedly "make good." But beyond that the professor does not think of him. The everlasting principle of equality has inserted itself in a place where it has no right to be, and where inequality is the breath of life.

American or Canadian college trustees would be horrified at the notion of professors who apparently do no work, give few or no lectures and draw their pay merely for existing. Yet these are really the only kind of professors worth having, — I mean, men who can be trusted with a vague general mission in life, with a salary guaranteed at least till their death, and a sphere of duties entrusted solely to their own consciences and the promptings（激起）of their own desires. Such men are rare, but a single one of them, when found, is worth ten "executives" and a dozen "organisers".

The excellence of Oxford, then, as I see it, lies in the peculiar vagueness of the organisation of its work. It starts from the assumption that the professor is a really learned man whose sole interest lies in his own sphere: and that a student, or at least the only student with whom the university cares to reckon seriously, is a young man who desires to know. This is an ancient medieval（中世纪的）attitude long since buried in more up-to-date places under successive strata（阶层）of compulsory education（义务教育）, state teaching, the democratisation（民主化）of knowledge and the substitution of the shadow for the substance, and the casket（精巧小盒）for the gem（宝石）. No doubt, in newer places the thing has got to be so. Higher education in America flourishes chiefly as a qualification for entrance into a money-making profession, and not as a thing in itself. But in Oxford one can still see the surviving outline of a nobler type of structure and a higher inspiration.

From *www. online-literature. com/stephen-leacock/my-discovery-of-england/6/*

Decide whether the following statements are True or False.

1. In Leacock's opinion, Oxford offers such education to students in the form that is matchless in American universities. (   )

2. Despite the poor building conditions, Oxford still achieved singular results. (   )

3. Oxford's greatness lies in its large student body, sufficient educational endowment, and the best models of university curriculum. (   )

4. Apart from the mechanical side of education, Oxford abounds in higher and more cultured studies. (   )

5. In Oxford, lectures are indispensible part of the university life and have much to do with the development of the student's mind. (   )

6. A professor of the English type was supposed to be a venerable kind of person, with snow-white whiskers reaching to his stomach and contian within him a reservoir of learning of such depth as to be practically bottomless. (   )

Unit 9

The Clash of Civilizations?

本单元课文综述

Text 精读　课文选自萨缪尔·亨廷顿（Samuel P. Huntington）的政论文《文明的冲突》。在文中，亨廷顿预言了文明冲突的到来，其中西方和伊斯兰文明的冲突将是焦点所在。

Passage One 泛读　为美国公共广播公司电视节目'思想库'主持人 本·瓦滕伯格（Ben Wattenberg）2002 年 1 月 24 日邀请《文明的冲突》一书作者亨廷顿做客'思想库'电视栏目，话题是文化冲突（When Cultures Collide）。

Passage Two 泛读　Naomi Klein 发表于民族杂志上的一篇文章。美国政府认为伊拉克战争是反恐战争的一部分，是拯救伊拉克人民于水深火热的正义之举。然而事实是否如此呢？

ext　　　　　**The Clash of Civilizations**?

Samuel P. Huntington

The Nature of Civilizations

During the Cold War the world was divided into the First, Second and Third Worlds. Those divisions are no longer relevant. It is far more meaningful now to group countries not in terms of their political or economic systems or in terms of their level of economic development but rather in terms of their culture and civilization.

What do we mean when we talk of a civilization? A civilization is a cultural **entity**. Villages, regions, ethnic groups, nationalities, religious groups, all have distinct cultures at different levels of cultural **heterogeneity**. The culture of a village in southern Italy may be different from that of a village in northern Italy, but both will share a common Italian culture that distinguishes them from German villages. European communities, in turn, will share cultural features that distinguish them from Arab or Chinese communities. Arabs, Chinese and Westerners, however, are not part of any broader cultural entity. They constitute civilizations. A civilization is thus the highest cultural grouping of people and the broadest level of cultural identity people have, short of that which distinguishes humans from other species. It is defined both by common objective elements, such as language, history, religion, customs, institutions, and by the subjective self-identification of people. People have levels of identity: a resident of Rome may define himself with varying degrees of intensity as a Roman, an Italian, a Catholic, a Christian, a European, a Westerner. The civilization to which he belongs is the broadest level of identification with which he intensely identifies. People can and do redefine their identities and, as a result, the composition and boundaries of civilizations change.

Civilizations may involve a large number of people, as with China ("a civilization pretending to be a state," as Lucian Pye put it), or a very small number of people, such as the **Anglophone Caribbean**. A civilization may include several nation states, as is the case with Western, Latin American and Arab civilizations, or only one, as is the case with Japanese civilization. Civilizations obviously **blend** and overlap, and may include subcivilizations. Western civilization has two major **variants**, European and North American, and Islam has its Arab, Turkic and Malay subdivisions. Civilizations are nonetheless meaningful entities, and while the lines between them are seldom sharp, they are real. Civilizations are dynamic; they rise and fall; they divide and merge. And, as any student of history knows, civilizations disappear and are buried in the sands of time.

Westerners tend to think of nation states as the principal actors in global affairs. They have been that, however, for only a few centuries. The broader reaches of human history have been the history of civilizations. In A Study of History, Arnold Toynbee identified 21 major civilizations; only six of them exist in the contemporary world.

The West Versus the Rest

The west is now at an extraordinary peak of power in relation to other civilizations. Its superpower opponent has disappeared from the map. Military conflict among Western states is unthinkable, and Western military power is unrivaled. Apart from Japan, the West faces no economic challenge. It dominates international economic institutions. Global political and security issues are effectively settled by a **directorate** of the United States, Britain and France, world economic issues by a directorate of the United States, Germany and Japan, all of which maintain extraordinarily close relations with each other to the exclusion of lesser and largely non-Western countries. Decisions made at the U. N. Security Council or in the International Monetary Fund that reflect the interests of the West are presented to the world as reflecting the desires of the world community. The very phrase "the world community" has become the **euphemistic** collective noun (replacing "the Free World") to give global legitimacy to actions reflecting the interests of the United States and other Western powers. Through the IMF and other international economic institutions, the West promotes its economic interests and **imposes** on other nations the economic policies it thinks appropriate. In any poll of non-Western peoples, the IMF undoubtedly would win the support of finance ministers and a few others, but get an overwhelmingly unfavorable rating from just about everyone else, who would agree with Georgy Arbatov's characterization of IMF officials as "**Neo-Bolsheviks** who love **expropriating** other people's money, imposing undemocratic and alien rules of economic and political conduct and stifling economic freedom. "

　　Western domination of the U. N. Security Council and its decisions, tempered only by occasional **abstention** by China, produced U. N. legitimation of the West's use of force to drive Iraq out of Kuwait and its elimination of Iraq's sophisticated weapons and capacity to produce such weapons. It also produced the quite unprecedented action by the United States, Britain and France in getting the Security Council to demand that Libya hand over the Pan Am 103 Bombing suspects and then to impose sanctions when Libya refused. After defeating the largest Arab army, the West did not hesistate to throw its weight around in the Arab world. The West in effect is using international institutions, military power and economic resources to run the world in ways that will maintain Western predominance, protect Western interests and promote Western political and economic values.

　　That at least is the way in which non-Westerners see the new world, and there is a significant element of truth in their view. Differences in power and struggles for military, economic and institutional power are thus one source of conflict between the West and other civilizations. Differences in culture, that is basic values and beliefs, are a second source of conflict. V. S. Naipaul has argued that Western civilization is the "universal civilization" that "fits all men". At a superficial level much of Western culture has indeed **permeated** the rest of the world. At a more basic level, however, Western concepts differ fundamentally from those prevalent in other civilizations. Western ideas of individualism, liberalism, constitutionalism, human rights, equality, liberty, the rule of law, democracy, free markets, the separation of church and state, often have little resonance in Islamic, Confucian, Japanese, Hindu, Buddhist or Orthodox cultures. Western efforts to **propagate** each ideas produce instead a reaction against "human rights imperialism" and a reaffirmation of **indigenous** values, as can be seen in the support for religious **fundamentalism** by the younger generation in non-Western cultures. The very notion that there could be a "universal civilization" is a Western idea, directly **at odds with** the particularism of most Asian societies and their emphasis on what distinguishes one people from another. Indeed, the author of a review of 100 comparative studies of values in different societies concluded that "the values that are most important in the West are least important worldwide. " In the political realm, of course, these differences are most **manifest** in the efforts of the United States and other Western powers to induce other peoples to adopt Western ideas concerning democracy and human rights.

　　The central axis of world politics in the future is likely to be, in Kishore Mahbubani's phrase, the conflict between "the West and the Rest" and the responses of non-Western civilizations to Western power and values. Those responses generally take one or a combination of three forms. At one extreme, non-Western states can, like Burma and North Korea, attempt to pursue a course of isolation, to **insulate** their societies from penetration or "corruption" by the West, and, in effect, to **opt out of** participation in the Western-dominated global community. The costs of this course, however, are high, and few states have pursued it exclusively. A second alternative, the equivalent of "**band-wagoning**" in international relations theory, is to attempt to join the West and accept its values and institutions. The third alternative is to attempt to "balance" the West by developing economic and military power and cooperating with other non-Western societies against the West, while preserving indigenous values and institutions; in short, to modernize but not to Westernize.

Implications for the West

This article does not argue that civilization identities will replace all other identities, that nation states will disappear, that each civilization will become a single coherent political entity, that groups within a civilization will not conflict with and even fight each other. This paper does set forth the hypotheses that differences between civilizations are real and important; civilization-consciousness is increasing; conflict between civilizations will **supplant** ideological and other forms of conflict as the dominant global form of conflict; international relations, historically a game played out within Western civilization, will increasingly be de-Westernized and become a game in which non-Western civilizations are actors and not simply objects; successful political, security and economic international institutions are more likely to develop within civilizations than across civilizations; conflicts between groups in different civilizations will be more frequent, more sustained and more violent than conflicts between groups in the same civilization; violent conflicts between groups in different civilizations are the most likely and most dangerous source of **escalation** that could lead to global wars; the paramount axis of world politics will be the relations between "the West and the Rest"; the elites in some torn non-Western countries will try to make their countries part of the West, but in most cases face major obstacles to accomplishing this; a central focus of conflict for the immediate future will be between the West and several Islamic-Confucian states.

This is not to advocate the desirability of conflicts between civilizations. It is to set forth descriptive hypotheses as to what the future may be like. If these are plausible hypotheses, however, it is necessary to consider their implications for Western policy. These implications should be divided between short-term advantage and long-term accommodation. In the short term it is clearly in the interest of the West to promote greater cooperation and unity within its own civilization, particularly between its European and North American components; to incorporate into the West societies in Eastern Europe and Latin America whose cultures are close to those of the West; to promote and maintain cooperative relations with Russia and

Japan; to prevent escalation of local inter-civilization conflicts into major inter-civilization wars; to limit the expansion of the military strength of Confucian and Islamic states; to moderate the reduction of counter military capabilities and maintain military superiority in East and Southwest Asia; to exploit differences and conflicts among Confucian and Islamic states; to support in other civilizations groups **sympathetic** to Western values and interests; to strengthen international institutions that reflect and legitimate Western interests and values and to promote the involvement of non-Western states in those institutions.

In the longer term other measures would be called for. Western civilization is both Western and modern. Non-Western civilizations have attempted to become modern without becoming Western. To date only Japan has fully succeeded in this quest. Non-Western civilization will continue to attempt to acquire the wealth, technology, skills, machines and weapons that are part of being modern. They will also attempt to **reconcile** this modernity with their traditional culture and values. Their economic and military strength relative to the West will increase. Hence the West will increasingly have to accommodate these non-Western modern civilizations whose power approaches that of the West but whose values and interests differ significantly from those of the West. This will require the West to maintain the economic and military power necessary to protect its interests in relation to these civilizations. It will also, however, require the West to develop a more **profound** understanding of the basic religious and philosophical assumptions underlying other civilizations and the ways in which people in those civilizations see their interests. It will require an effort to identify elements of commonality between Western and other civilizations. For the relevant future, there will be no universal civilization, but instead a world of different civilizations, each of which will have to learn to coexist with the others.

Retrieved from *http://history. club. fatih. edu. tr/103% 20Huntington% 20Clash% 20of% 20*

New Words and Phrases

entity	n.	thing with distinct and real exsistence 实体
heterogeneity	n.	varied in composition 异种,异质,不同成分
anglophone Caribbean		英语语系的加勒比海人
blend	v.	form a mixture 混合
variants	n.	变体,变型
directorate	n.	board of directors 董事会,理事会
euphemistic	adj.	委婉的
impose	v.	inflict 将某事物强加于
neo-Bolsheviks		新布尔什维克

expropriate	v.	没收,征用,剥夺
abstention	n.	abstaining, esp not using one's vote at an election 弃权,弃权票
permeate	v.	enter sth and spread to each part 弥漫,渗透,透过,充满
resonance	n.	共鸣,回声,反响
propagate	v.	spread more widely 传播,宣传
indigenous	adj.	native 本土的
fundamentalism	n.	原教旨主义(认为圣经的经文翔实无误,应构成宗教的理论或实践的基础)
at odds with		disagreeing or quarrelling with 与某人不合,争吵
manifest	adj.	clear and obvious 明白的,明显的
insulate sb./sth. from/against		protect sb./sth. from the unpleasant effects of sth 使某人(某物)与不良影响隔绝
opt out of		choose not to take part in 决定不参加
band-wagon		join others in doing sth fashionable 赶时髦
supplant	v.	take the place of, replace 取代,代替
escalation	n.	becoming more intense 逐步升级或加速
sympathetic	adj.	showing favour or approval 表示好感或赞同
reconcile	v.	使一致,和谐
profound	adj.	intense or far-reaching 深刻,极度

About the author:

Samuel P. Huntington is the Eaton Professor of the Science of Government at Harvard University, where Samuel spent most of his teaching career specializing in defense and international affairs. In 1993, Huntington ignited a debate with the publication of an extremely influential and often-cited article entitled *The Clash of Civilization* in which he predicted conflicts between the world's major cultures in the post-Cold War era.

Notes to the text

1. *The Clash of Civilizations*: Huntington later expanded the article *the Clash of Civilizations* into a full-length book, published in 1996, and entitled *The Clash of Civilizations and the Remaking of World Order*. The book articulates(清晰地表达) his views that post-Cold War conflict would occur most frequently and violently along cultural (often civilizational, e.g., Western, Islamic, Sinic, Hindu, etc.) instead of ideological lines.

2. **Huntington states his basic contention (论点) pretty concisely:** culture and cultural

identities, which at the broadest level are civilization identities, are shaping the patterns of cohesion (凝聚), disintegration (解体), and conflict in the post-Cold War world.

He breaks the world up into seven separate competing civilizations: Western; Sinic (roughly the Chinese); Japanese; Hindu; Islamic; Orthodox (东正教); Latin American; and offers the possibility that African civilization may be an eighth; and then goes on to elaborate his theory.

尽管实现不同民族、国家和宗教之间的和平共处一直是人类的共同理想,萨缪尔·亨廷顿在《文明的冲突》一文中却指出:冷战时代的政治意识形态对垒结束之后,世界冲突的主流将不再是政治冲突和经济冲突。在亨廷顿看来,中华文明和伊斯兰文明同西方基督教文明有很大的差异性,未来世界的冲突将是由此而起的。

3. **Lucian Pye 白鲁恂**: (1921 – 2008) a political scientist, was considered one of the most knowledgeable observers of China.

4. **Anglophone Caribbean 加勒比海英语作为母语的国家**: used to refer to the independent English-speaking countries of the Caribbean region. Upon a country's full independence from the United Kingdom, Anaglophone Caribbean traditionally becomes the preferred sub-regional term as a replacement to British West Indies, countries including: Barbados 巴巴多斯, Jamaica 牙买加, Saint Lucia 圣·卢西亚。

5. **Arnold Joseph Toynbee 汤恩比** (1889 – 1975): a British historian who wrote the famous twelve-volume analysis of the rise and fall of civilizations, *A Study of History*《历史研究》。

6. **Georgy Arbatov 阿尔巴托夫**: 曾任六位苏联首脑外交助理, a soviet politician, academic and political advisor.

7. **Pan Am 103 Bombing 洛克比空难 (泛美航空公司客机爆炸案)**: On December 21st 1988, the world was shocked at the downing of umbo jet Pan Am 103 at Lockerbie, Scotland. All 259 passengers and crew and eleven people on the ground were killed, including 189 Americans. Following that terrorist attack, international sanctions were imposed by the United Nations against Libya since Libya failed to deliver the two suspects in the bombing for trial.

Exercises

I. **Answer these questions based on Text and the words and expressions listed below are for your references.**

1. **According to Huntington, in what meaningful ways should the world be divided?**
   in terms of their political or economic systems/in terms of their level of economic development /culture and civilization

2. **What is Samuel P. Huntington's definition of a civilization?**
   a cultural entity/common objective elements/the subjective self-identification of

people/be dynamic as time flows

3. What is the euphemistic implication of the phrase "the world community"?

to give global legitimacy/reflect the interests of/at an overwhelming peak of power

4. What may be the sources of conflict between the West and other civilizations?

differences in power/struggles for military, economic and institutional power/ differences in culture

5. Comment on the possibility of one universal civilization.

a universal civilization that fits all men/differ fundamentally from those prevalent in other civilizations/have no resonance in other cultures

6. What are the possible responses of non-western civilizations to western power and values?

to pursue a course of isolation/to opt out of participation in the western-dominated global community/to join the West and accept its values and institutions/to balance the West by developing economic and military power and cooperating with other non-Western societies against the West

7. What does "to modernize but not to Westernize" mean?

develop their own economic and military power /establish cooperation within themselves /preserve indigenous values and institutions

8. Sum up the implications of the clash of civilizations for the West in your own words.

II. Further questions for discussion.

1. Do you have faith in a "universal civilization" in the end? Why or why not?

2. Can you cite any example to show that the United States and other Western powers try to induce the rest of the world to adopt Western ideas concerning democracy and human rights?

3. What is your attitude towards the Islamic fundamentalism? Is it justified ? Why?

4. Since Sept. 11, 2001, ideas about the nature of religious and cultural conflicts have been a subject of heated debates. Is the war in Iraq a war against Islam in the name of anti-terrorism?

5. What do you think of anti-Americanism?

III. Vocabulary study.

1. Word in Use.

1) **blend**：mix in order to get a certain quality 混合,掺和

Those cottages blend perfectly with the landscape.

The poem blends the separate ingredients into a unity.

Many animals can blend with their surroundings, owing to their protective colouring.

2) **impose**：try to make sb. accept an opinion or belief 将某事物强加于

She imposed her ideas on her children.

The government imposes additional tax on business expansion.

The abrupt earthquake imposes hardships on the population of the area.

3) **propagate**：to spread views, knowledge, beliefs more widely 传播观点，知识，信仰等

It is necessary to propagate scientific knowledge among farmers nowadays.

The farmer was hoping to propagate the best qualities of both types of sheep.

Hitler tried to propagate the myth of racial superiority.

4) **at odds with**：disagreeing or quarreling with 不和，争吵

The newly wed couple is constantly at odds with each other.

He was personally at odds with the new policy.

On many issues John and Mary found themselves seriously at odds.

5) **manifest**：clear or obvious 明白的，明显的

It is manifest to us all that she has little interest in this.

If she had inner doubts, it was not manifest to anyone else.

She heard the news of his death with manifest unconcern.

6) **opt out of**：choose not to take part in 决定不参加

I think I'd better opt out of the game.

Today there is a growing tendency for people to opt out.

Teachers must not be allowed to opt out of their responsibility.

7) **supplant**：replace; take the place of 取代

Machinery has largely supplanted hand labour in making shoes.

The tyrant managed to supplant the teachings of rule of love with the practice of the rule of fear.

The general plotted to supplant the king with the help of the army.

8) **sympathetic**：showing favor or approval 同情的，表示同情的

He's wrong; I am not sympathetic to him.

Public opinions seem sympathetic.

She found her boyfriend very sympathetic.

9) **reconcile**：make aims, statements agree when they seem to conflict 使一致，和谐

The policeman is trying to reconcile the evidence with the facts.

After each fight they are soon reconciled.

Since the couple could not reconcile their differences, they decided to get a divorce.

10) **profound**：deep, intense, very great 深的，深切的，深远的

His ignorance of economics is profound.

They listened to the speaker with profound interest.

Finally, we want to take this opportunity to beg him to convey our profound friendship and best regards to his people.

2. Word Distinctions.

1）**indigenous；native** 均表示'本土的'，在这个意思上，两个词可替代。

但 indigenous 强调'自然土生土长的而不是外地来的'（naturally existing in a place rather than arriving from another place）课文中'a reaffirmation of indigenous values'重新肯定本土价值。native 虽是出生本土但后来可能转而生活它乡. 如电影：*A Native of Beijing in New York.* 另外 native 还有 first, or coming before any others 的意思。

选择以上适当的词填空：

The Maori are the _____ people of New Zealand.

This was his first visit to his _____ land in 30 years.

His _____ language is Spanish, but he speaks English without a trace of an accent.

The horse is not _____ to America — it was introduced by the Spanish.

2）**tear sth；tear at sth**

tear：to pull or be pulled apart

tear at sth：to try to pull pieces off something in a violent way/to cause you to feel emotional

选择以上适当的词填空：

There are scenes in this movie that _____ my heart because they are just like scenes from my life.

I _____ my skirt on the chair as I stood up.

The wind _____ the newly planted trees.

The dog _____ the meat on the bone.

A couple of pages had been _____ from the book

She _____ the bandages until they loosened.

3. Decide the meanings of the following words from the context by matching each word in Column A with the word or expression in Column B that is similar in meaning.

A	B
1）be at odds with	a. take the place of；replace
2）manifest	b. showing favor or approval
3）insulate sb/sth from or against	c. clear or obvious
4）opt out of	d. place sth unpleasant on sb
5）supplant	e. deep, far-reaching
6）escalation	f. be disagreeing or quarrelling
7）sympathetic	g. protect from the unpleasant effects of sth.

8) reconcile sth. with sth.   h. decide not to take part in

9) profound   i. increase

10) impose   j. make sth. agree when they seem to conflict

4. Try to write a brief story with the following words and phrases.

science, democracy, terrorism, war,

the fundamental problems of mankind, a universal civilization

IV. Translation.

1. Put the following Chinese expressions into English.

1) 文明的冲突   2) 文化认同   3) 普世文明   4) 本土价值观

5) 原教旨主义   6) 文明实体   7) 世界共同体   8) 霸权地位

2. Put the following Chinese sentences into English with the words or phrases in the bracket.

1) 新建的办公大楼与周围的环境很不协调。(blend)

2) 我绝不会勉强别人接受我的意见。(impose)

3) 传教士到东方传播其信仰。(propagate)

4) 在政治上他总是和父亲意见不合。(at odds with)

5) 游行示威仅仅显示了人们对政府的不满而已。(manifest)

6) 要是我决定退出的话,该办理什么样的手续? (opt out)

7) 我们的主要出口货物已经由咖啡改为石油了。(supplant)

8) 我确信他一定会赞成你的建议。(sympathetic)

9) 我会让自己的想法和你的想法一致起来。(reconcile)

10) 那位知名科学家对宗教产生极大的兴趣。(profound)

3. Put the following Chinese paragraphs into English.

我们生活在一个与其他星球隔绝的美丽的小星球上,但是地球的人口已经太多;庞大的消费社会正在成长;科技也变得无比强大,足以毁灭这个星球。我们正疯狂地奔向一个极端的时代:极端的富有,极端的贫困,极端的科学技术,极端的科学试验,极端的全球化影响力,大规模的毁灭性武器,还有以宗教名义进行的恐怖活动。假如想要逃此一劫,我们就得学会如何驾驭这一形势。

我们正面临诸多难以克服的困难。但这是一本提出解决方案的书,一本提供许多解决方案的书。有了这些解决方案,我们将促成变化,修正航程。如果做的对,我们就会有美好的未来。如果做错了,人类的进程将受到干扰,其结果无法逆转,人类将因之倒退几个世纪。

4. Put the following quotes into Chinese.

1) Civilization begins with order, grows with liberty, and dies with chaos.

—— Will Durant

2) The true civilization is where every man gives to every other every right that he

claims for himself.   —— Robert Ingersoll

3）Every advance in civilization has been denounced as unnatural while it was recent.   —— Bertrand Russell

4）All our lauded technological progress — our every civilization — is like the axe in the hand of the pathological criminal.   —— Albert Einstein

5）The end of the human race will be that it will eventually die of civilization.

—— Ralph Waldo Emerson

5. Translate the following passage into Chinese.

We are all men with the same power of making and destroying, with the same divine foresight mocked by the same animal blindness. We ourselves may not be in fault today, but it is human being in no way different from us who are doing what we abhor and they abhor even when they do it. There is a fate, coming from the beast in our own past, that the present man in us has not yet mastered, and for the moment that fate seems a malignity in the nature of universe that mocks us even in the beauty of those lonely hills. But it is not so, for we are not separate and indifferent like beasts; and if one nation for the moment forgets our common humanity and its future, then another must take over that sacred charge and guard it without hatred or fear until the madness is passed. May that be our task now, so that we may wage war only for the future peace of the world and with the lasting courage that needs no stimulant of hate.

From *Sunday before the War* by *Arthur Clutton-Brock*,《中国翻译》2001 年第 5 期

V. Comment on the structure of the text.

The text is an abridged version of Samuel P. Huntington's political essay *The clash of Civilizations* which Huntington later developed into the book *The Clash of Civilization and the Remaking of World Order*. While the text from the essay chiefly focuses its attention on the nature of civilizations, the West vs the rest and the implications of the clashes for the West, the full length book comprise the following five parts：

Part I：For the first time in history global politics is both multipolar and multicivilizational；modernization is distinct from Westernization and is producing neither a universal civilization in any meaningful sense nor the Westernization of non-Western societies.

Part II：The balance of power among civilizations is shifting：the West is declining in relative influence；Asian civilizations are expanding their economic, military, and political strength；Islam is exploding demographically with destabilizing consequences for Muslim countries and their neighbors；and non-Western civilizations generally are reaffirming the value of their own cultures.

Part III: A civilization-based world order is emerging: societies sharing cultural affinities cooperate with each other; efforts to shift societies from one civilization to another are unsuccessful; and countries group themselves around the lead or core states of their civilization.

Part IV: The West's universalist pretensions increasingly bring it into conflict with other civilizations, most seriously with Islam and China; at the local level fault line wars, largely between Muslims and non-Muslims, generate "kin-country rallying," the threat of broader escalation, and hence efforts by core states to halt these wars.

Part V: The survival of the West depends on Americans reaffirming their Western identity and Westerners accepting their civilization as unique not universal and uniting to renew and preserve it against challenges from non-Western societies. Avoidance of a global war of civilizations depends on world leaders accepting.

Extended Exercises

1. Arrange the following paragraphs in a logical order.

Lessons of London: What's next in War on Terror

1) Ultimately, the only real defense from terrorist attacks is being able to find out about them in advance. Intelligence gathering has improved but needs to be even stronger, including consistently improving human intelligence and patrol. Police and ordinary citizens must be alert and encouraged to convey information.

2) London is one of the most secure cities in the world, steeped in years of dealing with terrorism. The city's preparation and resolve was evident on July 7. I am very impressed by London's reaction to the bombings. Both the emergency personnel and the citizens seemed prepared. The first responders were rapid, well-directed, organized and professional, in accordance with obviously well-tested plans.

3) Once a terrorist incident does occur, there is no such thing as a perfect response. By definition, a terrorist attack means people are being hurt or killed. But by studying the response to past attacks, we can better prepare to handle those in the future.

4) The effort must continue. As we learned on July 7, 2005 — and in Madrid and Bali — the enemies have not lost their resolve. We must not lose ours.

5) That is not only a realistic assessment; it also is a mindset that just might save lives. Political, business and community leaders are sometimes reluctant to talk about terrorism or stage drills to prepare their response because they don't want to frighten or upset people. But that's a mistake. People react to emergencies more effectively when they're not shocked by them.

6) As for the citizens, at least a dozen people told me in one way or another, "we know

this was going to happen; it was just a question of when. "

From *The World of English*, May 2006

2. In the following article, some paragraphs have been removed. Choose the most suitable paragraph from the list A-E to fit into each of the numbered gaps. There is ONE paragraph, which does not fit in any of the gaps.

Insignia: the Way You Tell Who's Who in the Military

From the earliest days of warfare to the present, special rank badges meant survival. In the heat of battle, knowing who to listen to was as important as the fighting skills soldiers and sailors developed. They had to know at a glance whose shouted orders to obey.

1) _____

As armies and navies started growing, however, that kind of intimacy wasn't possible. The badge of rank, therefore, became important. Today's Army, Marine Cops, Navy, Air Force and Coast Guard rank insignia are the result of thousands of years of tradition.

2) _____

The American military adapted most of its rank insignia from the British. Before the Revolutionary War, Americans drilled with militia outfits based on the British tradition. Sailors followed the example of the most successful navy of the time — the Royal Navy.

3) _____

To solve this, Gen. George Washington wrote, "as the Continental Army has unfortunately no uniforms, and consequently many inconveniences must arise from not being able to distinguish the commissioned officers from the privates, it is desired that some badge of distinctions be immediately provided; for instance that the field officers may have red or pink colored cockades in their hats, the captains yellow or buff and the subalterns green. "

4) _____

The use of most English ranks carried on even after the United States won the war. The army and Marine Corps used comparable ranks, especially after 1840. The Navy took a different route.

A: When the Air Force became a separate service in 1947, it kept the Army officers insignia and names, but adopted different enlisted ranks and insignia.

B: So, the Continental Army had privates, sergeants, lieutenants, captains, colonels, generals, and several now-obsolete ranks like coronet, subaltern and ensign. One thing the Army didn't have was enough money to buy uniforms.

C: Even during the war, rank insignia evolved. In 1780, regulations prescribed two stars for major generals and one star for brigadiers worn on shoulder boards, for epaulettes.

D: Through the ages, the badge of ranks have included such symbols as feathers, sashes, stripes and showy uniforms. Even carrying different weapons has significant rank. The badges of rank have been worn on hats, shoulders and around the waist and chest.

E: In the earliest times, rank was not an issue. "Do what Grog says" was enough so long as everyone knows Grog.

From *The English World*, March 2006

3. The passage contains TEN errors. Each indicated line contains a maximum of ONE error. In each case, only ONE word is involved. You should proofread the passage and correct it.

Man-made diamonds are nothing new — industry started making
them in the 1950s, and each year about 80 tons of high-quality　　　1) _____
synthetic diamonds are used in tools like drill bits and sanders.
High-quality crystals, though, open up huge possibilities, jewelry is　　2) _____
the least of them. Scientists are most excited about the prospect of
making diamond microchips. As for chips have shrunk over the　　　3) _____
years, engineers have struggled with ways of dissipating the heat　　4) _____
they create. Because silicon, the main component of
semiconductors, breaks out at about 200 degrees Fahrenheit, some　　5) _____
experts believe new material will be needed in a decade or so.　　　6) _____
Diamonds might pay the bill. They can withstand 1,000 degrees,　　7) _____
and electrons move through them so easily that they would tend to　　8) _____
heat up in the first place. Engineers could cram a lot more circuits　　9) _____
into a diamond-based microchip — so they could perfect a way of　　10) _____
making pure crystals cheaply.

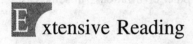

Extensive Reading

Passage One

When Cultures Collide
萨缪尔·亨廷顿(Sam Huntington)
谈文化冲突 (When Cultures Collide)

Ben Wattenberg:

Sam Huntington, welcome to Think Tank. Can you give us an short take (简要介绍) just to begin our conversation, on the thesis of The Clash of Civilizations?

Sam Huntington：

Well, I think the essence of the argument is that during the 20ᵗʰ century and the Cold War, ideology（意识形态）was a key factor in international relations. The wars were between fascists, communists and liberal democratic countries.

Ben Wattenberg：

Right, okay.

Sam Huntington：

And now ideology has faded from the scene and people no longer identify with ideologies; they identify with their cultures and cultures may exist at a very local level, but there are also broader cultural entities, and the broadest cultural entities are civilizations. And the argument of the book is that the most dangerous conflicts in the future will be between states and groups from different civilizations because these have a potential to escalate.

Ben Wattenberg：

Because they're dragging（卷入）their allies with them.

Sam Huntington：

Exactly. Following September eleventh, how did the world divide in terms of cultures and civilizations? The countries that are closest to us culturally — Britain, Canada, Australia — immediately came forward（挺身而出）, sent military forces to work with ours. The reaction in Europe, part of Western civilization as we are, was again enthusiastic sympathy and expressions of support. And then you have countries in the other civilizations, in some cases being rather surprisingly cooperative, like Russia.

Ben Wattenberg：

And now India.

Sam Huntington：

And China. But at a more modest level. And then we have the Muslim world which clearly is very ambivalent（心情复杂）about what happened to us and what has happened in Afghanistan. And so they divide very much along civilizational lines.

Ben Wattenberg：

Well, they do and they don't. I mean, if you put, as you do in your book, you put Russia in a separate civilization; you put India in a separate civilization. And now we have the situation where they're marching in lock-step (步伐一致).

Sam Huntington:

Well, lock-step is an overstatement.

Ben Wattenberg:

Well. But neither is France marching in lock-step.

Sam Huntington:

They are cooperating with us because we have defined this situation now as a war on terrorism. The interesting question is, to what extent is this a lasting coalition (联盟) against terrorism, and to what extent will it dissipate (逐渐解散).

Ben Wattenberg:

However, you say in your book that the West is in decline. And that East Asia is ascendant (上升). Since you wrote the article and then the book, Indonesia has come pretty close to collapsing, and Japan has been in a dozen year slump now from which it may never emerge. On the one hand you can say, Nine Eleven was a civilizational conflict. But the results of it don't seem to be in keeping with (一致) what you wrote.

Sam Huntington:

Well, first of all, I think one has to look at this as I tried to do it in the book in terms of a longer historical perspective. What could be considered the high point of the West was right after World War I, when Western countries ruled a huge portion of the world. And the world was colored, in large part, red as the result of the British Empire. And that has faded.

Ben Wattenberg:

Well, it has faded, but you mark that as an indicator, as you just did, of the peak of Western civilization.

Sam Huntington:

Well, of the peak of the political influence, rule of western civilization.

Ben Wattenberg:

On the other hand, the West saw the addition of a number of Eastern European countries and possibly Russia after the Cold War.

Sam Huntington:

Oh, come on, Russia isn't part of Western civilization in any meaningful sense of that term.

Ben Wattenberg:

You make the case (你想说明) that it's not only wrong-headed but dangerous to consider what we call 'Western values' as universally appealing. I don't buy that. I seem to think that my sense of the way the world works is that when given half a chance, people really do want liberty.

Sam Huntington:

I think people do want liberty, and what form of liberty they want is very important. And what key concept, particularly, in the United States, is individualism. And most of the world doesn't look at that as a prime value. They put much greater emphasis upon collectivities. People have the individual rights that are given to them by their tribe or their state or whatever.

Ben Wattenberg:

When you say that, it sounds to me as if you're saying 'things don't change', yet we have seen in recent decades there are more and more democratic societies. You look at economic liberty, market societies. And these are both sort of hallmarks (标记) of Western civilization. And it goes up and up and up... into well, China.

Sam Huntington:

The Chinese really had market economy at a primitive level, of course, long before Western civilization existed.

Ben Wattenberg:

Well, but their picking up (很快学得) of the market economy now is in some large measure due to the fact that they want to play in the Western game. They really have to.

Sam Huntington:

Well, they want to play in the global game. And everybody has recognized that a state-run economy is not a very efficient way to run an economy. I have never said there isn't change. I argue in my book that as civilizations evolve, interact with each other, of course there's change. And particularly the emergence of this multi-civilizational world where people in different civilizations, who historically have been pretty much isolated from each other, are now interacting with each other in a very intense fashion, in a way which never happened before.

Ben Wattenberg:

But I think that there is this tendency going on around the world, that the world is picking up the views and values of Western thought.

Sam Huntington:

What I think we have to get back to is a basic distinction, which I elaborate at some length (充分详细阐述) in the book, which is the difference between Westernization and modernization.

Ben Wattenberg:

Yes. That's important.

Sam Huntington:

All the world, obviously, or almost all the world certainly, wants to modernize, develop, become more prosperous and so forth. But that does not necessarily mean that they want to adopt Western culture. And in many cases, don't want to adopt Western values.

Ben Wattenberg:

Well, tell me the hallmarks of Western culture.

Sam Huntington:

Well, I mentioned one: individualism. There's the pluralism (多元), which has existed in the West as it has in no other civilization really. The idea of representation(西方代表权制) as existed in the West, and the distinction between the religious sphere and the political sphere. These are some of the distinctive characteristics of a Western civilization. Any one of these can be found in other civilizations, but the peculiar combination is unique to the West and this is the reason why, three or four centuries ago, the West took the lead in modernization and in economic development.

Ben Wattenberg:

I don't think that has stopped. And yet it seems to me that tendency is continuing, it is expanding.

Sam Huntington:

What tendency?

Ben Wattenberg:

The tendency of people to look at those, and to adapt, those hallmarks of Western civilization, freedom of expression, freedom of religion. People really do like individualism. And they want individual liberty.

Sam Huntington:

Look, Ben, you make these statements 'people like individualism'. Show me some hard data(确凿数据) that will support that. Now I look through the things, say, the World Values Survey, which has been done three times so far in the past couple of decades looking at different countries and it's very hard to find much evidence of that sort of change. It's, again, hard to find much in the way of change over time.

Ben Wattenberg:

Does voting count? It's individual action to shape their own destiny.

Sam Huntington:

Well, there has certainly been a spread of democratic regimes around the world. I think it is fair to say democracy has taken root successfully in countries where there was a significant Western influence.

Ben Wattenberg:

Now, Bangladesh has something like a democratic government. Pakistan had it for a while and who knows where it's going. So ...

Sam Huntington:

There's a very real distinction between electoral democracy and liberal democracy(选举民主与自由民主之区分).

Ben Wattenberg:

I understand.

Sam Huntington:

And Western democracy is liberal democracy. Now maybe a liberal democracy will follow the introduction of elections, but that hasn't happened yet. And law and order and the protection of civil rights, freedom of the press, minority rights, and a rule of law that you can trust ...

Ben Wattenberg:

Okay, now let's talk about America because that's what I really want to talk about. You seem to indicate in the book in these perilous times, internally America doesn't have the spine and the backbone to weather this storm. The case is made that America is internally weak, that we've lost our moral compass, that we have high crime rates, that we have the other form of multi-culturalism: Balkanization, separatism, and there's a high rate of illegitimate births, and that this weakens us.

Sam Huntington:

Well, I think those have been real problems in our society. I don't see how anybody could deny that. But I also have argued in the book that's the great characteristic of the United States, because we are such an open, pluralistic, competitive society, that when we develop problems, whether it's crime or birth control or education or poverty or whatever, we engage in a national debate. The press, political parties, intellectual leaders come up with solutions and, as a result, several of the problems which you mentioned have certainly been reduced in their severity now because of the nature of American society. And I think that is the great strength of this country. And I think that is more characteristic of American society than of a society anywhere else.

Ben Wattenberg:

Including our Western colleagues in Europe.

Sam Huntington:

Yes, definitely because they are also liberal democratic regimes but they don't have anything like the openness and the pluralism that we have.

Ben Wattenberg:

Do you think there's a good chance that there will be a war — as in real war — between civilizations, or is this more likely to be an on-going contest for ideas and loyalties?

Sam Huntington:

Well, it certainly will be the latter. It could be the former. We have all around the border of the Muslim world, you have Muslims fighting non-Muslims. We also have been on the verge of a major inter-state war between Pakistan and India. And that strikes me as a very dangerous situation as to how that might escalate in terms of involving other societies. And as I point out in the book, I think a major potential danger would be a conflict between China and the United States, because there are very real issues separating China and the United States.

Ben Wattenberg:

That's really the big one, isn't it?

Sam Huntington:

And while the Chinese have been cooperating with us, more or less, on the terrorist front, there is the big issue of who's going to be the dominant power in East Asia. Japan was once. We have been for the past fifty years. China was the dominant power for many, many centuries and the Chinese, quite naturally, think they ought to resume that position.

Ben Wattenberg:

Will America and the West prevail (胜出)?

Sam Huntington:

I think America will remain, by far and away, the single most powerful country. The West will remain the primary civilization. But I think there are powerful indigenous forces in many societies, not all societies, that are appealing to local traditions and values and customs and rejecting what they view as the cultural imperialism and arrogance of the West.

Ben Wattenberg:

Sam, thank you very much for joining us. And thank you. For Think Tank, I'm Ben Wattenberg.

Retrieved from *PBS' "THINK TANK WITH BEN WATTENBERG"* # 1005 *"When Cultures Collide" Broadcast* 1/24/2002

I. Reading comprehension.

1. According to Samuel Huntington, the most dangerous conflicts in the future will be
   _____

   A) between fascists, communists and liberal democratic countries.

   B) between states and groups from different civilizations.

   C) between countries with different ideologies.

   D) between Russian and the rest of western countries.

2. According to this passage, what distinguishes the United States from its Western colleagues in Europe?

   A) Openness and pluralism.

   B) The idea of democratic structure.

   C) Distinction between the religious sphere and the political sphere.

   D) A combination of above-mentioned characteristics.

3. What was Ben Wattenberg's attitude towards the views and values of Western civilization?

   A) He was neural in his statement.

   B) He agreed with Samuel Huntington.

   C) He believed that people would tend to pick up those hallmarks of Western civilizations.

   D) He argued that Western democracy would never be accepted by other civilizations.

4. Why did Huntington argue that a major potential danger would be a conflict between China and the United States?

   A) Because China did not support the United States on the terrorist front.

   B) Because China has its own views and values which differ from that of Western countries.

   C) Because of the big issue of who's going to be the dominant power in East Asia.

   D) Because China was sympathetic with Muslims.

5. Which of the following statements concerned with 9.11 is NOT TRUE?

   A) The world is already divided in terms of cultures and civilizations.

   B) Most of the countries of western civilization are sympathetic and supportive.

   C) Britain, Canada and Australia are closest to the United States in terms of culture.

   D) China seemed to be surprisingly cooperative.

II. Topics for further discussion.

1. Do you think mankind is facing a great chance of a Third World War? What do you think would be some of the possible triggers and underlying causes that may lead to another world war?

2. Can cultural differences be gradually erased with modernization and globalization?

3. What does the support for religious fundamentalism by the younger generation in non-Western cultures imply?

Passage Two

Let's Make Enemies(让我们成为敌人)

Naomi Klein

美国政府认为伊拉克战争是拯救伊拉克人民于水深火热的正义之举,然而事实是否如此呢?

"Do you have any rooms?" we ask the hotelier. She looks us over, dwelling on my travel partner's bald, white head. "No," she replies. We try not to notice that there are sixty room keys in pigeonholes(分类架) behind her desk — the place is empty. "Will you have a room soon? Maybe next week?" She hesitates. "Ahh. . . . No."

We return to our current hotel — the one we want to leave because there are bets on when it is going to get hit — and flick on the TV: The BBC is showing footage (片断) of Richard Clarke's testimony before the September 11 Commission, and a couple of pundits are arguing about whether invading Iraq has made America safer.

They should try finding a hotel room in this city, where the US occupation has unleashed (放开,去掉限制) a wave of anti-American rage so intense that it now extends not only to US troops, occupation officials and their contractors but also to foreign journalists, aid workers, their translators and pretty much anyone else associated with the Americans. Which is why we couldn't begrudge (不满) the hotelier her decision: If you want to survive in Iraq, it's wise to stay the hell away from people who look like us. (We thought about explaining that we were Canadians, but all the American reporters are sporting the maple leaf — that is, when they aren't trying to disappear behind their newly purchased headscarves (头巾).)

US occupation chief Paul Bremer hasn't started wearing a hijab yet, and is instead tackling the rise of anti-Americanism with his usual foresight. Baghdad is blanketed with inept (不熟练,不恰当) psy-ops organs like *Baghdad Now*, filled with fawning articles about how Americans are teaching Iraqis about press freedom. "I never thought before that the Coalition (联合政府) could do a great thing for the Iraqi people," one trainee is quoted saying. "Now I can see it on my eyes what they are doing good things for my country and the accomplishment they made. I wish my people can see that, the way I see it."

Unfortunately, the Iraqi people recently saw another version of press freedom when Bremer ordered US troops to shut down a newspaper run by supporters of Muqtada al-Sadr. The militant Shiite cleric has been preaching that Americans are behind the attacks on Iraqi civilians and condemning the interim (暂时,临时的) constitution as a "terrorist law". So far, al-Sadr has refrained from calling on his supporters to join the armed resistance, but many here are predicting that the closing down of the newspaper — a nonviolent means of resisting the occupation — was just the push he needed. But then, recruiting for the resistance has always been a specialty of the Presidential Envoy to Iraq: Bremer's first act after being tapped by Bush was to fire 400,000 Iraqi soldiers, refuse to give them their rightful pensions but allow them to hold on to their weapons — in case they needed them later.

I have gone to the mosques and street demonstrations and listened to Muqtada al-Sadr's supporters shout "Death to America, Death to the Jews," and it is indeed chilling (吓人的). But it is the profound sense of betrayal expressed by a pro-US businessman running a Pepsi plant that attests (证明了) to the depths of the US-created disaster here. "I'm disappointed, not because I hate the Americans," Khamis tells me, "but because I like them. And when you love someone and they hurt you, it hurts even more."

When we leave the bottling plant in late afternoon, the streets of US-occupied Baghdad are filled with al-Sadr supporters vowing bloody revenge for the attack on their newspaper. A spokesperson for Bremer is defending the decision on the grounds that the paper "was making people think we were out to get them."

A growing number of Iraqis are certainly under that impression, but it has far less to do with an inflammatory (煽动性的) newspaper than with the inflammatory actions of the US occupation authority. As the June 30 "handover" approaches, Paul Bremer has unveiled a slew of (许多) new tricks to hold on to power long after "sovereignty" has been declared.

Some recent highlights: At the end of March, building on his Order 39 of last September, Bremer passed yet another law further opening up Iraq's economy to foreign ownership, a law that Iraq's next government is prohibited from changing under the terms of the interim constitution. Bremer also announced the establishment of several independent regulators, which will drastically reduce the power of Iraqi government ministries. For instance, the *Financial Times* reports that "officials of the Coalition Provisional Authority said the regulator would prevent communications minister Haider al-Abadi, a thorn in the side of the coalition, from carrying out his threat to cancel licenses the coalition awarded to foreign-managed consortia (联营) to operate three mobile networks and the national broadcaster."

The CPA has also confirmed that after June 30, the $18.4 billion the US government is spending on reconstruction will be administered by the US Embassy in Iraq. The money will be spent over five years and will fundamentally redesign Iraq's most basic infrastructure, including its electricity, water, oil and communications sectors, as well as its courts and police. Iraq's future governments will have no say in the construction of these core sectors of Iraqi society. Retired Rear Adm. David Nash, who heads the Project Management Office, which administers the funds, describes the $18.4 billion as "a gift from the American people to the people of Iraq." He appears to have forgotten the part about gifts being something you actually give up. And in the same eventful week, US engineers began construction on fourteen "enduring bases" in Iraq, capable of housing the 110,000 soldiers who will be posted here for at least two more years. Even though the bases are being built with no mandate (授权) from an Iraqi government, Brig. Gen. Mark Kimmitt, deputy chief of operations in Iraq, called them "a blueprint (蓝图) for how we could operate in the Middle East."

The US occupation authority has also found a sneaky way to maintain control over Iraq's armed forces. Bremer has issued an executive order stating that even after the interim Iraqi government has been established, the Iraqi army will answer to US commander Lieut. Gen. Ricardo Sanchez. In order to pull this off, Washington is relying on a legalistic reading of a clause in UN Security Council Resolution 1511, which puts US forces in charge of Iraq's security until "the completion of the political process" in Iraq. Since the "political process" in Iraq is never-ending, so, it seems, is US military control.

In the same flurry (骚动) of activity, the CPA announced that it would put further constraints on the Iraqi military by appointing a national security adviser for Iraq. This US appointee would have powers equivalent to those held by Condoleezza Rice and will stay in office for a five-year term, long after Iraq is scheduled to have made the transition to a democratically elected government.

There is one piece of this country, though, that the US government is happy to cede (让予,放弃) to the people of Iraq: the hospitals. On March 27 Bremer announced that he had withdrawn the senior US advisers from Iraq's Health Ministry, making it the first sector to achieve "full authority" in the US occupation.

Taken together, these latest measures paint a telling picture of what a "free Iraq" will look like: The United States will maintain its military and corporate presence through fourteen enduring military bases and the largest US Embassy in the world. It will hold on to authority over Iraq's armed forces, its security and economic policy and the design of its core infrastructure — but the Iraqis can deal with their decrepit (破旧的) hospitals all by themselves, complete with their chronic (长期的) drug shortages and lack of the most basic sanitation capacity.

On nights when there are no nearby explosions, we hang out at the hotel, jumping at the sound of car doors slamming. Sometimes we flick on the news and eavesdrop on a faraway debate about whether invading Iraq has made Americans safer. Few seem interested in the question of whether the invasion has made *Iraqis* feel safer, which is too bad because the questions are intimately related. As Khamis says, "It's not the war that caused the hatred. It's what they did after. What they are doing now."

Retrieved from *http://www. thenation. com/doc/20040419/klein*10 – 23 – 2006

Decide whether the following statements are True or False.

1. The fact that the hotelier refused to let the American reporters check in indicates a sign of anti-Americanism. (   )
2. Paul Bremer makes great progress in tackling the rise of anti-Americanism. (   )
3. The author believes that a growing number of Iraqis tend to grudge against the United States because the inflammatory newspaper "was making people think we were out to get them". (   )
4. Iraq's future government will play an important role in the construction of the core sectors of Iraqi society. (   )
5. The US's efforts to free Iraq have not achieved what Iraqi people have expected. (   )

Unit 10

Professional Women and Domestic Violence

本单元课文综述

Text 精读　课文选自美国《职业妇女》杂志的一篇关于家庭暴力的文章。人们通常以为家庭暴力事件主要发生在下层社会的家庭里,而事实并非如此。家庭暴力超越社会经济阶层,上层与中层社会的妇女遭受家庭暴力的比例与低收入家庭妇女基本相同。这个结论似乎出人意料。

Passage One 泛读　文章的作者认为,对家庭暴力犯罪施于更加严厉的惩罚是制止家庭暴力的有效办法。

Passage Two 泛读　节选自英国约瑟夫·朗特利基金会(Joseph Rowntree Foundation)发表的一份报告:家庭暴力干预项目中的教训。参与该项目的有暴力倾向的男子与受害求助的妇女,配合妇女救助处共同阻止或减少男人的暴力。

ext　**Professional Women and Domestic Violence**

Hillary Johnson

For most people, the phrase "domestic violence" summons a stereotypical scene: police pounding on the door of a ramshackle house; a man loudly, perhaps drunkenly, declaring his innocence; a woman was crying. But for a vast number of middle-or upper-class women, many of them professionals, domestic violence is a secret, usually silent affair. They are prisoners of their world, but for many reasons they feel compelled to **don** a mask of **normalcy.** In spite of their bruises and scars, they may not even admit that they are victims. And until they fully acknowledge what is happening to them — a process that can take years — the very last thing they want to do is make their situation public.

Battering Crosses Class Lines

Definitive statistics on these white-collar victims are hard to come by, especially because shame or fear of reprisal makes them reluctant to report the crime. The Justice Department's 1994 National Crime Victimization Survey (NCVS) found that only about half the women who suffered domestic abuse between 1987 and 1991 reported it to the police. As incredible as it may seem, *Family Violence: Crime and Justice*, a 1989 book that reviewed the research on the subject, projected that one-fifth to one-third of all women could be assaulted by an intimate at some point. And the perception that most victims are poor and uneducated is clearly distorted. The NCVS found less than a 10% difference in the rate of family violence between those with household incomes of less than $10,000 and those earning more than $50,000. "Women of means are just as trapped as women on welfare," says Carol Arthur, the director of the Domestic Abuse Project in Minneapolis, Minnesota, a nonprofit program that aids victims. "The stories and issues are all the same. There are just different barriers to leaving the relationship."

Perhaps the greatest myth about white-collar domestic violence is that its victims should be able to arrange smooth, bloodless departures because, unlike poor women, they **are blessed with** financial and social resources. "The irony is how hard it can be even for women who earn more than the men they're involved with to leave," says Sharon Rice Vaughn, who co-founded one of the first battered-women's shelters in the country in 1972 in St. Paul, Minnesota. "It is particularly hard for professional, highly paid women to believe that battering is happening to them," One TV reporter was blind to the warning signs in her own relationship even though she had covered a number of domestic-violence cases. "I was in denial that I could be an abused woman because I'm smart, I'm professional, I know a lot of cops," she says. "And there was this constant self-questioning — is it really as bad as I think it is?" Experts say the confusion is compounded by a **Gaslight** (a movie by Alfred Hitchcock in which a husband schemes to convince his wife that she is going insane) effect created by the **sporadic**, random nature of the abuse; the victim wonders whether she really is being **brutalized** or whether the attacks are somehow her fault. The effect is even more potent when there's a strong desire to keep the relationship intact. "It's about wanting it to be a one-time thing," notes a domestic-abuse counselor.

Women's Success Breeds Targets

In addition, professional women are trapped by a fear of exposure. "That's the abuser's secret emotional blackmail," says Rice Vaughn. "If you have a reputation, your reputation will be ruined." In fact, women who earn more or are more successful than their partners can be more vulnerable targets than women of like status to their husbands', according to Evan Stark, co-director of the Domestic Violence Training Project in New Haven, Connecticut, 40% of whose clients are middle — and upper-class victims of domestic abuse. "Those men are compensating by resorting to socially **condoned** male dominance," explains Rice Vaughn. "It becomes their form of revenge. It's as though she is being blamed for his failures — if she weren't so successful, he wouldn't be seen as less successful. "

Lorraine Holmes, an attorney in Homestead, Florida, represents mainly women who have been battered or otherwise abused by their husbands. Holmes herself lived with an abusive man in South Florida for four years beginning in 1984 while attempting to build her law career. She was the wage earner, he the househusband who assured her he would soon "**make it big**" in the music business. "I always counsel women to make an escape plan," says Holmes. "If it means saving only $3 to $4 a week from the household money, do it. " Her own plan involved confronting her former husband — although she knew the result would be injury to herself — during an 18-month trial "pro-arrest period" in greater Miami. She arranged a two-week absence from work, then informed her husband of her intent to divorce him. "He dragged me across the floor, threw me into a wall and threatened to kill me. I had handprint bruises on my arms and an **abrasion** on my face, but I don't remember it was from him hitting me or slamming me into the wall. "

Subtle Manipulation

How did Holmes get involved with a violent man, and why did it take her four years to leave? Certainly, little about her suggests someone easily intimidated or willing to suffer abuse. During the 1970s, Holmes, who graduated in the top 7% of her law class, spent most of her time fighting for feminist causes. And her husband-to-be, like many abusers, showed no predilection toward violence throughout a five-month courtship; indeed, Holmes found him particularly seductive and charming. "He was the only man I had ever gone out with who was as smart as I was," Holmes says. "His sweet-talking got me hooked on the relationship. He had already started the crazy-making — convincing me I had no memory, that my recollections of conversations were wrong — but it was done very subtly. Despite one prior incident of abuse, I married him in May 1985. "

Aside from the subtle manipulation, there were no warning signs that he was capable of severe physical violence. The first blow enraged Holmes: "I told him to get out of my life. " Her reaction was typical of many women, says Evan Stark, "who have grown up with a certain level of entitlement — they're **incensed.** And at first they think they can control or change it. But with these manipulative men, you can be in a relationship for a long time before you get it together to leave. " Stark points out that in many white-collar households, the violence is not just sporadic but rare; rather, the abuser depends on "**coercive** strategies — the use of intimidation and threats — to gain and keep control. " Holmes allowed her husband to return when he convinced her that the violence had been a fluke. "When people like me, who are out to change the world, get into a relationship with someone who is so clearly disturbed, the crusading part of our personality comes out — we're going to fix that, too," she says.

Nevertheless, her husband steadily **escalated** the psychological harassment and abuse. "Butteries use the same techniques as terrorists," Holmes says. "Isolation, threats and random violence. I never knew whether I was coming home to a cooked meal and a bubble bath or to accusations and intimidating behavior, which may or may not have resulted in physical violence, like the meal being thrown in my face or him **jabbing at my gut with a two-by-four.** "

Holmes wanted out by the end of the second year of marriage, but like many in her situation, she was demoralized and discouraged, as well she might have been. Statistics indicate that women who leave their abusive partners are at a 75% greater risk of being killed by their abusers than those who stay. "I've followed the news and seen a lot of domestic-**homicide** reports in Miami," says Holmes. "No one cared ... — they were back-paged. I would just get up the courage to leave, and then I would read about another murder. " Holmes's **salvation** came when she began meeting other victims of domestic assault at a counseling service offered by Dade County. "Most of these women had gotten free, and they were able to help me objectively assess the risk of mortality. "

Suburban Isolation

Although Holmes and some other women interviewed for this article sought help through public agencies, many professional women suffer years of torment because they are isolated in their experience. Unlike poor women, who may have used other public services, professional, middle-class women can be loath to seek help from women's shelters. If they look for help, it is typically in the private offices of marriage counselors. But "marriage counseling assumes you're on a level playing field with your abuser," says Susan Neis, director of Cornerstone, an organization providing services to domestic-abuse victims in four affluent suburbs of Minneapolis. "You aren't. "

Professional women usually have a great deal to lose by **severing** ties with their abusers, often including an expensive home in an exclusive neighborhood, their social standing in the community, their financial security and a superior education for their children. Because so much is riding on the **perpetuation** of their marriage, they may lack supporters — even among their own families ... says Carol Arthur, "I have heard women weigh their safety with what they would give up. If the violence happens only three or four times a year, they barter. "

There is also the problem of a legal system that one victim characterizes as an "abuser's haven. " Women trying to divorce wealthy, established husbands typically find themselves **ensnarled** in court battles for years. Finally, the fact remains that when a man is intent upon killing his wife, there is no sure way to prevent it. One distinguished judge whose husband was arrested for assaulting her says, "I have not even tried to get a divorce, because I believe it would be fatal." She **stipulated** that she could not, under any circumstances, be identified.

Killing Their Careers

Aside from the physical and emotional **toll**, domestic violence can exert a crushing weight on a career. Holmes was just starting out in an elite Miami firm when her husband began his terrorist tactics. "He would physically restrain me from going to work," Holmes says. Once, stark naked, he pursued her out the front door and into the yard in order to pull her back inside. "Eventually," Holmes recalls, "I was barely out of the house before I would begin to be afraid of what would face me when I got home. It blew my concentration at work. In the corporate world, and certainly in the legal world, you're expected to perform at 120% no matter what. Toward the end, people were rewriting my briefs. I was told that I couldn't put together a **cogent** sentence."

Holmes discovered as well that a frank admission of an abusive relationship can **deter** prospective employers from hiring women. When she explained the gaps in her job history to employers, "they immediately assumed that if I was so weak as to allow myself to be abused, I would be a weak **litigator**," she says. It was one reason Holmes launched a solo practice.

Jeanne Raffesberger, a Wisconsinite, was an ambitious technical analyst in the insurance industry. Throughout a 15-year marriage, her husband repeatedly threatened her life with knives and, twice, with a 357 Magnum revolver. But, as with many working women married to abusers, it was the day-to-day psychological harassment that damaged her most. "He would call me stupid, tell me I was a miserable failure," she says. Some days her husband would prevent her from going to work by taking her car keys from her. Whenever she began to make progress in her career, he would demand that she quit her job, stay home and clean house — eight hours a day. At 2 p. m. she would fill the sinks and tubs with hot water. When her husband arrived home later to the wafting aroma of pine, he was reassured that she had fulfilled her wifely duty to him. Nevertheless, within days he would order her to "get off her ass" and find work. "It was a gradual, incremental slide into total chaos," she remembers. She abandoned her career . . .

Although domestic violence discriminates along gender lines rather than class lines, professional women have one advantage over poor women: their job skills and education. It is precisely because they have independent incomes, says Stark, that some white-collar women are able to extricate themselves.

Still, any advantages women of means may have over poor and blue-collar women are minimal, says Carol Arthur. "White-collar women are like all other women in terms of getting sucked into the psychological and emotional abuse that traps them," she says. "All the messages we got growing up taught us to define ourselves in terms of our relationships. " In the end, having the emotional strength to leave that notion behind is what really sets one woman apart from another.

From *Family Violence A. E. Sadler* 1996 *Greenhaven Press, Inc.*

New Words and Phrases

don	v.	put on (clothes etc.) 穿上,披上,戴上（衣服等）
normalcy	n.	state of being normal 常态;正常
batter	v.	hit (sb/sth) hard and often 接连猛击（某人,某物）
sporadic	adj.	occurring irregularly 偶发的;偶见的
condone	v.	overlook; forgive 容忍（过失）; 宽恕,原谅
jabbing at my gut with a two-by-four		hitting my gut with a heavy blow 猛烈击打我的腹部
abrasion	n.	scraping or wearing away; rubbing off 刮除;磨损磨掉
subtle	adj.	fine; delicate 难以察觉或描述的;细微的,精细的
incense	v.	make (sb.) very angry 激怒（某人）
coercive	adj.	using force or threat 强迫的,胁迫的
escalate	v.	become more intense 逐步升级,加剧
jab	v.	poke or push at (sb. sth.) roughly 刺,捅
gut	n.	internal organs of the abdomen（腹腔的）内脏
make it big		to succeed in starting and expanding (the music business)（美俚）成功,飞黄腾达
homicide	n.	killing
salvation	n.	saving of a person's soul from sin（对人的灵魂的）拯救
sever	v.	cut off 切断
perpetuation	n.	永存或持续
ensnarl	v.	to entangle in 使被纠缠
stipulate	v.	state 讲明;规定
toll	n.	loss or damage caused by (sth.) 损失或毁坏
cogent	adj.	convincing; strong 使人信服的
deter	v.	prevent; discourage 防止
litigator	n.	诉讼人
gaslight		电影"煤气灯下"

About the author:

Hillary Johnson is a frequent contributor to Working Woman magazine.

Notes to the text

1. **Domestic violence:** family violence, broadly refers to physical and/or sexual violence between people who are intimately associated. Spousal abuse, elder abuse, and child abuse are the types of violence most frequently falling under this label. However, the category is often expanded to include violence between gaymen, lesbians and unmarried heterosexual partners as well as siblings.

美国的家庭暴力发生于社会各个阶层。实际上美国大男子主义以及由此导致的家庭暴力由来已久。成立于100多年前的美国"基督教女青年会"其主要目的就是为了拯救受家庭暴力伤害的妇女。如今它在全美的分会达3,000个左右。美国主流社会的男女不平等现象依然严重。不少男子回到家中常把自己在外面所受的气发泄到妻子身上。

造成家庭暴力日益严重的因素很多,首先是来自家庭的影响,施暴者多生长于暴力充斥的家庭。他们从小目睹父亲殴打母亲,长大后效法;其次是社会因素,男人酗酒、吸毒、赌博是产生家庭暴力的温床;还有文化方面,特别是电影、小说对催生家庭暴力的负面影响;再就是经济因素,家庭生活拮据,尤其是在整个经济不景气的大环境下,家庭暴力会更多。美国家庭暴力主要有三种形式:一是丈夫为取得在家庭中的支配地位而对妻子采取的暴力行为;二是暴力从上一代传到下一代,即在暴力环境中长大的孩子,会受暴力环境的影响,认为愤怒和郁闷可以通过暴力来解决。这是从他们父母身上学到的,因而他们更倾向于用暴力的方式来解决问题;三是老年人也和妇女儿童一样是暴力的施加对象。近年来,研究人员和政府相关人员开始认识到家庭暴力的广度和严重性,特别是对儿童造成的影响。

2. **Minneapolis Minnessota:** 明尼苏达州明尼阿波利斯市

3. **St. Paul:** 圣保罗市

4. **New Haven, Connecticut:** 康涅狄格洲纽黑文

5. **Florida:** 佛罗里达州

6. **Miami:** 迈阿密

Exercises

I. **Answer the following questions based on Text and the words and expressions listed immediate below are for your reference.**

1. **What scene will usually appear in your mind when you come across the phrase "domestic violence"?**

   police/pounding on the door/a woman/crying

2. **Why does the author say that domestic violence is a secret for a large number of middle-or upper-class women, many of them professionals?**

feel compelled to/don a mask of normalcy/hate to admit they are victims

3. **What does the sentence "Women of means are just as trapped as women on welfare" mean?**

women who earn enough to support themselves/women of lower income/experience the same difficulties

4. **Why is it hard for professional women to believe that battering is happening to them?**

be in denial/smart/professional

5. **Can you give the reason why women who earn more or are more successful than their partners can be more vulnerable targets than women of like status to their husbands?**

compensate/resort to/socially condoned male dominance/form of revenge/blamed for

6. **How did Holmes get involved with a violent man?**

courtship/show no predilection/seductive and charming/sweet talking/get hooked on

7. **Give an account of how Holmes' husband abused her.**

drag her across/throw her into a wall/threaten

8. **Who are loath to seek help from women's shelters, professional women or poor women? Where do they usually look for help?**

private offices/marriage counselors

9. **What do professional women usually lose if they sever ties with their abusers?**

expensive home in an exclusive neighborhood/social standing/financial security/ superior education for their children

10. **What other harms can domestic violence bring to professional women aside from the physical and emotional toll?**

crush weight on a career

11. **Why do prospective employers of professional women hate to hire them if they make a frank admission of an abusive relationship?**

assume/weak/litigator

12. **Does the author believe that professional women are smarter in dealing with domestic violence than blue-collar women?**

II. Further questions for discussion.

1. What would you act if you happened to have married an abuser? What suggestions will you give to those who happen to have married abusive husbands?

2. Do you think a man will show his tendency toward violence before he gets married? If

yes, what might possibly be indications of a potentially abusive male?

3. Could you suggest ideas that may help women from being abused?

III. Vocabulary study.

  1. Word in use.

    1) **don**：*vt.* to put on 穿上, 披上, 戴上

      He quickly donned a welcoming smile as his guests arrived.

      You should don a wicker helmet on the construction site.

      Do all the students need to don school uniforms?

    2) **be blessed with**：to be fortunate in having sth/sb. 在某事物（某人）方面有福

      He is blessed with excellent health.

      You are certainly blessed with a glib tongue.

      May you be blessed with love and happiness forever!

    3) **brutalise**：*vt.* to make (sb.) brutal or insensitive 使（某人）变得残酷无情

      The soldiers brutalized by a long war showed no mercy to the injured girl.

      British troops brutalize Iraqi youth were caught on camera.

      The rot in learning is brutalizing our society.

    4) **condone**：*vt.* to treat or regard (an offence) as if it were not serious or wrong; overlook; forgive 容忍（过失）, 宽恕, 原谅

      I do not condone my husband's behavior.

      Not punishing them amounts to condoning their crime.

      I will condone your actions of negligence.

    5) **intimidate into**：to frighten (sb. in order to make sb. do sth.) 恐吓, 威胁（某人）做某事

      The suspect tried to intimidate the witness into silence by threatening him.

      Bob intimidated the witness into silence.

      They intimidated him into doing what they wanted.

    6) **incense**：*vt.* to make (sb.) very angry 使某人大怒, 激怒（某人）

      The decision to reduce pay levels incensed the work-force.

      The offensive answer incensed Mr. Smith.

      His failure to pass the examination incensed his father.

    7) **play (the) field with (infml)**：to avoid committing oneself to one person, activity etc 不对某人做出承诺, 不承诺参加某一活动等

      Can you assure me that your boyfriend is not playing field with you?

      Al has a steady girl friend, but John is playing the field.

      Jim is crazy about Mary, but she is still playing the field.

    8) **stipulate**：*vt.* to say that something must be done, when you are making an agreement or offer (在协议或提议中) 规定, 约定

Jack stipulated payment in advance.

The lease stipulates that the tenant's failure to pay rent by the end of the mouth may result in eviction.

We may wish to stipulate in advance that you pay the money for it.

9) **deter from**: *vt.* to make (sb.) decide not to do (sth.)使某人决定不做某事

I don't think that failure will deter him from making another attempt.

People cannot deter the manager from carrying out his plan.

The decision to jail music promoter Glenn Wheatley for tax evasion could deter others from committing the crime.

2. Word distinction.

1) **deter; defer** 两个词拼写相近,容易混淆.

deter: to prevent or discourage 阻止,威慑

defer: to put off; postpone. 推迟;延期

课文中 "a frank admission of an abusive relationship can deter prospective employers from hiring women" 坦率承认有受虐待的夫妻关系会阻碍再有老板招聘此类女性。

选择以上适当的词填空:

My bank has agreed to _____ the repayments on my loan while I'm still a student.

These measures are designed to _____ an enemy attack.

Can we _____ making a decision until next week.

High prices are _____ many young people from buying houses.

2) **be intent on/upon; with intent to do**

be intent on/upon 中作形容词"热衷于","专心致志于";

在 with intent to do sth 中作名词"意图","目的"。

选择以上适当的词填空:

He is _____ getting promotion, and no one is going to stop him.

The suspect fired a weapon _____ kill his wife.

The students were all _____ their preparation for the final exam.

He entered the building _____ to steal.

3. Decide the meanings of the following words, matching each word in Column A with the word or expression in Column B that is similar in meaning.

A	B
1) homicide	a. sudden attack
2) ramshackle	b. become completely committed to
3) assault	c. handle with skill
4) manipulation	d. killing of one person
5) get hooked on	e. thing that is accidentally successful

6）enrage　　　　　　　　f. break or separate by cutting

7）sever　　　　　　　　 g. make repeated attacks on

8）harassment　　　　　　h. make sb. very angry

9）fluke　　　　　　　　 i. attract or tempt

10）lure　　　　　　　　 j. almost collapsing

4. Try to write a brief story with the following words and phrases.

sweet-talking, get hooked on, courtship, batter, drag, throw, jab, counselor, domestic-abuse, barrier to, seek a divorce, meet at court

IV. Translation.

1. Put the following Chinese expressions into English.

1）反家庭暴力　　 2）婚姻暴力　　 3）自杀倾向　　 4）性侵害经历

5）妇女权益保护法　 6）冷暴力　　　 7）被虐妇女　　 8）婚内强奸

2. Put the following Chinese sentences into English with the words or phrases in the brackets.

1）尽管在婆家受到虐待,但每次她母亲来看她,她都装作没事一样。(don a mask of)

2）幸运的是,这座城市有许多文化古迹,它肯定能被评上魅力城市之一。(be blessed with)

3）有如此多的孩子暴力犯罪,是因为他们长年被虐待和忽视而变得残忍。(brutalize)

4）我无法原谅他在这种情况下使用暴力。(condone)

5）警察威胁我,不让我声张。(intimidated me into)

6）观众对裁判的判罚极为愤怒,冲进了球场。(incense)

7）我没见过玛丽专情于一个男人,她太喜欢同时与几个人恋爱了。(settle down with)

8）我们应该加强安全措施,制止商店扒手行窃。(deter)

3. Put the following Chinese paragraph into English.

美国社会学家 A. Straus 对家庭暴力现象做过许多调查研究。他发现,男性也会成为家庭暴力的受虐者。在过去的十年里,男性殴打女性的比例下降,而女性攻击男性的比率反而上升了。其它研究结果也表明了这点。据美国司法局统计,在 1994 年里,百分之五十五的家暴受害者是男性。第十三届世界社会学大会报告说,1992 年,美国丈夫虐妻的比率为百分之四点六,而妻子虐待丈夫的比率却为百分之九点五。

4. Put the following quotes into Chinese.

1）The family you came from isn't as important as the family you are going to have.

—— D. Herbert Lawrence

2）To make a lasting marriage we have to overcome self-centeredness.

—— Grorge Goreon Byron

3）The family is one of nature's masterpieces. —— George Santayana

4）Happy are the families where the government of parents is the reign of affection, and obedience of the children the submission to love. —— Francis Bacon

5）Marriage may be compared to a cage the birds outside despair to get in and those within despair to get out. —— Michel de Montaigne

5. Translate the following passage into Chinese.

Look at the world's worst trouble spots and you can't fail to notice they have one thing in common：tit-for-tat attacks between warring parties. Escalation of violence is incredibly destructive, yet we humans find it very difficult to break the vicious cycle. It seems we are not good at conflict resolution. Perhaps we could learn a lesson or two from the spotted hyena.

Spotted hyenas are highly sociable. Like other animals that live in close-knit groups, they don't always get along. But spotted hyenas don't hold a grudge. Within about 5 minutes of a fight, the erstwhile combatants can often be seen playing, licking or rubbing one another, or engaging in other friendly acts to dissipate the tension.

V. Comments on the structure of the text.

The text is a special feature, in which the writer probes into the issue that professional women are the victims of domestic violence.

Like other feature stories, the text consists of three elements of a feature, a headline, a body and a conclusion. The first paragraph is an introduction, which paints a setting to lead readers into the rest of the article. It is also called a lead which presents the writer's theme：the white-collar women in the United States are often the victims of family violence.

The body is a detailed presentation of facts. The facts are arranged according to their importance. The four subheadings provide readers with a clear picture of the arrangements of facts. In this part, the writer provides statistical information to convince readers that battering crosses class lines, and then, analyzes the causes behind；white-collar victims are in denial that they can be abused women because they think they are smart and professionals, and also their success breeds targets. The effective analysis is backed up by data the writer gathered through her interviews.

The conclusion is drawn with a quotation, which enforces the lead.

Extended Exercises

1. In the following article, some paragraphs have been removed. Choose the most suitable paragraph from the list A — F to fit into each of the numbered gaps. There is ONE paragraph which does not fit in any of the gaps.

Hair
By Marcia Aldrich

I've never seen my mother wash her own hair. After my mother married, she never washed her own hair again. As a girl and an unmarried woman — yes — but, in my lifetime, she never washed her hair with her own two hands.

1)_____.

Her appointment on Fridays at two o'clock was never cancelled or rescheduled; it was the bedrock of her week, around which she pivoted and planned.

2)_____.

With Julie my mother discussed momentous decisions concerning hair color and the advancement of age and what could be done about it, hair length and its effect upon maturity, when to perm and when not to perm, the need to proceed with caution when a woman desperately wanted a major change in her life like dumping her husband or sending back her newborn baby and the only change she could effect was a change in her hair.

3)_____.

Her voice was usually tense, on guard, the laughter forced, but with Julie it dropped much lower sounded at home. And most remarkably, she listened to everything Julie said.

4)_____.

Just as Mother seemed to like her latest color and cut, she began to agitate for a new look. She wanted her hair to be fashioned into an event with a complicated narrative past. However, the more my mother attempted to impose a hair style pulled from an idealized image of herself, the more the hair style seemed to be at odds with my mother.

5)_____.

A: The more the hair style became substantial, the more the woman underneath was obscured. She'd riffle through women's magazines and stare for long dreamingly hours at a particular woman's hair.

B: Upon marriage, she began weekly treks to the beauty salon where Julie washed and styled her hair.

C: That was what Julie called a "dangerous time" in a woman's life. When my mother spoke to Julie, she spoke in almost confessional tones I had never heard before.

D: These two hours were indispensable to my mother's routine, to her sense of herself and what, as a woman, she should concern herself with — not to mention their being her primary source of information about all sorts of things she wouldn't otherwise come to know.

E: As a child I was puzzled by the way my mother's sense of self-worth and her mood seemed dependent upon how she thought her hair looked, however, her search for the perfect hair style never ended

F: Each of my best friends was subjected to her mother's hair dictatorship, although with entirely different results.

From Best Contemporary American Essay 2003

2. **In the following article, some paragraphs have been removed. Choose the most suitable paragraph from the list A — F to fit into each of the numbered gaps. Arrange the following paragraphs in a logical order.**

When my mother, a Catholic schoolgirl from the South, decided to marry my father, a Buddhist gangster from the North, her parents disowned her.

1)_____

The year my mother met my father, there were several young men working at her house, running errands for her father, pickling vegetables with her mother.

2)_____

She treated these men as brothers, sometimes as uncle even, exclaiming in self-defense, "I didn't even know about love then."

Mother says love came to her in a dark movie theater.

3)_____

In the dark, she couldn't make out his face but noticing he was handsome. She wondered if he knew she was watching him out of the corner of her eye. Watching him without embarrassment or shame.

4)_____

Later, in the shadow of the beached fishing boats on the blackest nights of the year, she would call him to mind, his face a warm companion for her body on the edge of the sea.

5)_____

A: Watching him with a strange curiosity, a feeling that made her want to trace and retrace his silhouette with her fingertips until she'd memorized every feature and could call his face to her in any dark place she passed through.

B: Her father chased her out of the house, beating her with the same broom she had used every day of her life, from the time she could stand up and sweep to the morning of the very day she was chased away.

C: In the early days of my parents' courtship, my mother told stories. She confessed elaborate dreams about the end of war. Unlike the responsible favorite daughter or sister she was to her family, with my father, in the forest, my mother became reckless, drunk on her youth and the possibility of love, ignoring the chores to be done at home.

D: She doesn't remember what movie it was or why she'd gone to see it, only that she'd gone alone and found herself sitting beside him.

E: It was understood by everyone that these men were courting my mother. My mother claims she had no such understanding.

From Best Contemporary American Essay 2003

Extensive Reading

Passage One

Harsher Penalties Can Reduce Family Violence

Casey G. Gwinn

For more than twenty years in this country, many have grappled with (努力克服) the complex issue of family violence. In the 1970s, the shelter movement developed to provide safe shelter for battered women and their children. Then, in the early 1980s, the shelter movement exercised its influence in the courts and state legislatures (立法机关) across the country. Class action lawsuits on behalf of battered women and legislation mandating (授权) arrest and aggressive law enforcement responses became commonplace. By the mid-1980s prosecutors and judges began to address their role in the appropriate response of the criminal justice system to family violence. Most recently, medical professionals, therapists, pastors, and the military community have joined coordinated strategies in many jurisdictions (辖区).

Clear consensus (共同看法) has developed in many jurisdictions that not only points the way toward effective intervention but brings with it reliable statistics to back the claim of effectiveness. The consensus in the criminal justice system context focuses around this clarion (响亮的) call: Aggressive arrest and prosecution policies, coupled with strong advocacy programs, in the context of a coordinated community response, can lead to effective intervention. Effective intervention is being defined as stopping the violence, making victims safer, and holding abusers accountable (负有责任的,可说明的,可解释的). Jurisdictions such as San Diego, California; Duluth, Minnesota; Quincy, Massachusetts; Knoxville, Tennessee; Newport News, Virginia; Seattle, Washington and others have seen dramatic drops in recidivism (惯犯,累犯) and in domestic violence homicide rates through implementation of these strategies.

Many, however, believe that a gaping hole still exists in the intervention effort across the country. It is the role of the incarceration (被监禁的人) and jail system in stopping the violence, making victims safer, and holding abusers accountable. If domestic violence is to be treated as a serious crime, then jail staff must play a role.

The stark (明摆着的) reality of the need for the jail officer to do more faces off squarely (直接地) with the traditional reluctance of jail staff to be in the business of rehabilitation. But jail officers clearly must play a role in the effort to stop domestic violence in this country. It is time to propose the expansion of the role of the jail officer in domestic violence cases. It is time to call for proactive (积极主动) steps from the detention community to assist the domestic violence movement in our effort to stop domestic violence . . . .

More Serious than a Misdemeanor

The jail system plays a crucial role in society's decision to treat domestic violence as a serious crime. Historically, however, this message does not emanate (来自) from the jails of this country. If a domestic violence offender is booked and released simply because of the misdemeanor nature of the offense, the crime is minimized. We can say it is "serious crime" until we are blue in the face but if it is not treated as serious crime, the batter will not receive that message. We must not allow the phrase "just a misdemeanor" or "only a misdemeanor" to creep into our vocabulary when we talk about domestic violence.

Nearly 90 percent of all domestic violence offenses nationally are handled as misdemeanors (轻罪), yet the potential lethality (致死性杀伤性) and often the raw nature of the violence far surpass many felony offenses. Indeed, in ten years as a prosecutor handling both felonies and misdemeanors, I have never handled a felony domestic violence case that was as "serious" as many of the misdemeanor cases that I handle on a regular basis.

Policies which automatically allow domestic violence offenders to receive book-and-release simply because of the nature of the offense must end. Policies which make domestic violence offenders eligible (有资格的,合格的) for a "Sheriff's Own Recognizance Release" or some such similar policy should be reviewed. Across the country in recent years, many jurisdictions that I have trained in have identified policies in the jail system that return domestic violence offenders to the home with rarely even a judicial review. The result is the minimization of the offense and the increased likelihood of yet another violent episode.

A study by researcher Larry Sherman proves this point. Sherman's study in Milwaukee also highlights the fallacies (谬见) swirling around these issues. Sherman studied the effectiveness of arrest in domestic violence cases in Milwaukee between 1988 and 1992. He concluded that arrest was counterproductive because of the high level of recidivism following release from custody. His research, however, must be more carefully examined. It actually proves a quite different point.

In Sherman's study, the "long arrest" lasted only 12 hours, the "short arrest" lasted approximately 6 hours, and the control group was simply warned by officers at the scene not to commit another offense. Only 1 percent of the subjects in the study were prosecuted and convicted in court. It should come as no surprise that an individual held for only 12 hours, not provided with treatment, and not prosecuted would feel empowered to continue the violence upon release from "custody". His study actually proves the point made here. If the detention system minimizes the offense and is derelict(弃置的) along with the rest of the system, in treating domestic violence as a serious crime, then offenders will continue *and* escalate their behavior upon release from jail.

The challenge for the detention facilities therefore becomes identifying ways in which domestic violence offenses are minimized or virtually "decriminalized"(非刑事化的). Systems with extremely low bail amounts for domestic violence offenses often cause a similar result. But what of work furlough(休假许可) programs? Most jurisdictions do not allow work furlough for "violent" offenders. Yet domestic violence offenders routinely qualify for work furlough programs across the country. What message does this send to offenders? Every policy in a detention facility or jail that relates to domestic violence cases must be assessed in light of the question: "Is domestic violence treated as a serious crime by this facility?"

Making Victims Safer

Jail officers must also acknowledge their role in providing for the victim's safety in a domestic violence case. Nearly 4,000 women are killed in this country every year in domestic violence homicides. Nearly 75 percent of these women are killed after separation in the relationship. By definition, incarceration(监禁) creates separation in the relationship. It challenges the power of the batterer over the victim. Not surprisingly then, release from custody may well be the most dangerous time for victims of domestic violence. Unfortunately, many victims assume that when their attacker is arrested he will stay in jail. Sadly, we know this is not so . . . .

The jail system, therefore, must ask basic questions. What policies are in place for notifying a victim prior to the release of her assailant(攻击者,行凶者)? What policies are in place which triggers(引发) notification(通知,报告) if she requests it? What relationship exists between shelters and jails to allow safety planning and crisis intervention to occur during the critical period of incarceration? The answer to these questions, unfortunately, is usually "None".

These issues can often be addressed irrespective of fiscal constraints. Shelters, advocates, and volunteers exist in every jurisdiction who can assist in the creation and implementation of appropriate policies. Even putting aside the moral imperative for such policies, the potential liability for failure to notify and failure to protect in these circumstances looms（隐现）on the horizon. Aggressive work is now being done across the country to assist victims in planning for their own safety upon the release from custody of their assailants. Jail systems need to join in this effort.

What Works?

There is a pressing need nationally for the jail and detention system in this country to begin working with researchers and domestic violence movement professionals to determine what works with domestic violence offenders. Does early release combined with monitoring reduces recidivism while saving money? Is work furlough as effective a deterrent（起制止作用的）as full-time incarceration? Does the length of a sentence correlate to long-term reductions in recidivism?

These questions have answers. First, however, we must ask the questions and then we must work to answer them. Pilot projects and limited duration studies even with rudimentary（初步的）approaches can be extremely helpful in this process. In jurisdictions in which I consult across the country, I am challenging system professionals to start answering their own questions about effectiveness. For example, if a jurisdiction were simply to take a large sample of domestic violence offenders from work furlough and early release categories and study re-arrest rates over time it would have a basis for discussion. While researchers abhor（憎恨）such simplicity without control groups and the like, any data will elevate the discussion.

The potential for partnerships between local domestic violence community professionals and the jail system is significant. A jurisdiction that studied the significance of the length of a sentence in a domestic violence case, for example, would also find that incarceration may also increase the chances of the victim's seeking the assistance of an advocate and engaging in safety planning. It is common sense that an incarcerated batterer may have some level of diminished control over the contacts and conversations of a domestic violence victim, yet few jurisdictions study this interrelationship.

In San Diego, we have found that the victim is far more likely to talk to an advocate and begin the process of satiety planning if the abuser is still in jail. We know from experience that our best contact with the victim is during the period of incarceration of the batterer. Yet, nationally, most jail systems are not studying how their policies might affect this dynamic. By bringing together those within a system that can study this issue, the process toward coordinated community response is greatly enhanced.

Treating Violence as a Choice

Perhaps the most significant arena for jail staff to have an impact lies in the area of treatment programs for batterers. Across the country, a consensus is emerging that focuses on a psycho educational model of "treatment" for batterers. It was developed in Duluth,

Minnesota, by Ellen Pence and Michael Paymar and is gaining acceptance across the country. The "Duluth Model" approach moves away from individual psychotherapy and rejects anger/ stress management or substance abuse treatment as the core of the intervention. It focuses on violence as a choice, most often made by men in our society, and works at re-educating men to make different choices. It seeks to address issues of sex-role socialization and the related topics of male entitlement and male privilege.

The key component of the Duluth model program, however, triggers the consequences for making the wrong choices. Clearly, in domestic violence cases, the most significant negative consequence must be incarceration. If domestic violence is to be treated as a serious crime, and if offenders are going to be forced to make different choices, then the criminal justice system must impose serious consequences for continuing criminal behavior.

From *Family Violence A. E. Sadler* 1996 *Greenhaven Press, Inc. , PO Box* 289009, *San Diego, CA* 92198 – 9009 *Printed in the U. S. A.*

I. Reading Comprehension.

1. Which of the following is not mentioned as one of the forces to have joined coordinated strategies in many jurisdictions?
   A. Medical professionals.　　　　　B. Military community.
   C. Therapists.　　　　　　　　　　D. School personnel.

2. It can be inferred from the text that _____.
   A. domestic violence in the U. S. is often regarded as a misdemeanor
   B. domestic violence in the U. S. is not often regarded as a misdemeanor
   C. domestic violence in the U. S. is regarded as a felony
   D. domestic violence in the U. S. is regarded as a serious crime

3. The reason why 75% of the women who are killed in the U. S. every year in domestic violence homicide after separation is that _____.
   A. they think their attackers are arrested and stay in jail
   B. the jail officers protest the offenders
   C. release from custody is the most dangerous time
   D. they fail to see the danger

4. The word "escalate" in Paragraph 9 means "_____".
   A. decline　　　　　　　　　　　　B. drop
   C. increase　　　　　　　　　　　　D. fall

5. The author's attitude toward the harsher penalties is _____.
   A. positive　　　　　　　　　　　　B. critical
   C. tolerant　　　　　　　　　　　　D. indifferent

II. Topics for further discussion.

1. Do you think harsher penalties can reduce family violence?
2. What do you think of the low bail amount system for domestic violence in the United States?
3. Do you agree that most of domestic violence offenses are treated as misdemeanors?

Passage Two

Lessons from the Domestic Violence Intervention Project

Sheila Burton , Linda Regan and Liz Kelly

我们能在家庭暴力干预项目中获得什么启示?

Background

There is currently no national policy on domestic violence in the UK. At the most basic level preventing violence against women in the home involves two components: increasing safety for the woman and her children in the short term and ending the man's violence in the longer term. The Domestic Violence Intervention Project (DVIP) undertakes both kinds of work.

In Britain there has been a growth in work with violent men within both the voluntary sector and the Probation Service(监管署). Much of this work draws on(源于) a model, developed in Minnesota, encompassing (围绕,包含) women and children's safety and working with men to take responsibility for their behaviour. Some independent groups work with men who have voluntarily referred themselves to the project, others provide services only for men found guilty of a domestic violence related offence who have received a court order to attend as part of their sentence. The Probation Service can recommend various sanctions(处罚) to magistrates (治安法官), these include a probation order of between six and thirty-six months, which may include a condition to attend a specified programme.

The overall philosophy of DVIP begins from an understanding that men use violence to achieve and maintain power over their partner. It has two basic aims: to empower women and increase their safety; and to stop men's violence and abuse. In providing two linked services — a Violence Prevention Programme (VPP) which works with violent men and a Women's Support Service (WSS) — DVIP is a unique approach in Britain. This two-year evaluation (October 1994 to September 1996) studied DVIP as a whole, WSS and VPP.

Proactive (主动) support for women

The Women's Support Service provides: telephone advice; one-to-one counselling; group work; advocacy (支持); and ongoing telephone support. Individuals choose the particular combination of support they need.

Over two years, with a small resource base (two part-time workers and volunteers) WSS was in contact with 796 women. One-third were partners of men on the VPP programme, the majority made contact independently. WSS was effective in reaching women from ethnic minorities and women with professional qualifications, two groups which currently under-use other forms of provision (措施).

The proactivity of WSS has several elements:

the project makes initial contact with women whose partners are on VPP;

for all women WSS is persistent in continuing contact (this can involve making numerous telephone calls to make/renew contact, following women up at regular intervals, and having priorities for follow-up);

work with women uses goal-oriented and directive crisis intervention, including a strategy called 'safety planning'. This tool aims to enable women to move from reacting to events as they happen to anticipating (预见) and planning ahead.

The advantages of proactive work are:

someone else takes responsibility for naming the experience as violence;

women can be invited into a support network at a much earlier point than they might otherwise choose.

Women using WSS were overwhelmingly positive about the support they had received. The things they valued most were basic messages:

that this is violence;

that violence is unacceptable;

that violence is not the woman's fault.

Many women noted the importance of uncompromising (不妥协的) messages in enabling them to both see their situation differently and to take action. Women also benefited from the combination of forms of support, with support groups being the most effective in combating shame, self-blame and the destruction of self-belief which strongly inhibit (阻止, 抑制) women's attempts to end violence.

Challenging work with men

The Violence Prevention Programme offers structured group sessions designed to assist men in understanding why they use abusive behaviour, how they can change and work towards constructing respectful relationships with women. Whilst a significant proportion of men were referred (转交) to VPP by the Probation Service, the majority referred to the programme voluntarily — many of this group had been given some form of ultimatum by their partner.

The programme comprises a 12-week, first-stage group focused on physical violence and a 24-week, second stage addressing other forms of abuse and controlling behaviours.

Movement between the stages is neither fixed nor automatic but depends on the man's involvement with the programme, his motivation and behaviour. An optional fortnightly, third stage is available for men who want to reinforce any changes they have made.

Two basic conditions are set out for men being accepted onto the programme: some willingness on their part to question denying their own responsibility and blaming their partner; and at least some awareness that they alone are responsible for the violence.

Drop-out rate

VPP has a marked drop-out rate, especially between assessment and initial attendance. Over two-thirds of the 351 men referred to the programme failed to complete it: 12 per cent were not accepted onto it in the first place. Under half (43 per cent) of the men who were accepted actually completed the programme.

There is a significant loss in the early weeks of the first stage group. Most of these are 'voluntarily referred' men whose primary motivation in attending the programme may have been to prevent their partner leaving. If they are successful, or if the woman leaves anyway, they may see no further reason to continue.

High drop-out rates are reported features of men's programmes in the UK and USA, with an average loss of at least 50 per cent. Finding ways to decrease drop-out is a major challenge for all programmes working with violent men.

What works

Within VPP the combination of court-mandated (委托) and 'voluntarily referred' men was productive and facilitated enhanced motivation in some court-mandated men.

The most effective tool used by VPP was 're-enactments', where men have to act out an incident and go through it again in slow motion. The point of the exercise — to reveal that decisions are made at various points — was communicated to most group members.

However, 'time outs' (the man is supposed to take an hour away from the situation if he is about to be violent, informing his partner that this is what he is doing) were used in abusive and controlling ways by a number of men. 'Time outs' are an extremely common component of work with violent men; this finding suggests that alternatives to them and/or mechanisms for ensuring that they are not used as new forms of control should be urgently explored.

The content of the VPP programme was fairly effective in communicating its key messages and in offering men alternatives to violence. From men's own accounts, in some cases confirmed by information from their partners, there would appear to be some real change in their understanding of domestic violence.

Ending violence and ending relationships safely

The data from VPP, and some of the men's partners, suggests that where men can be held in the group, and especially if they complete both the first and second stage elements, physical violence decreases dramatically, and some men change in more fundamental ways.

A critical question is whether men changing should be the only criteria of 'success' for men's programmes. This study suggests that participation, especially where the project has a dedicated women's service, creates a window of opportunity for relationships to end safely. Men's programmes may make this possible because of the immediate reduction of violence, and through explicitly encouraging men to either leave themselves, or to not intervene or intimidate women when they decide to leave. The importance of this contribution to women's safety should not be underestimated, since leaving is the most dangerous time for women and children.

Voluntary or mandated entry

This study revealed that VPP's willingness to accept men who 'voluntarily' refer themselves was important to women in their struggles to end violence. A significant proportion of women demanded some combination of attendance, completion of the programme and change in behaviour as conditions for the relationship continuing. Moreover, where pro-active support for women is available, men's attendance can increase women's options and room for manoeuvre.

Conclusion

Towards the end of this study a new policy from the Inner London Probation Service (ILPS) signalled a shift from funding specialist agencies to work with violent men to running groups 'in-house'. Whilst the model ILPS proposes shares much with that currently used by VPP there will be no linked support for women and no provision for men who have voluntarily referred. It is unclear whether specialist agencies will be able to survive without partnership funding from the Probation Service, or other statutory (法定的) agencies. Interviews with probation officers highlighted both their limited awareness of local policy and lack of knowledge of domestic violence.

The researchers conclude that specialist projects have a number of advantages. They can:

have women and children's safety as a central philosophy;

provide reasonably sized groups with a rolling entry/exit so that no man has to wait long to attend;

provide an integrated model of staged groups including a follow-up group;

provide one-to-one work for men in particular circumstances;

create access for a combination of court mandated and voluntary participants;

encourage the development of specialism and expertise.

The single focus and higher level of work in specialist projects means that work can be regularly reviewed and where necessary adapted.

The debates surrounding work with violent men, in Britain and internationally, mean that gender issues, sexual politics, cannot be avoided: at the heart of programmes for violent men is a gender tension. This at times was reflected in, and played out through, the structures of DVIP. Towards the end of the evaluation a co-ordinator for the whole project was appointed in an attempt to bring cohesion to the organisation. Management of projects working in this field needs to be both strong and open enough to work creatively with 'gender agendas'.

WSS has demonstrated that pro-active approaches have a place in support for women suffering domestic violence. Few women resented an outsider making the first move and most welcomed support; they saw it as enabling them to make changes sooner and/or more definitely than they would have done otherwise. The potential of pro-active work is that through earlier intervention some women and children will suffer less violence and as a consequence be less affected over the longer term. Pro-active approaches are a form of provision that is both protective and preventative.

There are no simple solutions to domestic violence, or models of response which are effective for all abused women or all abusive men. This study suggests that there are significant dangers in undertaking challenging work with men without the addition of parallel support services for women. However, there does seem to be a place for work with men in the co-ordinated, multi-layered responses to domestic violence. When combined with pro-active work with women it actually increases the local resources available to women. But programmes for violent men are neither an answer, nor an alternative to other forms of sanction, and should not be used as a form of diversion.

Retrieved from *http://www. jrf. org. uk/knowledge/findings/socialpolicy/spr*338. *asp*

Decide whether the following statements are True or False.

1. One advantage of proactive work is to take responsibility for naming the experience as violence for a woman victim, which indicates that violent men are often more than happy to admit their abusive behaviour. (   )

2. The report suggests that women may experience shame, self-blame and the destruction of self-belief while suffering domestic violence abuse. (   )

3. One basic condition for accepting men onto the Violence Prevention Programme is some willingness on their part to admit their own responsibility instead of blaming their partners. (   )

4. A significant number of women require violent men to attend and complete the programme and to change in behaviour as conditions for the relationship continuing. (   )

5. The report concludes that Violence Prevention Programme is effective and it can be an alternative to other penalties for violent men. (   )

赠送课件说明

　　充实教学内容、丰富教学资源、改进教学方法是高校教师提高教学质量的基本思路，也是我们编写教材的宗旨。为方便教师教学，我们配套制作了本教材的教学课件，免费提供给使用本教材的教师。为保证教师获得课件，请授课教师填写如下开课情况证明并邮寄（或传真）至下列地址，我们将在 48 小时内寄出课件，或向教师提供用户名和密码，在本社网站上下载课件。

联系方式：

地址：对外经济贸易大学出版社市场营销部　　北京朝阳区惠新东街 10 号
邮编：100029
电话：(010)64492342，(010)64496374
Email：uibep@126.com

- -

证　　明

　　兹证明_____大学_____院_____系_____专业第____学年____学期开设的_____课程，采用对外经济贸易大学出版社出版的_____（书名、作者）作为本课程教材，授课教师为_____，共____个班，学生共____人。

　　授课教师需要获得与本书配套的教学课件。

　　授课教师联系方式：

地　　址：_____

邮　　编：_____

固定电话：_____

手　　机：_____

E-mail：_____

　　　　　　　　　　　　　　　特此证明

　　　　　　　　　　授课教师：　　　　　（签字）
　　　　　　　　　　院/系主任：　　　　　（签字）
　　　　　　　　　　（院/系办公室公章）
　　　　　　　　　　200　年　　月　　日